# Long-term Care for the Elderly in Europe

Long-term care is an increasingly important issue in many contemporary welfare states around the globe given ageing populations. This ground-breaking book provides detailed case studies of 11 EU-member states from different welfare regimes within Europe to show how welfare states organize, structure and deliver long-term care and whether there is a social investment perspective in the delivery of long-term care. This perspective is important because the effect of demographic transitions is often used as an argument for the existence of economic pressure on welfare states and a need for either direct retrenchment or attempts to reduce welfare state spending. The book's chapters will look specifically into how different welfare states have focussed on long-term care in recent years and what types of changes have taken place with regard to ageing populations and ambitions to curb increases in public sector spending in this area. They describe the development in long-term care for the elderly after the financial crisis and also discuss the boundaries between state and civil society in the different welfare states' approaches to the delivery of care.

**Bent Greve** is Professor of Welfare State Analysis at the Department of Society and Business, Roskilde University, Denmark.

**Social Welfare Around the World**
Series editor: Bent Greve
*Roskilde University, Denmark*

This series publishes high-quality research monographs and edited books that focus on development, change in provision and/or delivery of welfare with a primary focus on developed welfare states. The books provide overviews of themes such as pensions, social services, unemployment and housing, as well as in-depth analyses of change and impact on a micro level. The impact and influence of supranational institutions on welfare state developments are studied, as are the methodologies used to analyse the ongoing transformations of welfare states.

1 **The Transformation of the Social Right to Healthcare**
Evidence from England and Germany
*Katharina Böhm*

2 **Welfare State Transformation in the Yugoslav Successor States**
From Social to Unequal
*Marija Stambolieva*

3 **Long-term Care for the Elderly in Europe**
Development and Prospects
*Edited by Bent Greve*

# Long-term Care for the Elderly in Europe

Development and Prospects

Edited by Bent Greve

LONDON AND NEW YORK

First published 2017
by Routledge
2 Park Square, Milton Park, Abingdon, Oxon OX14 4RN

and by Routledge
711 Third Avenue, New York, NY 10017

*Routledge is an imprint of the Taylor & Francis Group, an informa business*

© 2017 selection and editorial matter, Bent Greve; individual chapters, the contributors

The right of Bent Greve to be identified as the author of the editorial material, and of the authors for their individual chapters, has been asserted in accordance with sections 77 and 78 of the Copyright, Designs and Patents Act 1988.

All rights reserved. No part of this book may be reprinted or reproduced or utilised in any form or by any electronic, mechanical, or other means, now known or hereafter invented, including photocopying and recording, or in any information storage or retrieval system, without permission in writing from the publishers.

*Trademark notice*: Product or corporate names may be trademarks or registered trademarks, and are used only for identification and explanation without intent to infringe.

*British Library Cataloguing in Publication Data*
A catalogue record for this book is available from the British Library

*Library of Congress Cataloging in Publication Data*
A catalog record for this book has been requested

ISBN: 978-1-472-48392-8 (hbk)
ISBN: 978-1-315-59294-7 (ebk)

Typeset in Times New Roman
by Apex CoVantage, LLC

Printed and bound by CPI Group (UK) Ltd, Croydon, CR0 4YY

# Contents

| | |
|---|---|
| *List of contributors* | x |
| *Foreword* | xiv |

**1 Long-term care: what is it about?**     1

BENT GREVE

*1.1 Introduction 1*
*1.2 What is long-term care and the quest for quality? 2*
*1.3 Overview of the book 3*
*1.4 Delimitations 6*

**2 Long-term care for the elderly in Hungary**     8

RÓBERT I. GÁL

*2.1 Introduction 8*
*2.2 Overview of the long-term care system 8*
*2.3 Being old 9*
*2.4 Demand and supply 12*
    *2.4.1 Eligibility 12*
    *2.4.2 Assessment of needs 13*
    *2.4.3 Available benefits and services 13*
    *2.4.4 Supply of public care 14*
    *2.4.5 Informal market for long-term care services 19*
*2.5 Projections 20*
*2.6 Conclusions 21*

**3 Long-term care: challenges and perspectives**     23

VIRGINIJA POŠKUTĖ

*3.1 Introduction 23*
*3.2 Organisations of long-term care 23*
*3.3 Formal LTC for the elderly 25*

vi  *Contents*

*3.4  Financing of LTC  32*
*3.5  Boundaries between state and civil society in the approach
to the delivery of care with an eye to the private sector's
ambition to provide and sell care  33*
*3.6  Informal care  33*
*3.7  Use of rehabilitation and welfare technology as ways to
improve quality of life and reduce the pressure on public
sector spending in the area  34*
*3.8  Conclusions  34*

**4  Long-term care for the elderly in Poland**                           38

ZOFIA CZEPULIS-RUTKOWSKA

*4.1  Introduction  38*
*4.2  New welfare state institutional context  38*
*4.3  Demand for long-term care  40*
*4.4  Supply of the long-term care  41*
  *4.4.1  Family  41*
  *4.4.2  Public sector  42*
  *4.4.3  Social sector  45*
  *4.4.4  Private sector and NGOs  49*
*4.5  Administration, financing and quality: challenges  51*
*4.6  Debate and reform proposals  53*
*4.7  Conclusions  55*

**5  Long-term care in Portugal: quasi-privatization
of a dual system of care**                                               59

ALEXANDRA LOPES

*5.1  Introduction  59*
*5.2  Historical trends in the consolidation of social care
for dependent elderly in Portugal: familism and
quasi-privatization of care  60*
*5.3  LTC in contemporary Portugal: provisions and
providers  61*
*5.4  The national network for long-term care: rehabilitation
and integration of health and social care in the new
millennium  65*
*5.5  The financials of care provision  68*
*5.6  Critical challenges for formal care provision in Portugal:
LTC staff shortage and absence of quality assessment
mechanisms  70*
*5.7  Conclusions  72*

*Contents* vii

## 6 Long-term care in Italy 75
EMMANUELE PAVOLINI, COSTANZO RANCI AND GIOVANNI LAMURA

6.1 *Introduction 75*
6.2 *Developments in long-term care policies for older people 77*
6.3 *The role of civil society in LTC delivery 80*
6.4 *Long-term care amid increasing individual needs and diminishing family capacity 81*
6.5 *A peculiar marketization: migrant care workers as the new cornerstones of the Italian LTC system 83*
6.6 *Use of rehabilitation and welfare technology 85*
6.7 *Quality measures and the quality of the Italian LTC system 88*
6.8 *Conclusions 89*

## 7 Greece: forced transformation in a deep crisis 93
PLATON TINIOS

7.1 *Introduction 93*
7.2 *The mixed system before the crisis 94*
7.3 *The crisis and the care economy 99*
7.4 *Conclusions: long-term care towards the end of the crisis 103*

## 8 Long-term care and austerity in the UK: a growing crisis 107
CAROLINE GLENDINNING

8.1 *Introduction 107*
8.2 *Long-term care: fragmented responsibilities 108*
8.3 *Recent developments in UK long-term care 109*
  8.3.1 *Personalisation and personal budgets 110*
  8.3.2 *Rehabilitation and reablement 111*
  8.3.3 *Reforming social care law and funding 112*
8.4 *Austerity policies 114*
8.5 *The impacts of austerity 116*
  8.5.1 *The impacts on long-term care services 117*
  8.5.2 *The impacts on older people 118*
  8.5.3 *Private care markets 119*
  8.5.4 *The impacts on family caregivers 119*
  8.5.5 *The impacts on care markets 120*
8.6 *Conclusions 121*

viii *Contents*

**9 Paradoxical decisions in German long-term care: expansion of benefits as a cost-containment strategy** 126

MARGITTA MÄTZKE AND TOBIAS WIß

*9.1 Introduction: the question of expansion 126*
*9.2 Design of an unwieldy long-term care system 128*
  *9.2.1 Benefits 129*
  *9.2.2 Financing 130*
  *9.2.3 Recipient rates 130*
  *9.2.4 Who cares? 132*
*9.3 Characteristics and governance structures in German long-term care 133*
  *9.3.1 The role of the market in long-term care 134*
  *9.3.2 Governance of long-term care 135*
*9.4 Recent long-term care reforms 137*
  *9.4.1 The broader concept of care 138*
  *9.4.2 Modernizing long-term care: reconciliation, monitoring quality, and promoting rehabilitation 139*
*9.5 Conclusions 139*

**10 Long-term care expenditures in Finland** 145

ISMO LINNOSMAA AND LIEN NGUYEN

*10.1 Introduction 145*
*10.2 Long-term care in Finland 146*
  *10.2.1 Long-term care and services for older people in Finland 146*
  *10.2.2 Organisation and financing of services for older people 147*
*10.3 Economic and demographic development in Finland 148*
  *10.3.1 Public sector surplus in comparison to European countries since 2008 149*
  *10.3.2 Demographic development in Finland 150*
*10.4 Expenditures on long-term care 152*
  *10.4.1 Total expenditures 152*
  *10.4.2 Expenditures on institutional care, home care and other services 155*
  *10.4.3 The share of private care 157*
*10.5 Financing of long-term care 160*
*10.6 Recent policy initiatives in Finnish long-term care 162*
*10.7 Summary and conclusions 163*

*Contents* ix

**11 Long-term care in Denmark, with an eye to the other Nordic welfare states** 168

BENT GREVE

11.1 *Introduction 168*
11.2 *Central issues 169*
11.3 *What is quality in long-term care? 171*
11.4 *Recent developments in the Nordic welfare state: an empirical focus 172*
11.5 *Development in elder-care policies: central changes 178*
11.6 *Conclusions: reformulation of welfare mix 181*

**12 Some concluding reflections** 185

BENT GREVE

12.1 *Introduction 185*
12.2 *Synthesis of development in long-term care 185*
12.3 *Trends in marketization of long-term care 188*
12.4 *Role of civil society 191*
12.5 *Austerity measures/change in financing 192*
12.6 *Rehabilitation and/or reablement: new trends 192*
12.7 *Quality measures including quality of life 193*
12.8 *Final concluding remarks 193*

*Index* 194

# Contributors

**Zofia Czepulis-Rutkowska** is a Senior Researcher in the Institute of Labour and Social Studies in Warsaw (Poland). Her research interests cover social policy institutions with a focus on pension systems and long-term care, social policy models and European social policy. She has participated in numerous comparative research projects. She has authored many publications on various aspects of social policy. Apart from her research activities, she worked for the Polish Social Insurance Institution from 2003 to 2010 as the Director of the International Co-operation Department, and in 2011 she worked for the Chancellery of the President of Poland as the director of the Social Policy Office. From 2007 to 2014, she was an expert in the Polish Senate working group preparing the law on long-term care.

**Róbert I. Gál** is a Senior Research Fellow at the Hungarian Demographic Research Institute, a Senior Extern at TARKI Social Research Institute, and an Affiliated Professor at the Corvinus University (CUB), all in Budapest. He holds his MSc in Economics from CUB and his PhD in Sociology from the University of Groningen, the Netherlands. His research interest is the regularities of lifecycle financing through intergenerational transfers. He is part of the global National Transfers Accounts project where he leads the intergenerational indicators working group. As a consultant, he has been repeatedly invited by the European Commission (as a member of the ASISP and ESPN expert networks), the International Labour Organisation as well as various government agencies and nongovernmental bodies in Hungary.

**Caroline Glendinning** is Professor Emerita, University of York (UK). Prior to retirement, Caroline had a long career of social policy-related research into disability, social gerontology, family care and adult social care. She led a large UK Department of Health-funded social care research programme at the Social Policy Research Unit, University of York, and was a founding Associate Director of the English NIHR School for Social Care Research. She also led the national evaluation of the individual budget pilot programme (IBSEN) and a large prospective study of home care reablement services. She has long-standing interests in policies, funding and organisation of long-term care in other countries. Caroline is a Trustee of the UK Thalidomide Trust. She is currently involved in

*Contributors* xi

local projects aimed at reducing social isolation among older people, and she contributes to EU social policy networks.

**Bent Greve** is Professor in Welfare State Analysis. He holds a master's degree in economics from the University of Copenhagen and a PhD and a doctoral degree in public administration from the Roskilde University (Denmark). His research on the welfare state covers areas such social security, the labour market, financing, tax expenditure, happiness and well-being. He has been the Danish expert to several European studies. He has published many books and articles, and he is currently the regional and special issues editor of *Social Policy & Administration*.

**Giovanni Lamura** works at the Department of Gerontological Research of the Italian National Research Centre on Ageing (INRCA), where he has gained experience in international research projects in the following fields: family care of the elderly, reconciliation of professional and caring responsibilities, migrant care workers, quality of life and well-being in older age, prevention of elder abuse and neglect, long-term care, and older workers. Currently he is involved in several cross-national research projects on elderly care.

**Ismo Linnosmaa** is a Professor and the Vice Director of the Centre for Health and Social Economics (CHESS) at National Institute for Health and Welfare. His research has focused on the economics of social and health care and pharmaceutical markets. His recent research has been on the cost-effectiveness of long-term care. He has managed large national and multinational research projects on the economics of social and health care and pharmaceutical markets, and he has participated in evaluations of policy reforms in social and health care in Finland.

**Alexandra Lopes** holds a PhD in social policy from the London School of Economics and currently works as a Senior Lecturer and Researcher in the Sociology Department of the University of Porto (Portugal). Her research interests and experience include the analysis of LTC systems from a comparative perspective and particularly on methods to monitor performance of LTC systems in familist settings. She has also been working on the topic of inequality in old age, with a particular focus on theoretical and methodological instruments to address poverty in old age and on theoretical developments in social class analysis in old age.

**Margitta Mätzke** is Professor at the Department of Politics and Social Policy at the Johannes Kepler University Linz (Austria). She completed her PhD in political science at Northwestern University, Evanston, Illinois (USA), and received the *venia legendi* in political science from the University of Göttingen (Germany). She currently works on comparative health and welfare state policy and has published book chapters and journal articles in the *Journal of European Social Policy, Journal of Health Politics, Policy and Law, Journal of Public Policy, Journal of Policy History, German Policy Studies, Social Politics, Social Policy & Administration*, and *Leviathan*.

xii *Contributors*

**Lien Nguyen** is a Senior Researcher at the Centre for Health and Social Economics (CHESS) belonging to the National Institute for Health and Welfare in Finland. Her research interests are economics of health and dental care, economics of smoking and public economics. Her recent research focuses on the cost-effectiveness of statin use by patients with myocardial infarction in Finland.

**Emmanuele Pavolini** is Associate Professor in Economic Sociology and Social Policy at the University of Macerata (Italy). His main field of research is welfare state policies. In particular, he has extensively published in the last 15 years in relation to elderly care and long-term care, looking at different issues from an international comparative perspective: main characteristics of different national long-term care (LTC) systems, institutional change and conciliation issues for working LTC carers, the functioning of the LTC labour market and LTC professionals, and inequalities in the access to LTC provision.

**Virginija Poškutė** is an economist and social policy analyst. Virginija acquired her academic degrees and qualifications at several educational institutions: Vilnius University (Lithuania), Roskilde University (Denmark), University of Bath (UK) and Tilburg University (The Netherlands). Virginija was Fulbright researcher at Darden Graduate School, University of Virginia (USA), and increased her academic qualifications at Harvard Business School (USA) and Fudan University, Shanghai (China). Virginija has extensive international job experience (UNDP/Lithuania; International Master's Programme "European Social Policy Analysis" by CEPS/INSTEAD, Luxembourg and Leuven University, Belgium; various projects for World Bank, UN, UNDP, European Commission) as well as experience in projects with national institutions (Ministry of Social Security and Labour, Ministry of Environment, Ministry of Economics, various NGOs) on economic and social policy issues. Currently, Virginija works for the ISM University of Management and Economics (Lithuania). Virginija's main research and teaching interests are within social policy, welfare economics, competitiveness, public and private sector integration, business ethics and corporate social responsibility.

**Costanzo Ranci** is a Full Professor in Economic Sociology at the Polytechnic of Milan, Italy. He is the Director of the Social Policy Research Unit (LPS). He has published extensively on long-term care, social inequality and welfare policy. Among his books (edited with E. Pavolini) is *Reforms in Long-Term Care in Europe: Investigating Institutional Change and Social Impacts* (Springer 2013).

**Platon Tinios** is Assistant Professor at the University of Piraeus (Greece). He studied at the Universities of Cambridge (MA, PhD) and Oxford (MPhil). He served as Special Advisor to the Prime Minister of Greece from 1996 to 2004, specialising in the economic analysis of social policy. He was a member of the EU Social Protection Committee from 2000 to 2004. His research interests include pensions, ageing populations, social policy, gender, labour economics and public finance.

*Contributors*  xiii

**Tobias Wiß** is a Postdoctoral Researcher at the Hertie School of Governance, Berlin (Germany). He received his PhD in Sociology from the University of Mannheim (Germany). His research focuses on comparative welfare state analysis and social policy, particularly pensions and family policy. He was the principal investigator of a project funded by the Austrian Science Foundation (FWF) about the politics of occupational welfare. His publications include articles in the *Journal of European Social Policy*, the *European Journal of Industrial Relations*, the *Politische Vierteljahresschrift*, and *Transfer: The European Review of Labour and Research*.

# Foreword

This book was written in an attempt to describe and analyse a latecoming area in social policy and an often neglected area in comparative welfare state analysis. Long-term care is at the same time an area with growing awareness due to demographic ageing and economic pressure in most welfare states.

Contributors to this book come from a variety of countries in Europe. Several of the contributors (from Denmark, Finland, Greece, Hungary, Lithuania, Poland and Portugal) are working together in the EU-supported Horizon 2020 project SPRINT (Social Protection Innovative Investment in Long-Term Care).[1] We acknowledge support received from this project, which has helped in writing this book. Naturally, the usual disclaimer exists that each author is responsible for his or her own work.

The book will play an important part in describing and analysing recent trends, since the financial crisis starting in 2008, in the development of long-term care. Further, it provides input to future understanding of the position of long-term care, including how and to what extent there will be a possible pressure on the welfare states due to demographic ageing.

Roskilde, May 2016
Bent Greve

## Note

1 Horizon 2020 Grant Agreement No. 649565.

# 1 Long-term care
## What is it about?

*Bent Greve*

## 1.1 Introduction

Long-term care is a rising and important issue in many contemporary welfare states around the globe given the demographic changes, expectations on size and quality of service, use of new technology in the years to come and the economic pressure on the welfare states.

This book will, for a selected group of EU-member states that covers all the classical depictions of welfare state regimes within Europe, present how welfare states organise, structure and deliver long-term care and also, albeit in a limited way, focus on whether there might be a social investment perspective in the delivery of long-term care.

This perspective is important as the demographic transitions' possible impact on public sector expenditures is often used as an argument for the (especially economic) pressure on the welfare states and a need for either direct retrenchment, increase in efficiency or at least attempts to reduce welfare state spending. The chapters in this book will look specifically into how different welfare states have focussed on long-term care (LTC) in recent years and what types of changes have taken place in the wake of the expected demographic changes and ambitions to curb increases in public sector spending in the area. The chapters will describe the development of long-term care for the elderly (mainly after the financial crisis) in different countries and also discuss the boundaries between state and civil society in the different welfare states' approaches to the delivery of care, with an eye to the private-sector ambition to provide and sell care. The distinction between state, market and civil society is also gaining importance in this field. The pressure has also raised the issue of how to ensure innovation in the area of social service (Sirovatka and Greve, 2014).

One central issue is what the individual responsibility is when elderly people are living together. Another is who takes care, and what is the implication for quality of life and labour market participation when civil society is doing the main part of the caring versus if relatives and/or friends. This will be discussed in the chapters. Has there been an increased role of families and private companies, and what might the implication be for the elderly and for society as a whole? Further, this book probes into how the welfare states use rehabilitation and welfare technology

## 2  Bent Greve

*Table 1.1* Spending on long-term care as a percentage of GDP in 2013

| Country | 2013 | Expected change 2013–2060 |
| --- | --- | --- |
| Denmark | 2.4 | 2.0 |
| Germany | 1.4 | 1.5 |
| Hungary | 0.8 | 0.4 |
| Greece | 0.5 | 0.4 |
| Italy | 1.8 | 0.9 |
| Lithuania | 1.4 | 0.9 |
| Austria | 1.4 | 1.3 |
| Poland | 0.8 | 0.9 |
| Portugal | 0.5 | 0.4 |
| Finland | 2.2 | 2.1 |
| UK | 1.2 | 0.4 |

Source: Eurostat, long-term care spending projection (http://ec.europa.eu/economy_finance/structural_reforms/ageing/health_care/index_en.htm).

to try to reduce pressure on public-sector spending in this area. Finally, the chapters discuss quality measures and how different approaches define and discuss what quality of care for the elderly means in different countries.

Chapter 12 will, using the information in the national chapters, sum up and try to depict commonalities and diversities in the development, and will include data related to selected aspects of long-term care.

At the outset, it can be seen that there are large differences in the spending on long-term care, (see Table 1.1) and differences in the projection of the development of spending.

Naturally, as the book also will show, these figures about public-sector spending do not inform about overall size, quality or actors in long-term care, where the split between state, market and civil society is important in all countries, although some countries rely more on civil society (especially the family) as a central and core provider of care. The data for the reference scenario are a clear indication that long-term care due to demographic changes, new technologies and continued expectations for better-quality long-term care will be important social policy areas in the years to come.

## 1.2  What is long-term care and the quest for quality?

Long-term care is a relative newcomer to the area of social policy. This is partly because historically care was provided by families and also because life expectancy (and hence more years outside the labour market) has increased over the last 50 to 60 years. This, combined with changes in family structure, has resulted in earlier access to informal care support for some. Looking for quality long-term care has therefore become more important (OECD, 2013). Although defining quality in health care might be possible (moving from sick to cured), this is more difficult in the area of long-term care. Long-term care involves assistance with

*Long-term care: what is it about?* 3

daily living, given that the ability to take care of ordinary daily tasks decreases over time. Long-term care also involves human contact and ensuring the best life possible for the individual. In many countries, long-term care has been and still is mainly an issue within the health care system. To put it simply, unless they are hospitalised due to illness, elderly people will largely have to take care of themselves with help from family and friends. This distinction between health care and long-term care is also one of the reasons why there is little comparative data in the area.

Having a good life is an old quest. However, with the change in family structure and longer life expectancy, this implies a risk that more elderly people will have fewer relatives to take care of them. This especially seems to be the case for women, given that they live longer than men. In the cases of couples living together, this means that men are more likely to have someone to care for them than are women.

Quality of care elements can include the following:

*   Effectiveness and care safety
*   Patient-centeredness and responsiveness
*   Care co-ordination

The many and varied approaches to measuring quality also imply that no common agreement can be found. For recent discussions, see Mot et al. (2012) and OECD (2013); see also Chapter 12. This lack of a common understanding of what quality is implies difficulties in measuring and analysing the impact of ongoing changes in long-term care and in evaluating long-term care (Rodrigues, 2017). Many elderly people want to stay in their own homes rather than in institutional care (Leichsenring, Billings and Henk, 2013). This also implies that support to the elderly will still be very different, given historical traditions in the different countries. Supporting the individual's ability to live at home as long as possible is a central aspect of quality of care; there is, however, a risk of individuals being lonely in this situation.

The mix between different actors involved in long-term care is a good reason also to look into state, market and civil societies' involvement in the financing and delivery of long-term care (Daly, 2012).

## 1.3 Overview of the book

The choice of countries in the book reflects classical analysis of welfare state clustering (Castle et al., 2010; Greve, 2013). It also reflects an ambition to cover the different geographical areas of Europe and the historical and current approaches to long-term care in selected welfare states. The following countries are included in the chapters:

Nordic welfare state model: Denmark and Finland
Central European model: Germany
Liberal model: UK

4   *Bent Greve*

Southern Europe: Greece, Italy and Portugal
Eastern Europe: Hungary, Lithuania and Poland.

The choice of countries examined in the book, with the exception of one country from the liberal model and the continental welfare state model, ensures a variety within the different welfare state models and a clear deviation between countries in historical and geographical positions to the provision of long-term care. Naturally, one can question whether Eastern Europe forms a specific cluster or it should be split among the other clusters given the development over the last 30 years. For the sake of simplicity, the choice has been to use this distinction among countries, but at the same time be open to the possibility of having three very different Eastern European countries depicted in the study. In the concluding chapter, similarities and varieties will be analysed.

Hungary, one country from the former Eastern European group of welfare states, is presented in Chapter (2) (by Gal). Long-term care seems to be of low priority compared to other central issues for the elderly, such as pensions. In the wake of the financial crisis, there has been a tightening of the conditions for receipt of long-term care. There is a strong expectation that the care will mainly be provided by members of the civil society, but here, as in the other welfare states, this has a disproportionately negative impact on the women's lives because they are usually doing the informal care.

Lithuania, one of the Baltic countries in Eastern Europe, is described in Chapter 3 (by Poskute). Lithuania has a strong growth in the number of dependent elderly, which implies a strong pressure on the long-term care system. Despite this, long-term care is not recognised as a separate social policy provision; there is some support, however, and there is an expectation that the elderly stay in their own homes as long as possible. There is also some institutional support for the very frail elderly. Due to the very fragmented approach, there is no clear knowledge of the level of spending on long-term care. The use of welfare technology is still in its infancy.

In Poland (Chapter 4 by Rutkowska), there is no clear definition of what long-term care is. The blurred boundaries between health and long-term care are an issue in Poland; here, members of civil society and migrant workers (for those who can afford to pay them) are used in the provision of long-term care. Thus, the official long-term care is limited and state involvement is fragmented; in addition, the boundaries to health care imply that for some in need of care, health care provision is the main possibility. The fragmented development also implies that welfare technology has limited implementation.

Portugal, an example of the Southern European welfare state model, is depicted in Chapter 5 (by Lopes). This chapter shows that there has been a rapid development of long-term care in Portugal, including higher coverage in formal care and a mixed system, in which the nonprofit sector is a strong actor in the provision of long-term care. This system, as in some other countries, is trying to integrate health and care while focussing on the role of the family. A combination of state financing and delivery from various actors are also characteristics of the system.

*Long-term care: what is it about?* 5

In Italy, which is analysed in Chapter 6 (by Pavolini, Ranci and Lamura), coverage is similar to that in Eastern European countries, but with a catching up towards continental welfare states' levels of provision. Here there is also a problem in defining when and to what extent individuals need public support and care and when the care can be done by the civil society. This is partly supported by individual cash allowances, but there is also an increased focus on market provision and migrants delivering care. Thus, a strong marketization is not the approach in Italy; instead there is adaptation of an informal based-family model.

Greece, another Southern European welfare state (Chapter 7 by Tinios), is an example in which the family plays the central role; for those without close family or friends, it might be difficult to get the care needed. The attempt to introduce a decentralised system of formal long-term care in the 2000s never had credible source of funding; as a result, the attempt was interrupted by the fiscal crisis. Greece also presents a case of retrenchment and cuts in the wake of the fiscal crisis, and inequality in access has probably widened, including differences in level of care dependent on geographic location.

In the liberal welfare state model of the UK, as analysed in Chapter 8 (by Glendinning), explicit austerity policies have led to major cuts in public spending that have increasingly impacted funding for, and the provision of, social care. Political devolution, both within and between countries in the UK, means the effects of these cuts are far from uniform; however, their impacts are probably most acutely felt in England. More and more care responsibilities are left to families, and people who need care (and their families) are under increased pressure to pay for care from their own private resources. The decline in public funding is also affecting the stability and quality of formal care services, with care providers struggling to meet minimum standards (including a new legal minimum wage requirement that affects many care workers). Meanwhile, new devolved funding responsibilities are likely to further increase variations between individual local authorities and hence widen geographic inequalities in access to publicly funded care.

Germany is presented in Chapter 9 (by Mätzke and Wiß). This chapter examines a latecomer in the long-term care system and also a paradoxical development including both retrenchment and a broadening of the scope of long-term care. Within residential care there are substantial user charges, implying inequality in access to care for the elderly. At the same time, there is a stronger focus in home-based care that the elderly should stay in their own homes longer.

Finland, discussed in Chapter 10 (by Linnosmaa and Nguyen), is a story about expansion of LTC provision until the financial crisis in 2008 and then overall retrenchment when taking the increase in the number of elderly into consideration. Finland has a lot of support from the informal sector and people are encouraged to live in their own homes as long as possible. The chapter also contains some information related to the other Nordic countries, including the increasing old-age dependency rate.

Denmark, as well as some information on other Nordic welfare states, is presented in Chapter 11 (by Greve). The chapter depicts the development of long-term

6    *Bent Greve*

care in Denmark, showing that two central issues have been at stake. One issue is an increased focus on the elderly living as long as possible in their own homes; another issue is a tendency towards marketization of care. Civil society still has a central role, but the use of rehabilitation, reablement and welfare technology are prominent features of the development.

Chapter 12 (by Greve) provides a comparative analysis of the countries presented in the book with the aim of looking for commonalities both from systemic and development perspectives. The chapter shows, for example, that there are strong differences in the use of marketization of long-term care, but there are also differences in retrenchment and in some countries no real retrenchment. Further, the ambition that elderly should have the option to stay in their own homes as long as possible, with the necessary support, is common among the countries. Finally, the chapter illustrates that use of informal care varies, as does the degree of use of welfare technology or ways of thinking about the possible impact of social investment in the field.

## 1.4  Delimitations

Given the size of the book, there are limitations in its scope and breadth. For example, the book does not try to present good examples of care, as this would require a framework where one could define what is a high level of quality and how has it been achieved. As the focus mainly is on long-term care for the elderly, issues of disability are only touched upon; see instead Gori and Wittenberg (2016).

Further, the book provides a limited look into good governance of long-term care and the different institutional structures in the welfare states; also discussed are the ways that welfare states have structured their responsibilities such that different, often local, actors are involved in decision making with regard to long-term care.

The possible impact on labour market participation (particularly for women) as a result of the lack of care is given only limited coverage.

## References

Castles, F.G., Leibfried, S., Lewis, J., Obinger, H. and Pierson, C. (eds) (2010), *The Oxford Handbook of the Welfare State*, Oxford: Oxford University Press.

Daly, M. (2012), Making policy for care: Experience in Europe and its implications in Asia, *International Journal of Sociology and Social Policy* 32(11/12): 623–635.

Gori, C. and Wittenberg, R. (eds) (2016), *Long-Term Care Reforms in OECD Countries: Successes and Failures*, Bristol: Policy Press.

Greve, B. (ed) (2013), *The Routledge Handbook of the Welfare State*, Oxon: Routledge.

Leichsenring, K., Billings, J. and Henk, N. (2013), Improving policy and practice in long-term care. In K. Leichenring, J. Billings, and N. Henk (eds) *Long-Term Care in Europe: Improving Policy and Practice*, Houndmills: Palgrave Macmillan, pp. 325–336.

Mot, E., Faber, R., Geerts, J. and Willeme, P. (eds) (2012), *Performance of long-term care systems in Europe*, Enepri Research Report no. 117, http://www.ancien-longtermcare. eu/sites/default/files/ENEPRI%20RR117%20_ANCIEN_%20Evaluation%20Final%20 Report.pdf).

OECD. (2013), *A Good Life in Old Age? Monitoring and Improving Quality in Long-Term Care*, *OECD Health Policy Studies*, Paris: OECD.

Rodrigues, R. (2017), Evaluating long-term care policies: Challenges and advancements. In B. Greve (ed) *Handbook of Social Policy Evaluation*, Cheltenham: Edward Elgar.

Sirovatka, T. and Greve, B. (2014), *Innovation in Social Services: The Public-Private Mix in Service Provision, Fiscal Policy and Employment*, Surrey: Ashgate.

# 2 Long-term care for the elderly in Hungary

*Róbert I. Gál*

## 2.1 Introduction

In sharp contrast with pensions, long-term care for the elderly is a low-priority sphere of public policy in Hungary that hardly receives attention or ignites debates. By tradition, growing old and becoming dependent is more a family than a social affair. This is reflected in the limited availability of public long-term care services, scarcity of related research and lack of relevant data. Despite this, the sector has seen a rapid expansion of home-based services since the start of the economic crisis.

The chapter starts with a brief overview of the LTC system (section 2.2). In section 2.3, I describe the process of becoming old. Section 2.4 gives a general description of both the demand and the supply sides. Section 2.5 contains projections. Section 2.6 concludes the chapter.

## 2.2 Overview of the long-term care system

Until recently, the Hungarian LTC system still bore the marks of central planning that was in effect in the country between 1950 and 1990. The organisational logic of the planner dictates centralisation (for it is easier to control fewer institutions); a preference for institutionalised care to managing personal networks (such as home-based care); and a kind of organisational blindness that does not notice needs beyond its sphere of operations. The consequence, as in other fields of activities, is a dual structure: a centralised system of institutions and a wide range of household activities by which people adjust to the situation. This structure is still recognisable, although it has changed due to the entrance of new providers (in particular charities) and, since the start of the economic crisis, a rapid expansion of home care.

Universal coverage, based on the principle of social equity, is an expressed policy goal of the Hungarian LTC system. Until 2008, age was the only prerequisite for entitlement. Anybody who was 62 years old, the retirement age at the time, was entitled. No means test was required and the extent of lost physical or mental capabilities was not checked. Personal insurance history was not controlled until 2006. Although the Health Insurance Fund (HIF) established personal health accounts in 2007, it was not meant to restrict entitlement but to increase revenues from the active-aged population. As a major change, in 2008 an eligibility test was introduced that evaluates the physical and social conditions of applicants. Conditions of the test were significantly tightened in 2015.

The country has no separate institutional structure for LTC in old age. LTC services are administered in the health care system and the social care system. Each branch has its own legislation, financing mechanism and services. They maintain parallel institutional networks both in institutional care and home care. Coordination between them is still weak despite some minor improvements over the last years due to the contraction of the health care and social affairs portfolios into one authority, the Ministry of Human Capacities (MHC).

The LTC system does not offer benefits for recipients to ease access to services. There is only one type of social allowance for relatives who provide for a disabled family member. All other expenses finance in-kind services. Generally speaking, the financial system of public LTC subsidises supply. Services are funded directly, and those in need of care do not get cash grants to buy services. Private insurance schemes are not involved. Operational costs are financed by the HIF for health care and the government, or local governments for social care. In addition, care providers may charge user fees.

Services provided through health care are nursing care in nursing departments of hospitals and home nursing care; the three main types of services in social care are home care (including meals-on-wheels services), day care and residential care. There are more than 50,000 authorised places for institutional care; these are all nearly full.

Most LTC activities are left to households or an informal market. Empirical evidence suggests that familial relations play an important role in long-term care for the elderly in Hungary (see the discussion of households for long-term care in section 2.4.4).

## 2.3 Being old

Available administrative data currently do not allow for a longitudinal analysis at the individual level or by cohort, and Hungary has no panel survey data on ageing. This makes it difficult to describe the process of growing old. The brief description here is cross-sectional. I will show four instances of what it means to be old at various ages. I will present period data on self-perceived health by age group in a European comparison; health status above various age limits; time transfers; and the rate of institutionalised population.

In every older age group, Hungarians report significantly poorer health than their European contemporaries. Nearly as many Hungarians complain about bad or very bad health among the 65- to 74-year-olds as in the 85 and older age group in the EU. In the EU, about one quarter of respondents still enjoy good or very good health among the oldest old; the corresponding Hungarian rate is a mere 5%. The rate of respondents reporting bad or very bad health grew from one third among the 65- to 74-year-olds to about one half in the in the same age group and to 57% among the oldest old (see Table 2.1).

10   *Róbert I. Gál*

*Table 2.1* Self-perceived health status in Hungary compared to the EU, 2013

| | EU28 | | | Hungary | | |
|---|---|---|---|---|---|---|
| | *65–74* | *75–84* | *85+* | *65–74* | *75–84* | *85+* |
| Self-perceived health (hlth_silc_01) | | | | | | |
| *Very good or good* | 45 | 30 | 23 | 16 | 9 | 5 |
| *Bad or very bad* | 17 | 28 | 37 | 33 | 48 | 57 |

Source: Eurostat. The code in parentheses is the Eurostat code for the question in EU-SILC.

*Table 2.2* Limitations due to health conditions

| | *65+* | *75+* | *85+* |
|---|---|---|---|
| Physical and sensory functional limitations (hlth_ehis_st9), 2008 | | | |
| Severe | 59 | 71 | 77 |
| Some or severe | 85 | 92 | 91 |
| Self-perceived long-standing limitations in usual activities due to health problems (hlth_silc_06), 2013 | | | |
| Severe | 22 | 30 | 43 |
| Some or severe | 63 | 74 | 84 |

Source: Calculations are based on the European Health Interview Survey (EHIS) wave 1 and the EU Survey on Income and Living Conditions (EU-SILC) wave 2013 (both by Eurostat). Codes in parentheses are Eurostat codes for the respective questions.

I combine Eurostat data on age groups above selected age limits in Table 2.2. In 2008, the large majority of people above the age of 65 (85%) faced some physical or sensory functional limitations. For 59% of them it proved to be severe. In the 85 and older age group, only 1 in 10 had no such limitations whatsoever, and about three quarters complained about severe functional constraints. In 2013, poor health created severe limitations in usual activities for 22% of those 65 years old and older. When narrowing down to the 85 and older age group, the corresponding rate is twice as high.

Declining health results in dependence and the need for care. Next I present two snapshots of the elderly receiving help while living at home or with family members or in institutions. In Figure 2.1, I present net time transfers by age. Time transfers are calculated from time use surveys. Time use surveys give an opportunity to identify activities of unpaid household labour and assign the services and goods produced by such labour to their consumer in the family. This information allows for drawing per capita age profiles of both consumption and production of unpaid household labour. In Figure 2.1, the two curves are netted out by deducing production from consumption. The resulting net values are called *net time transfers* because the non-zero values of the goods and services are provided by or for someone else of different age (Donehower, 2011). In the Hungarian context, net time transfers are almost exclusively intrafamilial and overwhelmingly take place within the household.[1]

Time transfers are provided and received between partners in retired households, but that hardly shows up in the figure because the age difference between the partners is small. Figure 2.1 focuses on intergenerational time transfers.

*Long-term care in Hungary* 11

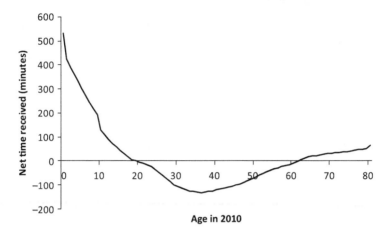

*Figure 2.1* Per capita net time transfers in minutes by age, 2010
Source: *Gál, Szabó and Vargha (forthcoming)*.
Note: Net time transfers are unpaid household labour consumed minus unpaid household labour produced.

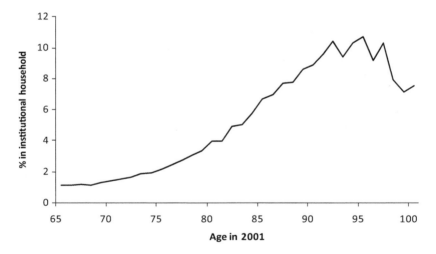

*Figure 2.2* Rate of population living in institutions by age, 2001
Source: Eurostat.

Accordingly, people become net receivers of time above the age of 62. At the age of 80 or beyond, the elderly receive more than 1 hour a day in net terms in the form of intrafamilial help.

More severe dependence results in institutionalisation. In Figure 2.2, I present the share of the population living in institutions by age. The curve starts at the age of 65 with 1%. This grows to around 10% among people in their mid-90s.

## 12 Róbert I. Gál

## 2.4 Demand and supply

Increasing limitations due to poor health create the need for help. In this section, I briefly describe the public long-term care system: the rules of eligibility, the extent of demand, the available benefits and services and the actual supply of public care.

### 2.4.1 Eligibility

There exists no national definition for the need of care. In 2008, an assessment process was introduced; however, this applies only to home care and institutional care but not to other segments of social care (such as meal provision) or health care.

The assessment process is initiated by the general practitioner and carried out by an expert committee appointed by the local notary, in the case of home care, or the expert committee of the National Institute for Rehabilitation and Welfare Affairs (*Országos Rehabilitációs és Szociális Szakértői Intézet*), in the case of institutional care. The criteria are national standards and they are binding but, as previously mentioned, they apply only to a segment of social care and not at all to health care. Eligibility for health care is insurance-based in principle, but it is nearly universal. In practice, almost every citizen holds the social insurance card, which is the condition for access to health care.

Since 2008, eligibility for institutional care has been restricted to those who need care for more than 4 hours per day. Need is established by a complex assessment process. Applicants are evaluated in 14 various activities, such as independence in daily activities (eating, bathing, dressing, toilet use, continence); self-reliance (dealing with household utilities and money, following therapy); walking; changing position; mental functions (orientation in space and time, communication, proper and reliable behaviour); eyesight; and hearing. Abilities are measured on a 0-to-4 scale and an algorithm translates the resulting values to time. The rules distinguish between help and personal care. A client is eligible for help if the score is 20 or higher or if the score is below 20 but the person meets some other conditions (such as various combinations of age and living conditions like living alone or living in dwellings with poor infrastructures). Help is complemented with care depending on the prevalence of certain combinations of age, health and living conditions. Personal care is provided only to people with an eligibility score of 20 or higher.

The first wave of restrictions diminished utilization by about 10% among new applicants in 2008. Access was further curbed by a recent modification (in effect since 2015) in the algorithm that converts needs to care time in the range giving access to home care. Only new applicants are affected; established eligibilities are not withdrawn. The effects are yet to be known at the time of writing this chapter. It is safe to say that even if the new measures prove to be strongly restrictive, the number of recipients will stay well above the level of less than a decade ago due to rapid expansion of home care. I will return to this process later.

As for health care, eligibility is universal.

### 2.4.2 Assessment of needs

Limitations in activities of daily living (ADL) or instrumental activities of daily living (IADL) can be estimated from the annual income survey of the Central Statistical Office (CSO), which is part of the EU-SILC comparative survey, and the Hungarian leg of the European Health Interview Survey (EHIS). The first wave of EHIS was conducted in 2009 in Hungary, and it reflected health conditions prevalent in 2008. The second wave was conducted in 2014. Only preliminary data from the latter had been published at the time of writing.

In total, 38% of the respondents aged 65 and older reported limitations in personal care activities in the first wave of EHIS (see Table 2.3). This is about 620,000 people. Household activities created problems for 48% in 2008 (780,000 persons). By the second wave of EHIS, the 38% share of ADL limitations decreased to 29% (CSO, 2015a), which is about 500,000 people. As expected, the frequencies are higher in older age groups: in the 85 and older age group, 55% are limited in personal care and 77% are limited in household activities. Severe limitations in personal care affected about 220,000 people (14% of the 65 and older age group); in household activities, the corresponding number was about 510,000 (31%). Based on different definitions, sources and estimation methods, projections of the 2009 and 2015 Ageing Reports (EC, 2015) were based on 594,000 and 788,000 dependents, respectively.

In light of the reach of the long-term care system (see section 2.4.4), these figures reflect significant unmet needs.

### 2.4.3 Available benefits and services

The nursing allowance (*ápolási díj*) is a social allowance; applications, based on the expert opinion of the general practitioner (GP) are evaluated by the local authority. The nursing allowance can also be claimed by relatives who are caring for a severely disabled or a permanently ill family member who is aged 18 or younger. That is, the nursing allowance is not specifically targeted to long-term care of the elderly. Depending on the health condition of the care recipient, the nursing allowance can be paid in increased amount (*emelt összegű ápolási díj*) or,

*Table 2.3* Limitations in daily activities in old age, 2008

|  | 65+ | 75+ | 85+ |
|---|---|---|---|
| Limitations in personal care activities (hlth_ehis_st10) | | | |
| Severe | 14 | 22 | 31 |
| Some or severe | 38 | 50 | 55 |
| Limitations in household activities (hlth_ehis_st11) | | | |
| Severe | 31 | 47 | 65 |
| Some or severe | 48 | 65 | 77 |

Source: Calculations are based on the European Health Interview Survey (EHIS) wave 1 (Eurostat). Codes in parentheses are Eurostat codes for the respective questions.

14    *Róbert I. Gál*

since 2014, as an extra nursing allowance (*kiemelt ápolási díj*). The amount of the new benefit is HUF 53,100, about €175, a month, which is 180% of the standard nursing allowance (HUF 29,500, about €95).

Social care services have three categories: basic services, institutions that provide daytime care and institutions that provide residential (long-term and temporary) care. Basic services are home care (*házi segítségnyújtás*) and social catering (*szociális étkeztetés*). Local authorities are obliged to provide home care and meals for those who need assistance at home in their everyday lives due to age, disability or poor health. Institutions that provide daytime care, such as clubs for the elderly (*idősek klubja*), aim to serve as a daytime substitute for family care by providing opportunities for the elderly to meet others, have meals and meet their health and hygienic needs, as well as to guard against loneliness. These clubs provide meals, various services and leisure activities for those who live in their own homes but cannot fully look after themselves.

Institutions for residential care (*időskorúak otthona, idősek gondozóháza*), mostly long term but occasionally temporary, are established for those who are not able to look after themselves or who need permanent help. Residential care centres serve meals three times a day, give clothes (if needed) and provide mental and physical health care.

Health care services have two main types: nursing care in nursing departments of hospitals and home nursing care. Most hospitals have some nursing beds for those who are in need of long-term nursing. These services include help in stabilising and improving health conditions, prevention of diseases and alleviation of pain, and preparation of relatives for participation in home care.

### 2.4.4 Supply of public care

Previous efforts to improve cooperation between health and social care in LTC have produced only preliminary results (SAO, 2008). The predecessor of the Ministry of Human Capacities launched a project called Homogenous Care Categories; its explicit aim was to survey nursing activity in residential homes and social care in hospitals in order to map the boundaries of social care and health care. Another project, the Integrated Social and Health Care System (ISZER by its Hungarian acronym), was initiated with the objective of maintaining and promoting the independence of older people and the optimal utilization of community, hospital and institutional resources by coordinating services. Key figures of coverage and other background information are presented separately for health care and social care in Table 2.4. In order to capture the effects of the economic crisis, I compare data for 2008 and 2014.

Table 2.4 reflects unmet needs. About 7% of the population aged 65 years and older received either home nursing care (2.19%) or home care (2.56%) or residential care (2.69%) in 2008. Against this share, the Hungarian sample of EHIS found 38% of the population aged 65 and older faced some degree of limitation in activities in their daily lives, and 48% had limitations in household activities, as shown in Table 2.3. Even simpler and cheaper services, such as meal provision or

*Table 2.4* Summary statistics of the long-term care system, 2008 and 2014

| | 2008 | 2014 | 2008 | 2008 | 2014 | 2014 |
| --- | --- | --- | --- | --- | --- | --- |
| | Total inhabitants | | Per 1,000 | Per 1,000 65+ | Per 1,000 | Per 1,000 65+ |
| **Health care** | | | | | | |
| Acute wards | 44,376 | 42,335 | 4.4 | | 4.3 | |
| Number of which are acute psychiatry | 2,894 | 2,905 | 0.3 | | 0.3 | |
| Chronic beds | 27,064 | 26,747 | 2.7 | | 2.7 | |
| Number of which are lasting care | 2,556 | 2,735 | | 1.6 | | 1.6 |
| Home nursing care patients | 52,053 | 63,820 | 5.2 | | 6.5 | |
| Number of which are 65+ | 35,601 | 46,499 | 3.5 | 21.9 | 4.7 | 26.8 |
| **Social care** | | | | | | |
| *In kind* | | | | | | |
| Recipients of home care | 48,120 | 132,985 | | 25.6 | | 63.5 |
| Home care nurses, total | 6,815 | 14,946 | | 4.2 | | 8.6 |
| Recipients of meals-on-wheels services | 107,803 | 171,998 | | 44.6 | | 69.8 |
| Recipients of alarm system-based assistance | 38,091 | 22,877 | | 21.2 | | 12.8 |
| Attendees of day care for elderly | 37,964 | 39,194 | | 16.4 | | 16.8 |
| Number of elderly homes | 969 | 1,008 | | | | |
| Residents in elderly homes | 49,894 | 53,540 | | 26.9 | | 27.6 |
| Unit cost of residential care (percentage of per capita GDP) | 26.0 | 20.0 | | | | |
| Unit cost of home care (percentage of per capita GDP) | 7.1 | 4.4 | | | | |
| *In cash* | | | | | | |
| Recipients of nursing allowance | 53,347 | 62,972 | 5.3 | | 6.4 | |
| Total spending on nursing allowance (percentage of GDP) | 0.06 | 0.08 | | | | |
| Nursing allowance per recipient (percentage of per capita GDP) | 1.0 | 1.0 | | | | |

Source: CSO (2009a, 2009b, 2015b, 2015c).

16  *Róbert I. Gál*

an alarm system-based assistance reached only 4.46% and 2.12%, respectively, of the reference population. The rest either had to pay full price for such services or get help from family, or their needs remained unmet.

Importantly, Table 2.4 hides a gender gap. In Table 2.5, I compare needs and access to public services and to spousal care by gender. Dependency rates are higher among women than among men both in terms of ADL and IADL in almost all older age groups. The female-to-male ratio is even higher in the take-up rates. Older women receive public care more frequently in every age group and type of service than men. However, women are more likely to live alone without access to spousal care. Among those aged 60 years and older, about three quarters of men but only about one third of women are married. In the 80 years and older age group, the male marriage rate is nearly six times the rate for females. So despite their higher coverage of public services, women are more likely to be left to rely on themselves or their families. It seems to be particularly pressing among the oldest people.

Total public spending on residential care decreased between 2008 and 2014 in real terms. Whereas number of residents in homes for the elderly increased from 50,000 to 53,500 (only about 7%), the unit cost of residential care lost about one quarter of its real value (see Figure 2.3). In order to top up their budget care, providers may charge user fees. Such fees depend on the cost of care and the assets of users. The exact amounts vary from service to service. Algorithms of the calculation are given by regulation, taking the user's personal income into account. Real estate assets are also part of the income calculation, but other types of assets are not. The availability of informal family carers is not taken into account. The maximum fee is 80% of monthly income for residential care and 50% for rehabilitative care. In addition, since 2015, providers of residential care can also charge an admission fee for new users. Its maximum amount is HUF 8 million (about €26,000). At least half of the places in a residential care centre must be free of admission fee.

*Table 2.5* Needs, access to public services and spousal care by gender and age, 2008

|  | *60–69* | *70–79* | *80+* |
|---|---|---|---|
| **Care needs, female/male** | | | |
| ADL | 1.29 | 1.36 | 1.47 |
| IADL | 0.94 | 1.16 | 1.16 |
| **Public care female/male** | | | |
| Domestic care | 2.37 | 3.15 | 3.37 |
| Social catering | 1.36 | 2.00 | 2.47 |
| Alarm system-based home assistance | 2.80 | 3.50 | 3.40 |
| Day care for the elderly | 2.19 | 2.66 | 2.64 |
| **Access to spousal care, male/female** | | | |
| Marriage rate | 1.42 | 2.35 | 5.70 |

Source: Author's calculation from CSO (2009b, 2013) and Czibere and Gál (2013, Tables 2 and 3).

Long-term care in Hungary  17

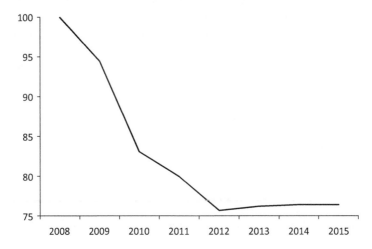

*Figure 2.3* Unit cost of residential care in real terms (2008 = 100)
Source: Calculation is based on legislation.

*Table 2.6* Dynamics of home-based care, 2008–2014 (2008 = 100)

|  | 2008 | 2009 | 2010 | 2011 | 2012 | 2013 | 2014 |
|---|---|---|---|---|---|---|---|
| Recipient of home nursing care, 65+ population | 100 | 97 | 99 | 106 | 110 | 121 | 131 |
| Recipients of home care | 100 | 132 | 156 | 183 | 260 | 274 | 276 |
| Nurses in home care | 100 | 138 | 156 | 176 | 240 | 203 | 219 |
| Recipients of meals-on-wheels services | 100 | 116 | 136 | 144 | 153 | 158 | 160 |

Source: CSO (2015b, 2015c).

Table 2.4 reveals a rapid shift in the institutional structure. The importance of home care increased rapidly over years since the economic crisis started. Whereas residential capacities remained practically unchanged, as shown previously, the number of home care recipients grew more than 2.7 times and meals-on-wheels services grew about 1.6 times by 2014 compared to their respective levels in 2008 (see Table 2.6; absolute figures are given in Table 2.4). Even coverage by the most expensive of such services, home nursing care, increased by 30% over the same period.

In order to contain the costs of expansion, the government reduced the per capita quota in 2013 (see later) and raised the eligibility criteria for new care recipients in 2015. The rapid increase in personnel also halted, although the drop in the number of nurses in home care (third row in Table 2.6) is partly due to a change in statistical definitions.

Unit costs of both residential and home care are low compared to Europe. In 2013, the method of calculation for the financial support of residential care changed. Instead of the per resident quota in effect until 2012, the government regulates the average wage of carers in residential homes. By applying further rules on the number of residents per carer and applying special multipliers for the difficulty of care (1.0 for regular elderly homes, 1.18 for dementia care and 1.19 for special elderly care), the normative support per resident can be calculated. Accordingly, the quota for regular care is HUF 651,510 per annum, unchanged since 2013 (currently about €2,100). The corresponding figure is HUF 145,000 (€470 or about 4% of per capita GDP) for home care, which was cut back from 166,080 (currently about €575) in 2012.

The expansion of coverage coincided with tensions in the labour market. As shown in Figure 2.4, the availability of home-based care increased faster in small settlements. In 2014, access to home care for people 65 years old and older averaged 7% (see Table 2.4). This hides 20% in small villages and 2% in Budapest. The relationship is more or less monotonous. Mid-size and larger towns (above 50,000 inhabitants) have somewhat denser service networks than smaller towns.

The two curves of Figure 2.4 reveal that the increase in the availability of long-term care is negatively related to the availability of jobs. The association suggests a connection between the increase in the availability of home-based care and the availability of jobs. Demand for labour is lower in smaller settlements, but home care is more easily available. As it seems, public long-term care is as much a job

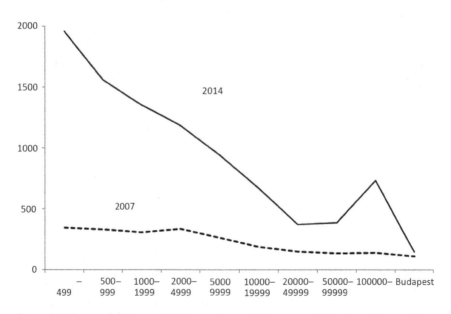

*Figure 2.4* Care recipients per 10,000 people aged 65 years and older by settlement size, 2007 and 2014

Source: CSO (2008, 2015c).

*Long-term care in Hungary* 19

opportunity as a relief for households and a resource that would increase labour force participation of relatives.

The bulk of care for the elderly is left to households or an informal market. Empirical evidence shows that familial relations play an important role in care for the elderly in Hungary. The 2012 wave of the European Quality of Life Survey (EQLS12) found that over 88% of respondents aged 65 and older said they would turn to a family member to get support if they needed help around the house when falling ill (see Table 2.7). This rate was the third highest among member states, higher than in the group of former socialist member states (81%) or the EU as a whole (76%). In contrast, Hungarians do not report turning to institutions at all (the corresponding rate is 9% in the EU and 15% in the three Nordic member states). Yet, the lack of use of institutions (or distrust of the people therein) does not mean the elderly are particularly isolated; the rate of those saying they had nobody to turn to was fairly low, 1.5%, the seventh lowest among member states.

Another piece of evidence pointing to the same direction is the 4th wave of SHARE (Survey of Health, Ageing and Retirement in Europe), which included Hungary. Analysing the survey Stoeckel and Litwin (2013) found that Hungarian elderly are by far the most likely to mention their children among their confidants they can rely on and second most likely, behind their Austrian fellows, to name their spouses.

### 2.4.5 Informal market for long-term care services

There is ample anecdotal evidence of a large grey are of elderly care between public services and familial care. People in need or their families buy services on an informal market, which is mostly out of sight of the authorities, is unregulated and tax evading, and is not supported by long-term care insurance.

Within the framework of the ANCIEN project (http://www.ancien-longtermcare.eu) Dandi et al. (2012) found that the Hungarian quality assessment system is based on input and process definitions and indicators in formal care. This puts the country in a group with Austria, Finland and Spain in contrast to systems, which are based on output indicators or have no quality assessment at all. The informal market for care, however, is largely unregulated and left unassessed.

*Table 2.7* From whom would you get support if you needed help around the house when ill? Responses from the 65 and older age group

|  | HU | HU rank | NMS11 | EU28 |
|---|---|---|---|---|
| A family member | 88 | Third highest | 81 | 76 |
| A service provider, institution or organisation | 0 | Lowest | 3 | 9 |
| Nobody | 1.5 | Seventh lowest | 2.6 | 2.0 |

Source: Eurofound (2015, Yl11_Q35a).

Notes: HU rank: Hungary's position in the rank order of member states. NMS11: BG, CZ, EE, HR, HU, LV, LT, PL, RO, SI, SK.

## 2.5 Projections

In Table 2.8, I show the key age-dependency rates in order to demonstrate the demography of the ageing process. It reveals a slow ageing through the second half of the 20th century, which will accelerate in the decades to come. Between 1960 and 2010, the population aged over 65 years nearly doubled from 0.9 million to 1.7 million. This age group grew much faster than the rest of the population. Over the same period, the population aged 19 and younger decreased sharply from 3.3 million to 2.1 million.

The baby-boom cohorts, born between 1953 and 1956, will reach the age of 65 between 2018 and 2021. Their children, who reached their peak number between 1974 and 1978, will follow between 2039 and 2043. By 2060, the total number of people above the age of 65 is expected to grow by more than 50% to over 2.6 million, which will account for one third of the total population.

The number of the oldest old (the 80 and older population) grew from 0.1 million (1%) in 1960 to 0.4 million (4%) in 2010. Projections indicate a significant increase up to 15% by 2060. The share of the oldest people increased not only in proportion to the total population but also among the elderly (65 and older), from 12% (1960) to about 25% (2010); it is expected to grow further to nearly half by 2060.

Ageing will inevitably add to the burden of old-age care. In the recent Ageing Report (EC, 2015) the European Commission expected an increase of 22.9% in the number of dependent old, which fluctuates between 10.5% and 36.4% depending on the underlying assumptions. The same projection predicts public LTC spending to grow from 0.8% of GDP in 2013[2] to 1.2% in 2060 (see Table 2.9). Under various demographic scenarios, the projected figure varies between 1.0% and 1.3%. If, everything else remaining unchanged, there is a gradual increase in the share of the disabled population receiving formal care (shift to formal care scenario), the expected spending in 2060 would be 1.9% of GDP. If the probability of receiving any kind of formal care catches up to the level of the EU28, average expenditures would grow to 3.5% of GDP, and if this convergence is combined with the convergence of costs to the European average public, LTC would consume 5.5% of the economic output.

*Table 2.8* Various age-dependency rates, 1960–2060

|                                 | *1960* | *2010* | *2060* |
| ------------------------------- | ------ | ------ | ------ |
| Younger than 19/total           | 33     | 21     | 18     |
| 20–64/total                     | 58     | 63     | 49     |
| 65+/total                       | 9      | 17     | 33     |
| 65+/20–64                       | 15     | 27     | 67     |
| 80+/total                       | 1      | 4      | 15     |
| 80+/65+                         | 12     | 24     | 46     |
| Total population (in millions)  | 10.0   | 10.0   | 7.9    |

Source: Population projection by HDRI (2015).

*Table 2.9* Projected public long-term care expenditure, percentage of GDP

|  | 2013 | 2060 |
| --- | --- | --- |
| Reference | 0.8 | 1.2 |
| High life expectancy | 0.8 | 1.3 |
| Constant disability | 0.8 | 1.0 |
| Shift to formal care | 0.8 | 1.9 |
| Coverage convergence | 0.8 | 3.5 |
| Cost and coverage convergence | 0.8 | 5.5 |

Source: EC (2015).

Note: Projections by the European Commission – Economic Policy Committee, selected scenarios.

This confirms the view that the main problem of the LTC system in Hungary is unmet needs, that is, quality of life in old age and adequacy rather than sustainability.

## 2.6 Conclusions

Long-term care is a backwater issue in Hungary that receives little public attention. Despite a rapid expansion of home-based care in recent years, the system is still underdeveloped in general, leaving a significant share of needs unmet. The bulk of long-term care activities are left to households or an informal market. Decision makers are still to internalise the increasing importance of the problem in an ageing society as well as the potential of government intervention for risk sharing and containing social costs.

## Notes

1 Details on net time transfers in the Hungarian context can be found in Gál, Szabó and Vargha (2015).
2 It has to be noted that the EC-EPC projection applies a different definition of LTC spending than the OECD. In the previous Ageing Report (EC, 2012), the point of departure, 0.8% of GDP in 2010, the same as in the new report, is only 0.3% in 2008 in the OECD analysis of LTC systems (Colombo et al., 2011).

## References

Colombo, F., Llena-Nozal, A., Mercier, J. and Tjadens, F. (2011), *Help Wanted? Providing and Paying for Long-Term Care*, Paris: Organisation for Economic Co-operation and Development (OECD).

CSO (Central Statistical Office). (2008), *Yearbook of Welfare Statistics, 2007*, Budapest: CSO.

CSO (Central Statistical Office). (2009a), *Yearbook of Health Statistics, 2008*. Budapest: CSO.

CSO (Central Statistical Office). (2009b), *Yearbook of Welfare Statistics, 2008*. Budapest: CSO.

## 22    *Róbert I. Gál*

CSO (Central Statistical Office). (2013), *Demographic Yearbook, 2012*, Budapest: CSO.

CSO (Central Statistical Office). (2015a), *European Health Interview Survey, 2014 (in Hungarian)*. Statisztikai Tükör 2015/29, Budapest: CSO.

CSO (Central Statistical Office). (2015b), *Yearbook of Health Statistics, 2014*, Budapest: CSO.

CSO (Central Statistical Office). (2015c), *Yearbook of Welfare Statistics, 2014*, Budapest: CSO.

Czibere, K. and Gál, R.I. (2013), The Hungarian long-term care system in micro data (in Hungarian). In É. Gárdos (ed) *Health Status and the Health Care System (in Hungarian) ELEF Tanulmányok 3*, Budapest: CSO, pp. 93–105.

Dandi, R., Casanova, G., Lillini, R., Volpe, M., De Belvis, A.G., Avolio, M., and Pelone F. (2012), *Long-term care quality assurance policies in European countries.* ENEPRI Research Reports 111. Brussels: ENEPRI.

Donehower, G. (2011), *Incorporating Gender and Time Use into NTA: National Time Transfer Accounts Methodology*, Berkeley: University of California, Department of Demography. Manuscript.

EC (European Commission). (2012), The 2012 Ageing report: Economic and budgetary projections for the 27 EU member states (2010–2060). *European Economy* 2.

EC (European Commission). (2015), The 2015 Ageing report: Economic and budgetary projections for the 28 EU member states (2013–2060). *European Economy* 3.

Gál, R.I., Szabó, E. and Vargha, L. (2015), The age-profile of invisible transfers: The true size of asymmetry in inter-age reallocations, *Journal of the Economics of Ageing* 5, 98–104.

Gál, R.I., Szabó, E. and Vargha, L (forthcoming), Invisible transfers: Who gives and who receives unpaid household labour? (in Hungarian). In K. Szép (ed) *Household Satellite Account, Hungary, 2010*, Budapest: CSO.

HDRI (Hungarian Demographic Research Institute). (2015), Population projection, 2015. Downloadable from http://demografia.hu/hu/tudastar/nepesseg-eloreszamitas (in Hungarian).

SAO (State Audit Office). (2008), *Report on the Hospitals and Residential Homes of Local Governments*, Budapest: SAO Reports 0820.

Stoeckel, K.J. and Litwin, H. (2013), Personal social networks in Europe: Do people from different countries have different interpersonal solidarities? In A. Börsch-Supan, M. Brandt, H. Litwin, G. Weber (eds) *Active Ageing and Solidarity between Generations in Europe: First Results from SHARE after the Economic Crisis*, New York: De Gruyter Online, pp. 277–287.

# 3 Long-term care
## Challenges and perspectives

*Virginija Poškutė*

## 3.1 Introduction

This chapter provides an overview on the latest developments and challenges of long-term care for elderly in Lithuania.

The issue of long-term care for the elderly has been becoming more and more critical over the last few decades in Lithuania. This is especially relevant given the rapidly worsening ratio of aged to working people in the population. Lithuania is the EU's fastest ageing country according to the EU Commission.[1] The Lithuanian population was made up of 19.1 percent retirement-age people in 1990, while there were 22.4 percent in 2014. By 2060, 37 percent of the population in Lithuania will be elderly, according to the forecast by Eurostat (see Figure 3.1).

Increase in average life expectancy (71.4 years in 1990 and 74.59 years in 2014)[2] implies that the number of elderly in the Lithuanian population will further increase. When the working-age population is rapidly shrinking due to negative natural growth and high emigration, especially of young working-age people, Lithuania faces even more challenges. If this negative demographic development will not change in near future, this is going to negatively affect not only sustainability of social security programs for elderly (pensions, long-term care for elderly, etc.) but it will also challenge all social security systems and the sustainability of long-term economic growth.[3]

## 3.2 Organisations of long-term care

LTC for elderly people in Lithuania is not recognised as separate public service or social policy provision. LTC for the elderly is provided within the national health care and social services systems (Figure 3.2). Nongovernmental organisations, together with informal private support and services, constitute a significant part of LTC provision for the elderly as well.

Long-term care for the elderly can be classified into formal and informal provisions. Formal LTC delivered via health and social systems includes the following services:

- Nursing (provided in institutions or at home)
- Permanent nursing
- Home care
- Care in day centres

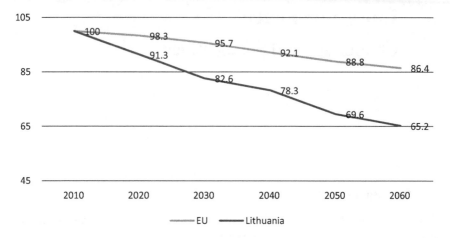

*Figure 3.1* Projection of working-age population aged between 15–64 years in E27 and Lithuania (2013 = 100)

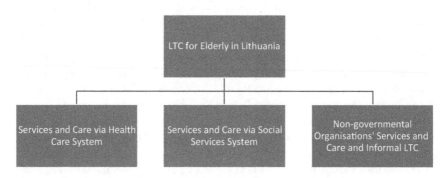

*Figure 3.2* Provision of LTC for elderly in Lithuania

- Care in social care institutions (health conditions of such persons are relatively better than those who are placed in nursing hospitals)
- Financial support to buy needed services from the private market.

There is no single central national or regional institution or unified national legal arrangements that coordinate LTC services for the elderly in Lithuania. Only one municipality (of Vilnius) recently approved the Strategy for Care of Elderly, 2012–2020.[4] Separate national laws regulate their respective areas (Law on Social Services, Law on Health Care Institutions). LTC policy changes so far were based on changes in the respective laws.

The Ministry of Health is responsible for the health care system policy. Main administrative institutions of social services provided by the social security sector are the Ministry of Social Security and Labour, the Department of Supervision of Social Services (under the Ministry of Social Security and Labour) and municipalities.

*Challenges and perspectives*   25

Health care-related LTC services are financed via various sources: the compulsory health insurance fund, the state and territorial self-government budgets, EU structural funds, private financial resources, charity and other sources (Marcinkowska, 2010a). Statistical data indicate that direct expenditures of private households on health (not specified by category) within the total expenditures on health are constantly increasing in Lithuania (they amounted to €0.7 billion in 2013 compared to €0.58 billion in 2008; direct expenditure of private households constituted 97.3% of all private expenditure on health). Private expenditure constituted 31.4% of total health expenditures in 2013. The social service sector-related LTC provision is financed from the local self-government budgets and target subsidies of the central budget assigned to municipal budgets.

It is recognised in the national programs and documents[5] that the system of social services for elderly shall be organised in such a way that persons would be enabled to stay as long as possible at home and with their families and that they be able to independently care for their private lives and participate in the society. Social services are aimed at securing safe and heathy environments for persons with disabilities, and assistance shall be provided to maintain human dignity and in coordination with individual health care, permanent nursing and permanent care (assistance). It is intended to create the system of integrated and individualised services in the community. The processes of transition from institutional care are given top priority. Only in cases when general social care services are ineffective and day care services are insufficient shall institutional social care be prescribed.

The measure 'Development of social service infrastructure' is implemented by regional project planning. Under the measure, a total of €17.2 million of European Regional Development Fund (ERDF) funds, €2 million of municipal funds and €1 million of state budget funds have been allocated to the development of infrastructure of noninstitutional social services and modernisation of homes for the elderly.

## 3.3  Formal LTC for the elderly

Health-related LTC services for disabled or chronically ill people are provided via the health care system, while social services oriented to provision of care for dependant people (elderly included) are delivered via the social services system.

LTC services via the health care system are targeted at those people who need support and care due to their long-term illnesses (mental or physical) in spite of their age. This means that elderly people might be staying for a long time in beds at a hospital instead of having long-term care.

Palliative care services are part of this system as well. Lithuania was the last country in the EU that legalised palliative care. Only 1 person out of 10,000 was receiving palliative care in 2008 and only 5 persons out of 10,000 were in 2011.[6]

Until recently, nursing services were mostly provided in residential care institutions (general or nursing hospitals) depending on health conditions (irrespective of age). Long-term medical treatment with nursing services in hospitals is financed for not more than 120 days. In 2014, nursing beds constituted 19.5% of all hospital beds (17.5 nursing beds per 10,000 population).[7] Such beds are nonexistent in most of the European countries. The number of such beds was increasing by 37.1% in Lithuania in 2014.

There were 48 nursing hospitals (providing nursing care, medical rehabilitation, follow-up treatment, palliative care and sanatorium treatment) in Lithuania (out of total 134 hospitals) in 2014.[8]

Since 2008, primary health care institutions are providing health-related nursing services at home (see also Figure 3.3). About €4.34 million are spent yearly on nursing services at home from the Compulsory Health Insurance Fund budget. Approximately 30,000 people (elderly included) were receiving such services at home in 2015.[9]

Social services at home, day centres or residential social care homes provided by the social security sector depend on a person's level of independency, need for services, level of income and the property held by an individual. Cash benefits available via the social system are not means tested.

Municipalities provide general (without permanent assistance by specialists) and special (social attendance and social care) social services for elderly (see Figure 3.4). General services include provision of information, consulting, intermediation and

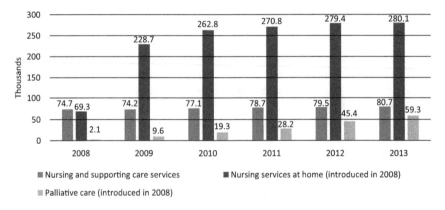

*Figure 3.3* Number of nursing services (cases), 2008–2013

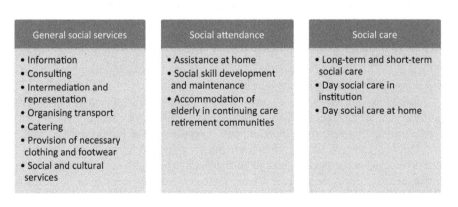

*Figure 3.4* Types of social services provided by municipalities

*Challenges and perspectives* 27

representation, organising transport, catering, provision of necessary clothing and footwear, and social and cultural services. Social attendance refers to the services aimed at providing a person with complex assistance, which does not require permanent attendance by specialists and which includes assistance at home, social skill development and maintenance, accommodation of the elderly in continuing care retirement communities and so forth. Social care refers to the services aimed at providing a person with complex assistance that requires permanent attendance by specialists. According to its length, social care may be classified as one-day, short-term or long-term care. Social care can be provided at home or in an institution.

There is no centralised publicly accessible information about availability of long-term social care institutions or services in the country, which makes it difficult for the elderly or their relatives to approach an institution for a LTC support. Eight out of 60 municipalities do not provide any information on availability of social services via their webpages, and one third of the municipalities provide inconsistent information that is not user friendly.[10] However, provision of the information on webpages is not sufficient, as most of the potentially needy persons might not be using the Internet.

There are no official statistics about the demand for LTC for the elderly in Lithuania. Only 11 percent of the elderly (69,700) were identified as having special needs or received special financial compensations for care or nursing in 2014.[11]

Thirty eight municipalities (out of 60) do not collect information on elderly people living in their territories, 15 municipalities collect information from the central population register and 7 municipalities collect information only about single elderly people.[12] Demand for social services is most often identified when elderly people apply for them or when someone applies on their behalf (relatives, neighbours). There is no legal requirement to visit the elderly at home and to identify elderly who are in need of care or to provide them with information on availability of the services.

An indication of the potential demand for help and care of the elderly might be received from the most recent survey by Statistics Lithuania (2015)[13] on persons who have difficulty performing self-care and home-care activities (see Figure 3.5): among those aged 65 to 74, 19 percent indicated that they are

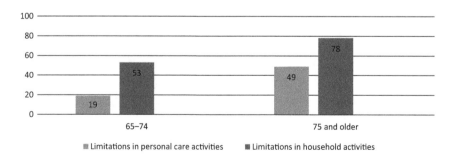

*Figure 3.5* Percentage of the population aged 65 years and older that has limitations in personal care and household activities (by age group), 2014[14]

experiencing difficulties in performing self-care, and more than half of them are experiencing difficulties in home care activities (see Figure 3.6). The situation is worsening among those aged 75 years and older: almost half of them (49 percent) experience difficulties in self-care activities, and 78 percent experience difficulties in home-care activities.

The situation gets worse with the age: among elderly aged 75 years and older, 45 percent indicated that they were having difficulties bathing or showering, 35 percent had difficulties getting in and out of a bed or chair and 30 percent had trouble dressing and undressing.[15]

The survey also revealed that among those aged 65 years and older who needed help in daily personal care activities, 50 percent were receiving some help (see Figure 3.7). Nevertheless, 31 percent of people who received such help indicated that the help was insufficient. Among the elderly who didn't receive any help in daily personal care activities, 24 percent indicated that there is a need for that. Females indicated a bit higher need for help than males.

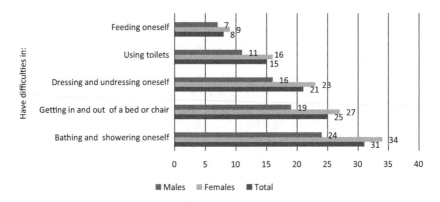

*Figure 3.6* Percentage of the population aged 65 years and older that has limitations in personal care activities, 2014[16]

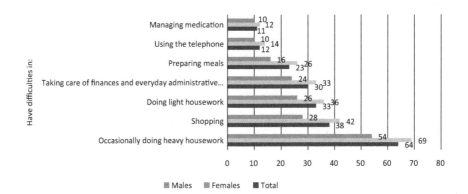

*Figure 3.7* Percentage of the population aged 65 years and older that has limitations in household activities, 2014[17]

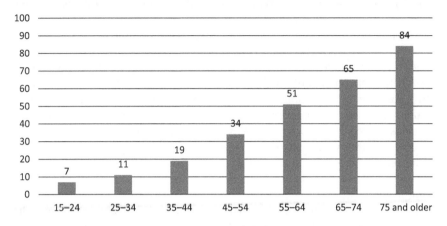

*Figure 3.8* Percentage of the population that experienced long-standing limitations in their activities due to health problems (by age group)[18]

The survey[19] revealed information about available help for people aged 65 years and older experiencing difficulties in performing household activities. Sixty-seven percent of the elderly experienced such difficulties and had some help. Nevertheless, almost one third of them (29 percent) indicated that the help was insufficient. Among elderly who didn't receive any help, 17 percent indicated need for help. Females again indicated higher demand for help than males.[20]

Another indication about potential demand for LTC for the elderly can be based on a study performed in one district of Lithuania that evaluated the needs of the elderly (aged 65 and older) for outpatient nursing and social services.[21] The respondents of the study indicated that 71.3 percent needed nursing and 58.2 percent needed social services. The need for the services was increasing with the age. The rural elderly reported higher need for social services (64.3 percent) than the urban elderly (49.6 percent). The majority of the respondents (86.4 percent) pointed out that those who took care of them had no special medical training. Respondents who were completely or almost completely dependent (groups by the Barthel Index) needed social (88.0 percent) and nursing (96.0 percent) services. The majority of respondents (79.2 percent) preferred to be cared for at home. The study concluded that more than half of the elderly needed both nursing and social services.[22]

In spite of the fact that the information is not organised on a central level and there is lack of information on available services in municipalities, the number of provided social services for the elderly is increasing in Lithuania. There were 13,200 social services cases for the elderly provided in 2012, and there were 13,800 in 2013 (66 percent of all social services provided by municipalities).[23] Assistance at home constitutes the biggest part (57 percent) of all social services provided for elderly, while short-term and long-term social care make up 29 percent and day social care at a person's home makes up 7 percent of all the services.[24] In spite of increasing numbers of the people provided with social care,

30    *Virginija Poškutė*

only 1 percent of all elderly people receive services at home in Lithuania. Even fewer are in LTC institutions.[25]

As for the residential care, 4,800 persons lived in care institutions for the elderly in 2014 (the number increased by 9 percent from 2010). Around 6,000 residents lived in care institutions for disabled adults, and 400 people lived in continuing care retirement communities in 2014 (increase of 3 percent and 77 percent from 2010, respectively, see Table 3.1). The number of the residents in nongovernmental, parish and private care institutions is also increasing: there were 1,879 residents in such institutions (an increase of 74 percent from 2010).

As responsibility for LTC for the elderly is spread among health care and the social sector, there is insufficient sharing of information among various institutions on elderly who need LTC (even if there is a legal requirement to share such information).[26]

Demand for a specific social service is assessed individually. The person in need of social services can be described as self-sufficient, partially self-sufficient or dependent. While identifying the demand, a person's physical and social self-sufficiency are assessed. The assessment of need is performed by social workers. The National Audit Office of Lithuania concluded in its report[27] that social workers were unable to determine people's needs for social services properly in 2015. Very often the assessment performed by social workers was subjective.[28] When assessing the need for LTC, the option of alternative care that would allow the elderly to stay at home at long as possible was not always offered by social workers. Thus, it is necessary to improve legislation regulating determination of the demand for social care in order to satisfy the needs of the elderly better and ensure that persons stay in their homes as long as possible.

*Table 3.1* Care institutions and continuing care retirement communities for the elderly and disabled adults[29]

|  | 2005 | 2010 | 2011 | 2012 | 2013 | 2014 |
|---|---|---|---|---|---|---|
| **Care institutions for the elderly, total** | 97 | 105 | 100 | 104 | 102 | 108 |
| **Residents in them** | 4,927 | 4,476 | 4,414 | 4,514 | 4,665 | 4,829 |
| **State (county) care homes** | 8 | 3 | 2 | 2 | 2 | 2 |
| **Residents in them** | 1,764 | 213 | 112 | 113 | 114 | 104 |
| **Municipal care homes** | 55 | 57 | 55 | 55 | 50 | 51 |
| **Residents in them** | 2,158 | 2,702 | 2,846 | 2,829 | 2,543 | 2,429 |
| **Other care institutions** | 2 | 3 | 2 | 2 | 2 | 2 |
| **Residents in them** | 200 | 482 | 315 | 357 | 384 | 417 |
| **Nongovernmental, parish and private care institutions** | 32 | 42 | 41 | 45 | 48 | 53 |
| **Residents in them** | 805 | 1,079 | 1,141 | 1,215 | 1,624 | 1,879 |
| **Care institutions for disabled adults, total** | 27 | 29 | 36 | 38 | 39 | 41 |
| **Residents in them** | 5,412 | 5,883 | 6,061 | 6,118 | 6,052 | 6,055 |
| **Continuing care retirement communities, total** | — | 12 | 10 | 14 | 21 | 20 |
| **Residents in them** | — | 227 | 212 | 262 | 449 | 402 |

*Challenges and perspectives* 31

The decision by the municipality to provide a person in need with a specific social service also depends on the infrastructure of the services in the municipality, which means that the application of social care does not include the priority of giving the person an opportunity to stay at home as long as possible (see Figure 3.9).

There is a lack of qualified employees who provide social care and day care services in people's homes, which has a negative impact not only on the availability of services but also on their quality. There is no efficient control of the quality of social services provided.[30]

In order to receive institutional LTC, individuals have to cover part of the related institutional expenses. Financial means (retirement pension, savings etc.) and property of elderly are assessed when establishing the copayment for LTC. The copayment for LTC shall not exceed 80 percent of the person's income.[31] There is no good system for evaluation of people's financial capabilities to pay for LTC. Employees of municipalities are not able to identify all the financial assets of the elderly, and the elderly applying for LTC do not provide full or correct information.

Despite the increasing scope of services (Table 3.2), there remains unsatisfied demand for them. The biggest unsatisfied demand is for assistance at home. There were elderly waiting for social services in 48 municipalities (out of 60) at the end of 2014. There were 1,222 persons waiting for various social services in municipalities (47 percent of them were applying for short-term and long-term social care, 33 percent for assistance at home).[32]

The National Audit Office[33] concluded that the organisation of social services for elderly people in municipalities of Lithuania is inefficient and cannot satisfy the increasing demand; there is not a single municipality that can provide all types

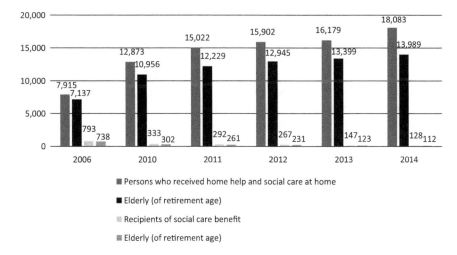

*Figure 3.9* Persons receiving social services at home[34]

## 32   *Virginija Poškutė*

*Table 3.2* Social services provided by municipalities in 2012–2014 and data on unsatisfied demand for them[35]

| Social services | Number of recipients | | | Unsatisfied demand (number of persons) | |
|---|---|---|---|---|---|
| | *2012* | *2013* | *2014* | *2013* | *2014* |
| **LTC** | 5,624 | 5,923 | 6,629 | 420 | 360 |
| **Short-term social care** | 1,232 | 1,192 | 711 | 14 | 12 |
| **Day social care in institutions** | 1,383 | 1,454 | 1,327 | 20 | 29 |
| **Social attendance in social attendance centres** | 1,437 | 1,570 | 714 | 31 | 0 |
| **Day social care at home** | 867 | 1,172 | 1,873 | 43 | 88 |
| **Assistance at home** | 9,034 | 9,012 | 9,075 | 402 | 312 |
| **Accommodations in continuous care retirement homes** | 336 | 468 | 477 | 27 | 6 |
| **Total** | **19,913** | **20,791** | **20,806** | **957** | **807** |

Source: The Public Audit Report, p. 21.

of social services for elderly people and that complies with the declared aspirations by the government to take care of the elderly.

### 3.4  Financing of LTC

There is no single estimation of expenditures related to LTC provision in Lithuania. Due to very complex, scattered and nonunified financing, it is not possible to distinguish the total amount of money spent on LTC in Lithuania.

Lithuania still has one of the lowest expenditures on health. Expenditure on health care as a percentage of GDP was 7.45 percent in 2009. In 2013, with the growth of GDP, this percentage has decreased to 6.5. Calculating expenditures on health by purchasing-power standard, Lithuania spent €1,192.5 per capita in 2013.[36] Expenditure for LTC within health sector comprised 7.6 percent of all health care expenditures in 2013.[37]

Statistical data indicates that expenditures on LTC within the health care system are increasing: they totalled €97.42 million in 2007, €163.26 million in 2013 and €198.4 million in 2014.[38]

Financing for all social services (including LTC for the elderly) within the social sector in 2012 to 2014 shows a gradual increase as well: €63 million were allocated in 2012, €68 million in 2013 and €81.8 million in 2014.[39]

The state does not control the costs of services provided by municipalities.

## 3.5 Boundaries between state and civil society in the approach to the delivery of care with an eye to the private sector's ambition to provide and sell care

Until recently, mostly public LTC institutions were active in the sector. Recently, LTC institutions in the private sector and community initiatives are being established more often. Licences to provide LTC services for private institutions are issued by the Department of Supervision of Social Services under the Ministry of Social Security and Labour. It can be stated that even with appearance of private LTC institutions, still there is no competition in the social services market. With unsatisfied demand for various services for elderly, there are queues of elderly persons waiting for a place in LTC institutions (public and private).

The price for private care is much higher than for care in public sector. In spite of higher price, the number of residents in nongovernmental, parish and private care institutions is continuously increasing.

## 3.6 Informal care

There were no national attempts to evaluate long-term care for the elderly provided informally in Lithuania (Marcinkowska, 2010b). Only the recent Survey of Health by the Department of Statistics included a few questions about that.[40] As the results of the survey showed, 14 percent of the population aged 15 years and older (16 percent of females and 12 percent of males) looked after or helped at least one person with problems due to old age or health problems at least once a week. The highest share of population providing such support was among the population aged 35 to 64 years (see Figure 3.10).

The same survey revealed that 60 percent of people who provided such help did so no more than 10 hours per week; 14 percent indicated they helped 10 to 20 hours a week and 26 percent indicated 20 or more hours per week. Two thirds of people taking care of others (65 percent) indicated that mostly they look after their family members.

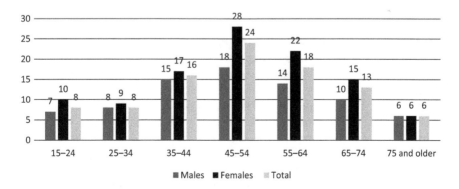

*Figure 3.10* Percentage of the population that has been providing care or assistance to other people with health problems by age group, 2014[41]

34    *Virginija Poškutė*

Next to increasing expenditure via health care and social systems, there is a strong indication that LTC provision by the informal sector (family members, neighbours and friends) comprises the most significant part of the support for the elderly and disabled in Lithuania. It is still very often perceived that to care for the elderly is the primary responsibility of a family. Institutional LTC for the elderly is still biased in society and is often perceived as insufficient care by the families of the elderly. In the study performed in one district of Lithuania that aimed to evaluate the needs of the elderly (aged 65 and older) for outpatient nursing and social services,[42] the majority of respondents (79.2 percent) indicated that they preferred to be cared for at home, which also gives an indication about the prevailing expectations for family members' responsibilities to each other.

## 3.7  Use of rehabilitation and welfare technology as ways to improve quality of life and reduce the pressure on public sector spending in the area

Rehabilitation and welfare technology for elderly are not being considered or discussed in Lithuanian social policy so far. Nevertheless, there is interest in involving the private sector or community initiatives as much as possible in order to reduce pressure on the public sector.

There some national initiatives to encourage the private sector to step into areas that were previously considered public. For example, the concept of social business was approved by the Ministry of Economy in 2015. It is expected that social business initiatives that encompass public-private partnerships will encourage social innovations. Pursuing a solution to prevailing social issues in society through a private-public partnership would provide opportunities to shift some social problems solutions from the public to the private sector.

## 3.8  Conclusions

LTC for the elderly in Lithuania is not recognised as separate public service or a social policy provision. LTC for the elderly in Lithuania is provided via health care and social security systems. Health-related LTC services for disabled or chronically ill people are provided via the health care system, while social services orientated to provision of care for dependant people (elderly included) are delivered via social services systems.

The need and level of dependency to qualify for LTC is different in health and social care sectors. Health condition-related LTC for the elderly is provided via long-term medical treatment in ordinary hospitals or in nursing hospitals. Only recently (2008) have nursing services at home within health care system been introduced as an option for LTC in Lithuania.

LTC for the elderly via the social security system is available depending on a person's self-sufficiency, need for services, level of income and held property.

Formal long-term care and home-based care for the elderly are still rather underdeveloped. There is insufficient infrastructure for provision of LTC for the elderly; there is no proper control of the quality of provided LTC services; and there is an insufficient number of qualified and decently remunerated employees working in LTC institutions or providing LTC services at home.

Informal care providers (family and friends) still remain the most significant providers of LTC for the elderly in Lithuania.

There are national initiatives to develop LTC for the elderly in such a way that most of the services would be provided via home-based care instead of institutional care. Such an approach is applied in order to enable a person to stay in their home as long as possible.

One of the main challenges of LTC for the elderly is the fact that there is no proper integration of the all LTC providers into one system. There is little sharing of the information among different stakeholders (municipalities, health and social care institutions, police, local communities) involved with or responsible for LTC provision for the elderly in Lithuania. There is still no public debate about policy initiatives regarding the overall system of LTC for the elderly and its challenges.

## Notes

1  http://ec.europa.eu/europe2020/pdf/csr2015/cr2015_lithuania_en.pdf
2  Statistics Lithuania: http://osp.stat.gov.lt/statistiniu-rodikliu-analize?portletFormNam e=visualization&hash=e6729112-922a-475f-b90c-716dab8a2f26
3  http://ec.europa.eu/europe2020/pdf/csr2015/cr2015_lithuania_en.pdf
4  Strategy for Care of Elderly 2012–2020. Approved by the Board of Municipality of city of Vilnius, Decision no. 1–707. July 18, 2012.
5  National Strategy for Overcoming Consequences of Aging of Population; The Law on Social Services; The Action Plan of the Transition from Institutional Care to the Provision of Services in a Family and Community for the Disabled and Children Deprived of Parental Care 2014–2020.
6  National Health Council's Annual Report, 2012, p. 52.
7  Health Statistics of Lithuania, 2014, p. 47.
8  Ibid.
9  Data from the Ministry of Health webpage: https://sam.lrv.lt/lt/veiklos-sritys/ asmens-sveikatos-prieziura/slauga-asmens-sveikatos-prieziura
10  The Public Audit Report.
11  The Public Audit Report, p. 11.
12  The Public Audit Report.
13  Results of the Health Interview Survey of the Population of Lithuania 2014. Statistics Lithuania. Vilnius, 2015.
14  Ibid.
15  Ibid.
16  Ibid.
17  Ibid.
18  Ibid.
19  Ibid.
20  Ibid.
21  Hitaite, L. and L. Spirgiene (2007), "The need of the elderly for nursing and social services in the community of Kaunas district", *Medicina (Kaunas)*, Vol. 43, No. 11 (http://medicina.kmu.lt).
22  Ibid.
23  The Public Audit Report.

36  *Virginija Poškutė*

24  Ibid.
25  Long-Term Care for the Elderly. Provisions and providers in 33 European countries, p. 71.
26  The Law on Social Services (Lietuvos Respublikos socialinių paslaugų įstatymas, 2006–01–19 Nr. X-493, 15 str. 4 d.)
27  The Public Audit Report, p. 12.
28  The Public Audit Report, p. 7.
29  Ibid.
30  The Public Audit Report, p. 8.
31  The Law on Social Services.
32  The Public Audit Report, p. 22.
33  The Public Audit Report.
34  Source: Statistics Lithuania.
35  Ibid., p. 21.
36  Health Statistics of Lithuania, 2014.
37  Ibid.
38  Statistics Lithuania: http://osp.stat.gov.lt/web/guest/statistiniu-rodikliu-analize?portlet FormName=visualization&hash=4dc94bc1–7d68–4e3e-b3f6-d79b5a3ad873
39  The Public Audit Report, p. 13.
40  Results of the Health Interview Survey of the Population of Lithuania 2014. Statistics Lithuania. Vilnius, 2015.
41  Ibid.
42  Hitaite, L. and L. Spirgiene (2007), "The need of the elderly for nursing and social services in the community of Kaunas district", *Medicina (Kaunas)*, Vol. 43, No. 11 (http://medicina.kmu.lt).

## References

The Action Plan of the Transition from Institutional Care to the Provision of Services in a Family and Community for the Disabled and Children Deprived of Parental Care 2014–2020. Ministry of Social Security and Labour. No A1–83, 14th February, 2014.

Health Statistics of Lithuania. (2014), *Lithuanian Ministry of Health, Health Information Centre of Institute of Hygiene*, Vilnius: Lietuvos statistikos Departamentas. 2015.

Hitaite, L. and Spirgiene, L. (2007), The need of the elderly for nursing and social services in the community of Kaunas district, *Medicina (Kaunas)* 43(11): 903–908. http://medicina.kmu.lt.

The Law on Social Services of the Republic of Lithuania, 19–01–2006, No. X-493.

Marcinkowska, I. (2010a). The Lithuanian Long-term care system. *CASE Network Studies and Analyses*. No. 414/2010. Warsaw, Bishkek, Kyiv, Tbilisi, Chisinau, Minsk. http://www.case-research.eu/sites/default/files/publications/31396313_CNSA%20414%20final_0.pdf.

Marcinkowska, I. (2010b). *The long-term care system for the elderly in Lithuania.* ENE-PRI Research Report No. 82. http://www.ancien-longtermcare.eu/sites/default/files/ENEPRI%20_ANCIEN_%20RR%20No%2082%20Lithuania.pdf.

National Strategy for Overcoming Consequences of Aging of Population, approved by the decision No. 737 of the Government of Lithuania, June 14th, 2004 (Nacionalinė gyventojų senėjimo įveikimo strategija, patvirtinta Lietuvos Respublikos Vyriausybės 2004–06–14 nutarimu Nr. 737).

Report by the National Audit Office on compliance of existing social services with increasing needs of elderly in Lithuania (No. VA-P-10–9–10, 30 June 2015; "Ar teikiamos socialinės paslaugos tenkina didėjančius senyvo amžiaus asmenų poreikius"); (Do the social services available satisfy the increasing needs of elder persons. *The Public Audit Report*, 30 June 2015 No. VA-P-10–9–10).

Results of the Health Interview Survey of the Population of Lithuania 2014. (2014 m. Lietuvos gyventojų sveikatos statistinio tyrimo rezultatai). Vilnius: Lietuvos statistikos Departamentas. 2015.

Statistics Lithuania. (2015). Official Statistics Portal, http://osp.stat.gov.lt/statistiniu-rodi kliu-analize?portletFormName=visualization&hash=e6729112-922a-475f-b90c-716dab8a2f26.

Strategy for Care of Elderly 2012–2020. Approved by the board of municipality of city of Vilnius, Decision no. 1–707.18 July 2012. (VYRESNIO AMŽIAUS ASMENŲ PRIEŽIŪROS 2012–2020 METŲ STRATEGIJA, 2012 m. liepos 18 d., Nr. 1–707).

# 4 Long-term care for the elderly in Poland[1]

*Zofia Czepulis-Rutkowska*

## 4.1 Introduction

There is no long-term care system in Poland under one heading. There are, however, numerous benefits and institutions that could be and are treated as long-term care by the experts and policy makers. The lack of a single definition of long-term care in the Polish law leads to differences in understanding of what is and what is not a part of the long-term care system. This ambiguity comes to the surface not only in the Polish research presentations, but also in the international benchmarking studies that need to be standardised in order to receive some, even if only linguistic, clarity. This problem of clear definition is relevant to many countries, if not all.

Poland is a new EU member state and a country that in the last two decades has undergone economic and political transitions. This has caused significant consequences for the welfare state[2] development in general and for long-term care in particular. These specific institutional circumstances, for a country like Poland, need to be looked at in order to understand the current status and debate on long-term care as well as the future developments and possible reforms.

The chapter consists of five sections. The new member state welfare system context is analysed in the first section. The demand for long-term care will be described in the second. The third section is dedicated to the institutional supply side of long-term care. Administrative and financing issues are addressed in the fourth section. The current policy debate is presented in the fifth section. The paper ends with conclusions.

## 4.2 New welfare state institutional context

Literature on the welfare state models in the new member states, or CEE states, is much scarcer than on the well-established Western European welfare states. Still, there is a growing recognition of the importance of the new welfare state models (Fenger, 2007; Tache and Neesham, 2011).

Poland has been undergoing significant political and economic transformation since the early 1990s that (with some simplification) could be described as moving from the centrally planned economy to the free market-driven economy. The transformation has influenced social institutional setup and many following reforms.

Some factors relevant to the topic that have influenced the introduction and changes in the social institutional landscape along with the transformation process are listed herein. The selection of the factors is not by all means complete. However, the GDP (lower) level, growing unemployment,[3] the social expenditure level and the labour market activity (low) level are important factors that shaped social policy from the onset of the transition process.

Currently, GDP per capita in purchasing power parity (PPP) in Poland is much lower than in the old member states. This indicator is of importance for possible social policy spending such as long-term care. Lower GDP obviously leaves less space for extra spending. This low income aspect is unfortunately often put aside in international benchmarking studies where basically relative indicators are used.

The economic transition process led to unemployment on a massive scale fuelled in particular by layoffs from the previously state-owned enterprises. This development, which left the working-age population (and among them many families with young children) with inadequate income, made the authorities allocate monies to the programmes dedicated to the support and activation of these social groups. The working-age groups had priority in social policy, not the frail elderly.

In the early 1990s it was noticed and it became an issue for high-profile debate that pension spending was very high both in terms of overall spending as a percentage of GDP and very high replacement rate that was considered unfair when many working-age people suffered from unemployment (as a result of economic transition). A lot of efforts were targeted at the reduction of pension spending (or at least slowing the growth rate) and resulted in a thorough pension reform in 1999. The pension reform faced much resistance from the stakeholders, and only well-orchestrated effort paved the way for its introduction. For example, an extra ministerial institution[4] was set up then in order to coordinate the reform.[5] Anyhow, the time of declining pension spending was – at the political level[6] – not the time when extra money could have been targeted at the introduction of a new social system like long-term care.

Unemployment, which was very high at the onset of the transition process, declined over the years as a result of various developments and policies. Still, the labour market activity level for people over 55 years of age is low compared to the old EU Member States.[7] The employment rate for people aged 55 to 64 is around 40%, whereas it exceeds 60% in Germany and is above 70% in Sweden. The labour market activity level is particularly low for women aged 55 years and older, and it declines from around 61% of the population at the age of 55 to 32% at the age of 60 (GUS, 2014b). Many policies and government initiatives have been aimed at improving this, but there are no significant results yet. It is hoped that by 2020 it should increase because of special activation programs, economic development and demographic trends. In social policy terms, there is much ambiguity about the evaluation of the availability of women aged 55 and older for care obligations at the family level. On the one hand, it could be assumed that they deliver long-term care for the family members, and on the other hand, bearing in mind population aging, it seems much better for the whole society and economy that their labour market participation rate increases in the near future, especially

40　*Zofia Czepulis-Rutkowska*

in anticipation of labour shortages as a result of the population aging. Also there is an argument that family are often not able to provide professional enough care for the dependent elderly in the households.

In the process of significant welfare state changes in the times of economic transition, the long-term care system (especially when the population ageing process was not still so well recognised as nowadays) was not a high-calibre issue or even an issue at all. Over the years, however, due to many factors, the long-term care and other institutional issues connected with the ageing process have become more debated.

## 4.3 Demand for long-term care

The demand for long-term care in whatever form (family, public or private) is determined by two intertwining factors: population ageing and the health status of the elderly. As for population ageing, the age structure of the elderly is important. The more elderly there are above 80 or 85 years of age, the higher the demand for long-term care. The healthier the elderly are, the less need there will be for long-term care.

It is difficult to assess the demand precisely as many elderly live in families and they receive the necessary help on regular family life basis, not often realising what is and what is not long-term care.

According to the statistics, there is a significant increase in the number of very old persons in the Polish population.

In 2012, Poland was still a young population compared to the average EU median age that was then 41.9 years; some countries, like Germany, were much higher above the median age. According to projections, the median age for both genders will be 52.5 in 2050; this number will be higher for women and lower for men (see Table 4.1).

The ageing index (relation of people aged 65 and older to people aged 0 to 14) demonstrated that the intergenerational relationship equalled 0.983 in 2013, and this is expected to increase to 1.271 in 2020, 1.966 in 2035 and to 2.693 in 2050 (GUS, 2014). This projection illustrates not only the dynamic growth of the elderly population but also the shrinking (at least relatively) of the younger population who would hypothetically be carers.

*Table 4.1* The median age for the population

| Year | Total | Men | Women |
|------|-------|-----|-------|
| 2013 | 38.6 | 36.9 | 40.4 |
| 2020 | 41.4 | 39.8 | 43.1 |
| 2035 | 48.1 | 46.2 | 49.9 |
| 2050 | 52.0 | 49.6 | 54.3 |

Source: GUS (2014a).

*Table 4.2* Percentage of disabled respondents who need help by frequency and age group

| Age | Constant | A few times a day | Once a day | A few times a week | Once a week | Less than once a week |
|---|---|---|---|---|---|---|
| 55–59 | 27.7 | 12.8 | 4.3 | 17.0 | 17.0 | 21.3 |
| 65–69 | 37.4 | 15.2 | 9.1 | 10.1 | 8.1 | 20.2 |
| 70–74 | 29.4 | 22.1 | 6.7 | 19.6 | 11.7 | 10.4 |
| 75–79 | 43.7 | 16.2 | 7.4 | 14.8 | 8.7 | 9.2 |
| 80–84 | 41.2 | 18.7 | 10.4 | 16.3 | 8.6 | 4.7 |
| 85–89 | 51.0 | 18.2 | 11.6 | 11.6 | 4.7 | 3.0 |
| 90+ | 59.4 | 22.6 | 5.7 | 8.4 | 2.5 | 1.3 |
| Total | **47.7** | **19.4** | **8.5** | **12.7** | **12.7** | **5.5** |

Source: Błedowski (2013).

Not only is the population ageing, but the structure of the subpopulation of the elderly is changing. The share of people aged 80 and older in the 65 and older age category was 26.3% in 2013. This share is not going to grow evenly, but according to the projection, it is going to reach 32.2% in 2035 and 35.8% in 2040.

Having in view the long-term care, two statistical indices are important: potential support ratio that shows the number of people 15 to 64 years old to the number of people aged 65 and older and the parent support ratio showing the relation of those aged 85 and older to those aged 50 to 64. According to the projection, the first index will decline in the period from 2013 to 2050 (from 4.58 to 1.69) and the second index will increase (from 0.08 to 0.38).

Whereas the population ageing statistics are available, it is much more difficult to obtain relevant information about the need for long-term care for people with poor health. One piece of data could be the number of persons considered disabled according to disability assessment. There are three levels of disability under the assessment system. The number of disabled people is growing with age.

According to comprehensive health and social research on the ageing population and the elderly, PolSenior (2012), the demand for help from others is growing with age. Table 4.2 shows how the demand for care and help is diversified. The first column shows how the constant need for care grows with age.

## 4.4 Supply of the long-term care

Suppliers of the long-term care include family, public institutions, social care and private institutions (and NGOs).

### 4.4.1 Family

Families are major long-term care providers in Poland (Golinowska, 2010). This is so because, as already mentioned, the labour market participation rate of women aged 50 and older is comparatively low. These women are natural resources for care workers in their own families. Here we focus on long-term care, but it should

## 42   Zofia Czepulis-Rutkowska

be noted that women aged 50 and older often take care of their grandchildren. The phenomenon of the "sandwich generation" – those who are looking both after their parents and their grandchildren – is well known in Poland.

The reasons that people – mainly women – are engaged in taking care of their families are unemployment and the low pension age. These reasons have been losing their impact over time. The unemployment rate has recently been decreasing, so women aged 50 and older will be probably less willing to give up their presence in labour market, if they are not pushed out. Also, the retirement age according to the still-prevailing law was increased, which limits the availability of the women as carers. Women's involvement in long-term care is, however, not only a Polish issue (Bettio and Verashchagina, 2010).

There have been many governmental initiatives aimed at labour market activation of people, especially women aged 50 years and older. It is still difficult to assess their efficiency by giving figures that would show the direct effects of these initiatives, but they have, by all means, contributed to changing attitudes of people over the age of 50 towards leading more active lifestyles. It seems that they have contributed to changing the lifestyle of the 50+towards being more active at least socially, for example through the so-called third-age universities. This may facilitate being more active at the labour market too.

Family carers face many financial and health problems. A survey of the family carers (Kosinska, Kułagowska, Niebrój and Stanisławczyk, 2013) showed that the carers themselves were not young (in their mid-50s); they spent around 5 hours caring if they were employed and twice that if they were not employed, but a nurse would come for only 1 hour. The physical strain was too heavy, leading to the carer's health status deteriorating, and they also needed to financially support the persons they cared for because the financial public support (in the form of pension or other benefits) was insufficient. In this context, it should be indicated that the rate for the long-term care nurse financed by the health care sector has declined in the recent years (Opiece długoterminowej grozi zapaść, 2015). This illustrates one way of transferring costs in long-term care from the health care sector to the families. This transfer may, however, lead to reverse financing back to hospital care.

In the literature it is often claimed that the Polish tradition breeds high family involvement in care for family members. There is some evidence, however, that if public institutions were more available, many families would be happy to use them. Some qualitative research pointed out that families would be happy to provide care but on a smaller scale (Czepulis-Rutkowska, 2015). To sum up, the family as care providers might be less available in the future.

### 4.4.2 Public sector

The public sector is the main formal long-term care provider. There are various services and benefits available. As already stated, there is no separate public long-term care system. Rather, segments of the already-existing welfare state play the role of long-term care. Traditionally the health care sector and the social sector are the managers and providers of long-term care.

The health care sector is administered by the Ministry of Health and social care is administered by the Ministry of Family, Labour and Social Policy.

Prior to the transition period, the Health Care Ministry was called the Ministry of Health and Social Care. The name of the administration represented its role within the overall government but also the welfare state paradigm connected with the ideology of the centrally planned economy.

Social assistance was called social care and was under the health administration. The social assistance system in the modern meaning was absent. Poverty or social exclusion were not acknowledged politically, and social care was aimed at mainly poor elderly or disabled people. In reality, the administrative bodies exercising the health and social care played the role of public long-term care providers.

It is important to reflect on this historical institutional setup because some experts and stakeholders suggest that the administrative reforms were disadvantageous for long-term care and they might be reversed for the benefit of long-term care. It should be noted, however, that the welfare state reforms were driven by many other considerations that are not less important than long-term care. Back in those days, the demographic changes such as population ageing did not seem that significant as they do a quarter of a century later.

Social care was renamed social assistance, had an entirely new rationale and was transferred to the Ministry of Labour and Social Policy. This will be described in section 4.4.3. The important reform of long-term care provision within the health care sector took place in 1999 as a result of a health care system reform going from the budgetary system to the insurance system. This reform in the health care system was driven by the examples of two European countries: Germany and the UK. The first one had the social insurance method for health care and the second had introduced semi-market rules in health care. Both countries' solutions seemed attractive for a countries in transition searching for efficient health care systems. It should be noted here that countries in transition, such as Poland, that were trying to find the right institutions for themselves perhaps focused too much on the overall performance in particular countries and not on actual reasons for such performance. In my view, this represents one of the significant features of the transition period and its various consequences for the long-term care system. This does not, however, mean that there were better means available for institution building capacity; this characterises only the process of building and reforming the welfare state institutions and indicates the difference between the new EU member (post-transition) state and the old member states with more stable institutional frameworks.

The significant health care reform (along with other important reforms) took place in 1999 and involved the implementation of the health insurance system. The idea was that a separate budget made up from health insurance contributions would allow for guaranteed access to necessary means and also efficient economic management of the funds. Not all plans were implemented, but one important outcome of the reform was higher cost awareness. The experts and policy makers started counting the health care costs on a much bigger scale than before, and they became much more aware of the underlying economic mechanisms.

In early 2000, a concept of long-term care was introduced in the health care sector. This distinguished between long-term care patients and those in "regular" hospital wards. Two types of these new long-term care institutions were established: care and treatment facilities (*zakłady opiekuńczo-lecznicze*) and care and nursing facilities (*zakłady pielegnacyjno-opiekuńcze*). The intention was that the first type of facility should differ from the second one with more focus on treatment activities, but in reality they function in a very similar manner.

Care facilities within the health care system are intended for relatively short-term stays – optimally 30 days. In reality, the stay is often prolonged. The Supreme Chamber of Control indicated that often people who should not be eligible stay in the care facilities, and there are many cases when persons who should be eligible are denied access to health care facilities (NIK, 2010).

It should be also noted here that, apart from this institutional separation, some hospital wards still provide long-term care in situations when the patient has nowhere to go or the treatment is not relevant because of a serious condition. These kind of stays are, however, shorter than they used to be. All the same, the accurate calculation of real costs of long-term care in the health care sector is difficult.

Apart from this residential form of long-term care within the health care system, there is also help at home available that is provided by specially trained long-term care nurses.

The health care services are financed through the Health Care Budget. The nurses are employed on a contract with the National Health Fund and are remunerated accordingly.

The so-called hotel accommodation costs in the care and nursing facilities should be covered by the residents themselves. There are, however, limits as to what part of resident income should be allocated to the accommodation costs. The qualitative research shows that this regulation, aimed at protection of the dependent person's income, could in some cases adversely impact the access to residential care. The administration of the facilities might avoid (although not officially) the beneficiaries with lower incomes, as they might not be able to cover the costs of the accommodations (Czepulis-Rutkowska, 2015a). The health care costs in these facilities are covered by the National Health Fund.

In recent years in Poland, as in other countries, there has been a growing interest in geriatrics, a medicine specialisation that can influence both long-term care (dealing with patients that already need constant care) and prevention that will slow the ageing process and may help limit long-term care costs. From 2010 to 2014, the number of geriatricians rose from 97 to 135, which led to an increase in the indicator of the number of geriatricians per 100,000 people aged 65 year and older from 1.9 to 2.3 (GUS, 2015). All in all, the numbers are insufficient. According to the Supreme Audit Office, there is no integrated system of geriatric care in Poland, although many activities to this end have been planned, for example, in the Long-Term Policy for Seniors. The Supreme Audit Office indicated that a well-organised health care system for the elderly would allow for more efficient and less costly care (NIK, 2014). Some experts take a position that what could make a difference is not so much the number of geriatricians or the focus on geriatrics, but rather a better education of general practitioners (GPs) to deal with elderly.

People who need round-the-clock care, nursing, rehabilitation and treatment continuation in residential form, but do not need hospitalisation, are eligible for residential care in the health care sector. The medical doctor and a nurse make the assessment of the relevant need. They use the Barthel scale to this end. If the patient scores 40 points or less on the Barthel scale, they are eligible. The Barthel scale measures activity of daily living (ADL) with a maximum score equal to 100. In this context, a score of 40 points is widely considered very low and results in refusal to help some people with real need. The final decision regarding receipt of a patient is comes from the medical doctor employed in the facility and its director.

### 4.4.3 Social sector

As already mentioned, as a result of institutional transition, the social assistance system as such was implemented in the Polish welfare state in the early 1990s. Before that, due to some ideological and other factors, poverty and unemployment, were not officially recognised.

The beginning of the economic transition saw swelling unemployment and poverty. The new institution then, social assistance, was initially focused on addressing the needs and situation of the unemployed. Social assistance helped people affected by unemployment such that they could provide for themselves.

This was the priority, although other issues were being addressed too. The social assistance care homes needed thorough change: improvement of living conditions, standardisation of quality across the country and so on (Grabusińska, 2013).

The benefits in the social sector were financed from the general budget, from local budgets and, to some extent, from social insurance contributions. The beneficiaries or their relatives were another source of financing.

Care homes are for people who cannot live by themselves due to various types of disabilities: physical, psychiatric, intellectual or a combination of these. In the 1980s, different types of care homes were aimed at specific groups of people, such as the elderly, the chronically ill, the mentally ill, intellectually disabled adults, intellectually disabled children and young persons and the physically disabled. The differences between them, as can be easily imagined, are blurred from time to time. Therefore, individuals with different needs are combined in one home.

Accommodations and care services are provided in care homes. Health care services were provided at homes until 1999, the year of health care reform when social insurance was introduced. Since then, the residents of care homes are covered by health care like all other citizens. The administrations of care homes often try, however, to build a special connection with GPs and specialists to guarantee the residents' access to the health care system (Czepulis-Rutkowska, 2015b). The qualitative research showed that apart from regulatory changes, the institutions have adopted new (often informal) institutional setups. It is especially important in a country like Poland that has frequent regulatory changes. In practice, however, in spite of their originally defined function, care homes accept various beneficiaries. In 21st century the different types of homes were merged. Residential care is not necessarily dedicated to the elderly; nonetheless, in most care homes the majority of clients are elderly.

## 46   Zofia Czepulis-Rutkowska

In 2014 there were 782 residential care homes in Poland; 53.6% of residents were 61 years of age or older, which was up by 50% compared to 2010. The highest increase of the elderly residents was among people aged 65 to 74 (15.6%) and 80 and older (8.4%). The majority of elderly residents stayed in homes for the elderly (39.6%) or for the chronically physically ill (31.1%). Many elderly also stayed at homes for chronically mentally ill (GUS, 2015).

As mentioned, the care services are financed from the lower administration (municipality) budget. All in all, however, the financing system is mixed and includes funds from the state budget, the private incomes of beneficiaries and family members' incomes. State subsidy is an important source for financing care homes, and it accounts approximately for 75% of the total costs. Residents are to pay for their stay in the care homes, but only up to 70% of their income. Their families are obliged to participate, too. If this is not enough, then the local government is obliged to pay the rest. In practice, the families frequently do not participate, since there is a family income threshold above which the family is obliged to pay.

According to the effective law, care homes may be public or private. Both types need to comply with set care standards. Because of that, private homes are being set up under different names and laws on economic activity. It is therefore difficult to estimate the real number of care homes and the number of beneficiaries staying there.

The number of care homes has increased significantly since the beginning of the transition in the early 1990s, but access is still unsatisfactory because the care homes are not evenly accessible throughout the country. For example, in 80 counties there is no care home at all, and the county self-government tends to use care homes for their own county residents.

As a result of already-mentioned changes introduced in the 1990s, care homes in Poland have undergone significant transformation during the last 25 years towards the improvement of service quality and living conditions: lower numbers of residents per room, getting rid of architectural barriers and so on. The attitude towards beneficiaries, such as respecting their dignity and autonomy, still needs to be improved (Grabusińska, 2013).

Community care services provided within the social care sector consist of "regular" care services and specialist care services. They are provided at the place of residence of the beneficiary. The social assistance centre decides whether services will be granted and determines their scope, time and place. The social assistance centre can deliver the services themselves or outsource their delivery.

Persons living alone and in need of help because of old age, illness or disability are eligible. People living with families who are not able to help could also be eligible. The services cover activities such as cleaning, shopping and meal preparation. They can be provided at full price, partial price or free of charge, depending on the financial standing of the person in need. The prices of the services, how they are organised and the payment are decided at municipality level. The municipality covers the cost if the beneficiary is unable to do that.

Specialist care services are for persons who need special services because of specific health conditions; persons with adequate professional qualifications have to be employed in order to deliver these services.

*Table 4.3* Care homes in 2014

| Care home type | Public and nonpublic care homes | | Self-government care homes | | Nonpublic care homes | |
|---|---|---|---|---|---|---|
| | Number of homes | Number of beds | Number of homes | Number of beds | Number of homes | Number of beds |
| Total | 782 | 77,368 | 580 | 63,960 | 202 | 13,408 |
| For the elderly | 117 | 8,591 | 80 | 6,639 | 37 | 1,952 |
| For chronically ill somatic patients | 156 | 15,850 | 131 | 14,114 | 25 | 1,736 |
| For chronically mentally ill patients | 164 | 20,687 | 141 | 18,781 | 23 | 1,906 |
| For intellectually disabled adults | 134 | 12,318 | 103 | 10,698 | 31 | 1,620 |
| For intellectually disabled children and young people | 69 | 5,410 | 20 | 2,058 | 49 | 3,352 |
| For the physically disabled | 8 | 901 | 3 | 290 | 5 | 611 |
| For the elderly and somatic chronically ill patients | 75 | 7,437 | 58 | 6,253 | 17 | 1,184 |
| For the chronically ill and physically disabled | 9 | 1,246 | 9 | 1,246 | — | — |
| For the elderly and physically disabled | 14 | 1,488 | 12 | 1,365 | 2 | 123 |
| For intellectually disabled adults and children | 36 | 3,440 | 23 | 2,516 | 13 | 924 |

Source: Ministry of Family, Labour and Social Policy (2016).

48 *Zofia Czepulis-Rutkowska*

*Table 4.4* Number of care services

| Year | Care services | | Specialist care services | |
|------|---------------|---|--------------------------|---|
| | *Number of persons* | *Expenditures (thousands PLN\*)* | *Number of persons* | *Expenditures (thousands PLN)* |
| 2005 | 81,993 | 266.2 | 4,571 | 10.1 |
| 2008 | 92,420 | 342.4 | 5,619 | 15.7 |
| 2014 | 88,880 | 385.5 | 4,410 | 14.7 |

Source: Ministry of Family, Labour and Social Policy (2016).

\*PLN: Polish Currency (Zloty).

The specialist care services, with the exception of those aimed at persons with psychiatric or poor intellectual condition (financed from general budget), are financed from the municipality budget.

The number of services rendered are considered to be unsatisfactory, given the growing demand for them in relation to the ageing population. Also, the quality of services is questioned now and then. The community services are of utmost importance due to the widely promoted trend of prolonging a person's stay in his or her own home. Separation of care services from other services financed at the municipality level might help to better manage their delivery. It also seems that increasing public financing towards care services might lead to their higher utilization and possible lower utilization of residential care as a result.

The family care home is a special form of long-term care that is not well developed in Poland. It is a form of day and night care at a home for three to eight persons, and care is provided in a way similar to care in real families. This seems to be an attractive form of care that pays more attention to an individual's situation and needs. The number of family care homes is very low; there were around 10 in 2008.

The community support centres basically offer day care. Various services are provided there. The beneficiaries receive meals, which is a great help for the families. The centres, with the exception of those for persons with psychiatric conditions or who are intellectually disabled, are financed from the municipality budgets.

In 2011, there were 1,380 support centres with 68,000; 100,000 people received services at these centres.

In the pension social insurance system, there is a carer's allowance (*dodatek pielęgnacyjny*) that is available for everyone over 75 years of age. The amount of the carer's allowance is comparatively low and by no means can cover the cost of long-term care service even at a basic level. It was PLN 208.00[8] in 2015 (whereas the minimum pension was PLN 880.45). Efforts were taken to limit the right to this allowance to only those in real need of long-term care. This was met with such criticism on the pensioners side that it had to be stopped. Elderly pensioners claim that this is a "pharmaceutical supplement", even though it was never stated officially. The problems around proper (according to the original intention) use of this benefit once again indicate how difficult it is to withdraw a benefit once granted.

Another cash benefit, the attendance benefit (*zasiłek pielęgnacyjny*), is paid to persons over 75 years of age (and others). The aim of this benefit is to cover part of the expenditure connected with dependency in daily life. Its amount is even lower: PLN 153. The attendance allowance is in the competence of the municipality social assistance centres. These two described benefits are additional sources of income with no real impact on ability to obtain long-term care.

Another benefit that is aimed at helping families with a disabled child is the attendance allowance (*świadczenie pielegnacyjne*), which is granted to family members who resign or cannot take employment because of a need to take care of the disabled relative. This allowance amounts to PLN 1,300 plus social insurance contributions for parents of disabled child (up to 18 years of age). This benefit was increased recently as a result of protest action taken by the parents. Arguments were raised in discussion that followed that perhaps similar solutions should be made available to the elderly members of a family, for whom the allowance is lower. In fact, the previous parliament started a debate on covering carers of the dependent elderly through this benefit. In the future, such a solution should be expected.

### 4.4.4 Private sector and NGOs

The private sector provision does exist in Poland in many forms. Residential care and home care are both available. Some parts of private care are a subject to public regulation, whereas other parts are not regulated because they function under something other than the long-term care definition or are in shadow economies.

The private care homes' management is regulated by social assistance law. Such care homes have to follow all rules and quality standards. Sometimes the homes are run under a different heading as a regular private enterprise. Then they do not need to follow the standards and they are not subject to administrative control.

The private market offers also luxury services and care at very high prices.

There are also many care homes run by religious, mainly Roman Catholic, organisations. The home care is provided by private agencies and informal care workers who are often from abroad (mainly Ukraine).

The private market for care services plays a supplementary role. It is aimed at the well-off members of the society and at those who are not covered by the public sector because of its limited availability. Very few could afford high prices in some of the private care homes, whereas home care delivered by emigrant care workers is much more financially accessible (Toruńczyk-Ruiz, 2014). The care quality issue is not raised here, though.

The civil society can be defined in various ways. Sometimes it is understood as all institutions outside the government, including the family. It can be also defined as an activity space between family and the government. In this text, the concept of civil society is understood in a practical and somewhat simplified manner, that is, in the context of division into private and public institutions and private or public objectives of their activities. According to this concept, there are three sectors. In the first sector, market, the subjects and the objectives are private. In the

## 50    *Zofia Czepulis-Rutkowska*

second sector, government administration, the subjects and aims are public. The third sector is civil society, with private subjects and public objectives.

The civil society is closely related to democracy, which allows for a certain degree of autonomy in the social activities. The members of civil society are able to organise themselves to articulate and realize various social aims with support from the state.

Understandably, civil society does not develop well in nondemocratic states that try to control the majority of social activity. This was the case in Poland until 1989. The civil society was not totally absent, but whereas in the West society and the state were supporting each other, in countries like Poland, the two subjects were often in conflict (if the sector existed at all). In Poland, the third sector was present, but it was quite limited. The Roman Catholic Church and its organisation was almost the only channel for civil society activity. The sociologists claim that in Poland (as in other postcommunist countries) the family, often the extended family, fills the gap of other civil society institutions. The transition from centrally planned to market-driven economy allowed for civil society development, and in fact, this was very much encouraged by various government initiatives and regulations. But civil society does not emerge and develop as a sheer result of regulation; rather, it is very much established in a tradition and its building is still underway (Kancelaria Senatu, 2014). Therefore the post-transition countries cannot be easily compared to the Western countries in terms of civil society development. In fact, the third sector institutions have been facing numerous problems; one of them is their operation close to major cities where various state organisations and services are also available.

Speaking about civil society's role in long-term care provision, one needs to bear in mind these circumstances of civil society development. If the family is included in the civil society concept, then Poland would be a country with a well-developed civil society. However, by the same token, the other elements of civil society would be underdeveloped.

Therefore, here I would like to focus on other nonfamily civil society institutions. Some of them were present even in the communist era; many of them were connected with the Roman Catholic Church. In the field of long-term care, there are religious organisations, which are mainly the care homes. According to the Ministry of Family, Labour and Social Policy, in the category of the third sector organisations, 24% were dedicated to social help that can include long-term care and 4.1% to health care. One of the institutions with a very long tradition is Caritas Polska, which was reactivated in 1990.

The institutions present in the communist times include the Polish Red Cross (*Krzyż Polski Czerwony*) and The Polish Committee of Social Assistance (*Polski Komitet Pomocy Społecznej*) (established in 1958).

There are also other civil society institutions that target their assistance toward the elderly. Here two examples of such institutions will be presented. One is Little Brothers of the Poor, and the second Syntomia. The first one is focused on fighting loneliness among the frail elderly. There are many different activities envisaged to this end with participation of voluntary workers. One of the most recent initiatives is the invitation of lonely elderly for Easter breakfast. Another project is concerned with learning about Alzheimer's disease. There are not long-term care activities; however, they are closely connected and could help the frail elderly and their carers. This association is active in three cities: Warsaw, Lublin and Poznan.

Syntomia is an association concerned with psychological aspects of ageing and care. It organises various workshops for both the frail elderly and their carers. One example is memory training for the elderly. An important activity is the support group for the carers.

Important issues connected with civil society organisations for the elderly are as follows: the short and not well-rooted tradition of civil society, concentration of their activities in cities even though there is big demand for help with long-term care in the rural areas and in small towns, dependence on scarce and uncertain financing and dependence on government grants (might undermine the organisation independence).

## 4.5 Administration, financing and quality: challenges

The system of administration and financing of long-term care is a complex one, as discussed. This characteristic makes this segment of the welfare state difficult to manage or reform. The financing system is mixed, with a big part of private funds channelled to long-term care. The private means are used for accommodation at care homes, for home care and also in the private care service market. It should be researched what part of the long-term care cost is being covered by society members with private funds and what part is being covered with public sources.

In the public sector, the financing system can be defined as means tested, although not in a traditional way. The funds of the prospect beneficiary are taken into account not at the entry point but at the payment point. The beneficiaries are made to pay according to their financial standing.

The benefit that can be treated as universal is the service of the long-term care community nurse. Also, the cash benefit within the social insurance system is paid without any test.

The total expenditure spent on long-term care is difficult to calculate due to the absence of one definition of this benefit. Only in the health sector is there a clear definition used for long-term care. Still, this definition, as mentioned, does not cover hospital departments of internal medicine that are still used as long-term care facilities to some extent. In the social sector, the extent of long-term care services for the elderly can be estimated by taking into account the number of elderly beneficiaries.

As already stated, two ministries are responsible for administration of the long-term care: the Ministry of Health Care and the Ministry of Family, Labour and Social Policy. It was decided, as a result of the country administration reform leading to much decentralisation in 1999, that local authorities and communities are the most competent bodies for both assessment of needs and provision of care. It was also decided that the local government should decide on the local budget appropriation. The local governments are obliged to prepare the projections of changing demand for care in their region or community. These are, however, being prepared on a general basis and can hardly be used for adequate preparation for future care needs.

The social sector administration is delegated to lower administration levels, but not all parts of it are financed from the local budget.

The care homes and home care for persons with psychiatric conditions or intellectual disabilities are financed from the general budget, whereas all other types of care should be financed from the local budget. This obviously creates different set of incentives for different categories of disabled and dependent people. At the local budget level, there is always competition between all different needs that exist in the local community.

In view of the growing number of psychiatric conditions, such as dementia, care in this area is of great importance. It seems to be a positive feature of the system.

The local authorities may take a different approach to similar situations, thereby creating unequal treatment across the country. For example, it depends on the local authority to what extent the family is charged for care provided to their relatives. Also, local authorities decide the price of the home care provided.

So, on the one hand, the decentralisation of social assistance (among other things) has brought about more flexibility and better possibility to tailor the services for those in need of long-term care, but on the other hand, it has created a situation where the elderly in need of long-term care could be treated differently depending on the place of their residence.

Quality of the services is an issue present in the debate on long-term care. As the system is segmented, the same concerns the debate and the law. Generally speaking, the law both in the social sector and the health sector stipulates observing standards in accommodation, care hours and personnel number and structure.

In the social sector, the poor quality of care homes was recognised early on and addressed. The standards concerning living conditions and personnel numbers and structure were introduced gradually. According to research, these goals connected with standards have been generally achieved. Still, issues concerning dignity and autonomy of clients lack enough attention and realisation (Grabusińska, 2013). There were several scandals reported in care homes. The recent one was in a private home for Alzheimer patients. This development calls for solutions that would protect the patients in homes in general and in homes for intellectually or psychologically sick patients in particular.

The need for quality and standardisation is also recognised in case of care services rendered at home. However, in this case the social assistance law only enlists the available services and eligibility criteria, leaving more detailed decisions to local governments and municipalities. Still, in the first decade of the 21st century, the standards of these services were defined only in half of the social assistance centres and only on a very general level. A monitoring of care services in the form of an opinion questionnaire is allowing for evaluation of the quality. Interestingly enough, the questions do not concern dignity or autonomy issues.

Also, the questions are framed in such a way that it would be difficult for persons with dementia or Alzheimer's disease to answer them.

Also in the health sector, the standards are defined in concerning the education structure of personnel, health equipment and accommodations. It is also stipulated that the personnel represent positive and understanding attitudes towards patients.

According to the High Chamber of Control, the standards are not often observed (NIK, 2010).

According to Polish law, quality is understood mainly as realising the standards that are different in different segments of long-term care. The realisation of these standards depends on financing and administration efficiency. Also, the issue of wider understanding of quality of life that is already present in the academic and social debate should somehow be translated into the rules of segmented long-term care regulations.

## 4.6 Debate and reform proposals

The debate on the long-term care system started to develop in the 21st century. At the onset of the transition period, the focus of the debate and reforms was on social assistance and later on both old age pensions and health care. After introducing radical reforms in those two segments and recognising the demographic challenges, long-term care started to become a social issue.

There are many stakeholders involved in the discussion on various aspects of population ageing. Many initiatives and meetings were taken and organised in the last decade. Also, there are many publications resulting from these initiatives and research.

Apart from general discussions, there have already been two legal initiatives providing for the long-term care system establishment in recent years. The first proposal was drafted by the Ministry of Health in 2007 by the interdisciplinary committee. The fact that the proposal was prepared by the Ministry of Health was connected with the cost burden on the health care side. The basic idea was to increase the contribution towards the health social insurance system by 2%. The contribution was to create a special fund dedicated to care needs. The economic rationale was to increase the health fund. It was widely recognised that the health fund money was, in general, insufficient and the long-term care introduction would allow an increase in the amount of money dedicated to health care. The same government was searching for other ways to increase the fund or transfer the costs of health care to other institutions.

It was claimed that money for care services should have been separated from the money for treatment services. It was expected that care services market would have developed as a result of employing professionals prepared to provide care services. Highly qualified medical personnel would have been freed from care responsibilities.

Cash and benefits in-kind were envisaged. Home care was to take precedence over institutional care. This proposal was strongly criticised by the Ministry of Finance and the employers who were opposing extra tax/contribution burdens,

## 54   Zofia Czepulis-Rutkowska

claiming that this would undermine their competitive edge. The argument was that the old age pension reform stabilised the contribution level and later increase of the social contributions should not be raised somewhere else.

This proposal was not turned into law not only because of the criticism but also because the government was changed. The next government, however, recognised the need for a long-term care system. The institutional setup was different. A partisan working group to work on the law to help dependent people was established in the higher chamber of the Polish Parliament (Senate). The leader of this body was governing party politician Senator Mieczyslaw Augustyn. The senator had a professional experience from the social assistance side (he was director of a social assistance care home). The parliamentary working group was therefore also taking into consideration the social sector as a long-term care provider. The working group leader had referred to the experience of Germany in this context where it was social assistance administration that wanted to introduce a separate long-term care system.

Still, the work followed the German regulation to a great extent. It was often claimed that one separate long-term care system would be able to solve the problems connected with long-term care needs. It was claimed by the majority of the working group members that a separate fund for long-term care needs created by contributions would be better than financing from the general budget. As an expert of this working group, I took a position that with changing labour market and working careers financed from contributions connected with formal employment might not be reliable.

The work of the second working group lasted for two government terms of office. The draft law was created, but not implemented.

Two questions emerge in this context. Is a single long-term care system instrumental towards efficiency? And if so, why was the draft law elaborated by the ruling party working group not put through?

As for the first question, it seems that many experts reached a consensus that it would be beneficial to have a single long-term care system because it seemed that it would allow for more effective use of the resources and for better integration of various services (Błędowski and Wilmowska-Pietruszyńska, 2009).

The second question should be answered in the institutional and economic context. The institutions within the health and social sectors represented their interests, and it was not easy to change this established situation after the initial stage of social reforms was undertaken in the 20th century.

Another reason for encountered difficulties was that there was no strong stakeholder to push the reform. The frail elderly can hardly play such a role. The working group was aware of this necessity to mobilise support and some initiatives towards this end were undertaken. Several high-profile conferences were organised. The society of supporters of the dependent people was established; many organisations have joined this association. This pressure turned out to be insufficient.

Another explanation may be that the reform momentum was lost. At the beginning of the transition process, the society believed that it would be possible to achieve the situation in the old member state countries by just changing their

Long-term care in Poland    55

institutional framework design. This obviously turned out not to be true, so the reform enthusiasm was lower.

A strong reason for failure to implement a new social costly institution was also the economic crisis. Although Poland was less struck by the economic crunch than many other countries, it made the implementation of the costly new social program very difficult without powerful stakeholder support.

The EU initiatives have played an important role in the Polish debate and policymaking. The incorporation of long-term care into the Coordination Regulation and also the Open Method of Coordination (FreSsco, 2015) has contributed to attaching more importance to long-term care in Poland.

The EU's Year for Active Aging and Solidarity Between Generations (2012) gave a boost to various events and discussions connected with population ageing and long-term care, among other issues.

The government document (in the form of a decree of the Council of Ministers) on the assumption of long-term policy for seniors for 2014 to 2020 was adopted in 2013. This document defines the policy for seniors as various activities of the government administration along with other organisations and institutions that create the conditions for healthy ageing with dignity. It aims, in particular, at allowing for independent life even with some functional limitations. Accordingly, this document focuses on the health of the elderly. There are three policy priorities enlisted. The first priority concerns the systemic solutions allowing for health care services for the elderly. Geriatric specialty is singled out as an institution in deficit. The second priority is about health promotion and prevention. The third priority is about social and care services for the elderly.

At the Ministry of Labour and Social Policy (now Ministry of Family, Labour and Social Policy), the Seniors Policy Department was created in 2013. This institutional move has ambiguous consequences for long-term care. It gives more prominence to the problems of the elderly and supposedly also the need for long-term care. It seems, however, that the program is much more aimed at elderly persons who are still in good shape. The program of the government policy is designed for prevention and provides for establishing centres and clubs to activate the elderly socially (Breza, 2014). A lot of effort has been also put into supporting the so-called third-age universities aimed at organising time for the retired elderly who are not yet in need of long-term care.

After some years of discussion on long-term care systems, it seems that a shift in policy can be identified: from trying to establish a system along with old age or disability addressing an extra social risk of dependency to mobilising all possible resources to prevent the need for long-term care.

It seems it was so far too difficult both institutionally and economically to implement an integrated reform of long-term care.

## 4.7 Conclusions

The current landscape of the long-term care in Poland is a complex one, and the future of this institution is unclear. Family is the main care provider. The public

## 56  *Zofia Czepulis-Rutkowska*

sector offers long-term care services and, to some extent, cash benefits via the health care sector and the social assistance sector.

The main problems to address include injecting more resources into the system, integration of the system and continuation of care, equal access in terms of place of residence and economic situation, quality of services in public as well as private providers and ensuring that informal carers, both paid and unpaid, comply with the basic care standards.

The policy makers are certainly more aware than before of the need to provide care for the frail elderly. It is yet to be seen how the new government (the Law and Justice party) will address the problem. At this stage, it seems that in terms of resources there is a small margin (if at all) for improvement as the Law and Justice party went to power with an expensive social scheme for introducing a universal child benefit. The law was already introduced.

There are other expensive social reforms not yet introduced: lowering the retirement age to 60 years for women and 65 for men. (Currently, according to law, the retirement age is to be gradually increased to 67 for both genders: for women in 2040 and for men in 2020).

As already stated, before efforts were taken to define the welfare state in Poland (new member state and after political and economic transition) in terms of welfare state models. It was determined that the path dependency perspective or policy diffusion policy is more adequate in explaining the new welfare state development and prospects (Frel de, 2009).

I would like to point out that, apart from what is presented in the literature features, the political and policy swings might be more pronounced in countries such as Poland with positive and negative consequences for the policy development. These are two sides to the same coin. As it was easier to introduce social policy changes in Poland, it is also somewhat easier to reverse them. This has happened to some extent to the old age pension system and the health care system.

Long-term care is one of the issues discussed as a part of policies connected with the population ageing process. Its significance in the debate has somewhat shifted from dedication to introducing the German-like long-term care system to more interest in a social activation, on the one hand, and geriatrics development programs, on the other (Derejczyk, Bień, Kokoszka-Paszkot and Szczygieł, 2008). All these initiatives compete for policy focus and resources.

Long-term care will have to be seriously addressed yet again in the near future in order to help the very old and frail.

## Notes

1 This article is based on research carried out as part of a research project: OPUS 5 No. 2013/09/B/HS5/00039 "Social Security Institutions for the Elderly in the Context of Social Policy Models", which was financed by the Polish National Research Center.
2 It is open to debate whether social systems under communism should (and if so to what extent) be treated as welfare state institutions (Barr, 2004).
3 Earlier the phenomenon of hidden unemployment was observed.
4 The office of the Government Representative for Social Security Reform Implementation was established.

Long-term care in Poland 57

5 This may be relevant experience for the implementation of any thorough social reform, a long-term care system being one of the examples.
6 It was claimed that a decline in social spending was absolutely necessary. Another argument was that people should be more responsible for their own well-being and that private institutions might be helpful to this end.
7 The labour market activity indicator including employed and unemployed is not high in Poland, but it has been increasing in recent years. Between 2010 and 2013, for women of working age it increased from 66.8% to 69.7% and for men it increased from 76.2% to 77.6%. The employment indicator was lower: 62.2% for women and 70.4% for men in 2013 (GUS, 2014b).
8 In March 2016, PLN 208.00 equaled €48.4. In 2015, the average wage in Poland was PLN 3,900.

## References

Bettio, F. and Verashchagina, A. (2010), Long-Term Care for the Elderly. Provisions and Providers in 33 European Countries, EU Expert Group on Gender and Employment (EGGE), http://ec.europa.eu/justice/gender-equality/files/elderly_care_en.pdf.

Błędowski, P. and Wilmowska-Pietruszyńska, A. (2009), Organizacja opieki długoterminowej w Polsce – problem I propozycje rozwiązań (Organization of long-term care in Poland – problems and solutions proposals) in: *Polityka Społeczna* (Social Policy), Nr 7, Warsaw.

Błędowski, P. (2013), Opieka długoterminowa w Polsce w świetle najnowszych badań (Long-term care in Poland according to current research, presentation delivered at a conference in Parliament based on PolSenior [2012]).

Breza, M. (2014), *Long-Term Care – Main Challenges in Time of Aging*. Comment paper Poland, Peer Review on Financing of Long-Term Care, Slovenia 2014.

Czepulis-Rutkowska (2015a), *Focus Group Interview with Long-Term Care Providers*, Katowice, April 2015, not published material.

Czepulis-Rutkowska (2015b), *IDIs with Social Care Homes Administrators in Bialystok and Olsztyn*, unpublished material. IDIs carried as a part of research project "Social security institutions for the elderly in the context of social policy models" financed by the Polish National Research Centre.

Derejczyk, J., Bień, B., Kokoszka-Paszkot, J. and Szczygieł, J. (2008), Gerontology and geriatrics in Poland against Europe – is it necessary to invest in? *Gerontologia Polska* 16(3). pp. 149–159.

Fenger, H.J.M (2007), Welfare regimes in central and Eastern Europe: Incorporating post-communist countries in a welfare regime typology. *Contemporary Issues and Ideas in Social Sciences* 3(2). pp. 1–30.

FreSsco (2015), FreSsco seminar (Poland): Practical problems connected with the application of the Social Security Coordination Regulations in the field of long-term care and posting, 19/06/2015, ec.europa.eu/social/main.jsp?langId=pl&catId=1098.

Golinowska, S. (2010), *The long term care system for the elderly in Poland*, ENEPRI Research Report No. 83.. www.ceps.eu, and ANCIEN website http://www.ancien-longtermcare.eu/node/27 (Access: 10 January 2015).

Grabusińska, Z. (2013), Domy pomocy społecznej w Polsce (Social assistance care homes in Poland), projekt "Koordynacja na rzecz aktywnej integracji" współfinansowany przez Unię Europejską ze środków Europejskiego Funduszu Społecznego.

GUS (Central Statistical Office) (2014a), Population Projection 2014–2050. Statistical Analyses and Studies, Table No 21, p. 127, Warsaw [2014].

## 58  Zofia Czepulis-Rutkowska

GUS (Central Statistical Office) (2014b), Kobiety I meżczyzni na rynku pracy (Women and men at the labour market). Warsaw stat.gov.pl/download/ . . . /pw_kobiety_i_mezc zyzni_na_rynku_pracy.pdf chart "labour market activity indication according to gender and age" (wspolczynnik aktywnosci zawodowej ludnosci wedlug plci i wieku), p. 3 (Access: 21 March 2016).

GUS (Central Statistical Office) (2015), Zdrowie i ochrona zdrowia w 2014 (health and health care in 2014), *Statistical Information and Elaborations*, Warsaw.

Kancelaria Senatu (Senate Chancellery) (2014), Społeczeństwo obywatelskie I jego instytucje (Civil society and institutions), OT-627, January 2014. www.senat.gov.pl/gfx/ senat/pl/senatopracowania/. . . /ot-_627_internet.pdf (Accessed: 13 February 2016)

Kosińska, M., Kułagowska, E., Niebrój, L., and Stanisławczyk, D. (2013), Burdens of caregivers of patients classified for long-term home care, *Environmental Medicine* 16(2): 59–68. www.enviromental-medicine-journal.eu (Accessed: 19 August 2015).

Ministry of Family, Labour and Social Policy (2016), statistics on social assistance https:// www.mpips.gov.pl/ (Accessed: 21 March 2016).

NIK (Supreme Chamber of Control) (2010), Informacja o wynikach kontroli funkcjonowania zakłądów opiekuńczo-leczniczych (Information of control of the care facilities), KPZ-410-09/2009. https://www.nik.gov.pl/plik/id,1874,vp,2244.pdf (Accessed: 19 February 2016).

NIK (Supreme Chamber of Control) (2014), Opieka medyczna nad osobami w wieku podeszłym (Health Care for Elderly), Health Depatrement, KZD-4101–003/2014. www. nik.gov.pl (Accessed: 21 March 2016).

Opiece długoterminowej grozi zapaść (Long term care in danger of collapse) (2015), Portale Medyczne 16.06.2015. http://www.portalemedyczne.pl (Accessed: 19 August 2015).

Tache, I. and Neesham, C. (2011), The performance of welfare systems in post-communist Europe: *The Cases of Romania and Bulgaria.* www.ijeroline.com.

Toruńczyk-Ruiz, S. (2014), Neighbourhood ties and migrant Networks: The case of circular migrant in Warsaw, *Central and Eastern European Migration Review* 3(1), Warszawa: Centrum Badań nad Migracjami WNE UW

Uchwała Nr 238 Rady Ministrów w sprawie przyjęcia dokumentu Założenia Długofalowej Polityki Senioralnej w Polsce na lata 2014–2020 (Resolution of the Cabinet of Ministers on the document Assumption of the Long Term Care policy for seniors 2014–2020 in Poland) (2014); Monitor Polski, Dziennik Urzędowy Rzeczypospolitej Polskiej (Official Journal of the Republic of Poland), 14 February 2014, Poz 118.

# 5 Long-term care in Portugal
## Quasi-privatization of a dual system of care

*Alexandra Lopes*

## 5.1 Introduction

This chapter addresses long-term care arrangements in Portugal. It focuses primarily on the recent trends in LTC provision in Portugal and looks at those from an institutionalist approach. The main goal is to discuss the underlying logics of the different arrangements that have been developing in Portugal to tackle the growing demands for LTC and to discuss some of the implications of the chosen paths of policy design.

Just two decades ago, Portugal was as poor in LTC infrastructures as some of the new member states are now. In a relatively short period of time, it managed to implement a national system of social care services that displays coverage rates close to the European Union average, although remaining as one of the least generous countries in the EU in what concerns the percentage of GDP allocated to elderly care and one of the countries with the lowest number of formal LTC workers. In its effort to build up supplies of home and residential services, Portugal has pursued its own preferred path of policy development. One could broadly describe that as a path of mixed LTC, with flexible residential care flanking home care services, and oriented toward the quasi-privatization of services provided by a powerful nonprofit sector that is financially supported by the state. Recent reforms have introduced a dual approach to LTC. Traditionally, LTC was confined to provision of help for activities of daily living without any component of health care. This is why for many years the LTC system has been designated as social care system. In the middle of the first decade of the new millennium, a new system was implemented that integrated health and social care. Set up as a network of services providing continuous care between hospital care and community-based care, it did not replace the existing social care sector and rather introduced a new branch that operates as a parallel system.

Long-term care is understood in this chapter as comprising all care services and benefits for people requiring support in essential facets of daily living as a consequence of illness, both physical or mental, or frailty occurring as a consequence of old age.

The chapter provides some analysis on the legislative developments in the LTC sector in Portugal and draws on administrative data collected from official national sources, such as the Ministry of Social Affairs or the Ministry of Health, and from

60 *Alexandra Lopes*

international bodies such as the European Commission (EU), the International Labor Organization (ILO) and the Organization for Economic Co-operation and Development (OECD). It is organized into five sections following this introduction plus some concluding remarks. The first section includes a brief review of the history of LTC provision in Portugal. In the second section we move to the analysis of the current provision of LTC, including a discussion about the roles of different stakeholders and about levels of achievement of care provision. The third section will focus on the more recent branch of LTC that was implemented in the middle of the financial crisis and will analyze what it brought to the existing LTC landscape both in terms of innovation and continuity. The chapter continues analyzing the financials of LTC provision in Portugal in view of discussing the implications of the chosen model of financing for the organization and the performance of the system. This is done in section 5.4, which will open the way for the last section of the chapter, where all that is presented before will be resumed in order to address the challenges and the anticipated future trends of LTC provision in Portugal.

## 5.2 Historical trends in the consolidation of social care for dependent elderly in Portugal: familism and quasi-privatization of care

To discuss issues of welfare state provision in Portugal, as in other Southern European countries, the background conceptual approach that is usually found in the literature is that of familism (Naldini, 2003). This is a term that is used in a rather consensual manner to describe the welfare state dynamics of this part of Europe and to describe in particular a policy setting that relies heavily on families as the main locus for care provision (not only for older people but also for children and those with disabilities), leaving for the state the role of income insurer and for charities the role of poverty alleviation and assistance to all those unable to secure their needs by activating family resources (Ferrera, 1996; Rhodes, 1997). *Familism* refers to a model of social organization based on the prevalence of the family group and where the family is the unit of account for the policymaking process. Policies therefore tend to take as a goal the well-being of the family as a group rather than the interests and necessities of each one of its members. The norm rests on resilient intergenerational exchanges sustained by a wealth of social values that reinforce and naturalize kinship obligation and reciprocity and that operate as the cement that keeps everything together (Lopes, 2006).

Overall, one could argue that the Portuguese welfare state has followed a model of development in all areas of provision that require the delivery of care services more or less aligned with the *Bismarkian* approach. This means it has traditionally emphasized income protection mechanisms with the state showing little interest in expanding coverage of public servicing.

The absence of infrastructures of care has been historically compensated by the assistance offered by nonprofit organizations with a religious Catholic foundation. It has been like that throughout the centuries; it was like that throughout

*Long-term care in Portugal* 61

the dictatorship period between 1933 and 1974 and it remained like that after the implementation of the democratic institutions and the expansion of a national social security system in the last quarter of the twentieth century. Confronted with increasing pressures from an ageing population, but without the inclination or the financial capacity to implement a full-fledged public LTC system, the option was to turn to the existing institutions providing assistance and integrate them in a care-provision system regulated by the state. To expand services, a new private/ public mix centered on public subsidies to nonprofit institutions was built up in the late 1980s. It was implemented through new legislation, published in 1983, that would set the contours of the activities offered by nonprofit institutions and would establish a specific statutory category – *Instituições Particulares de Solidariedade Social* (IPSS) – that of private nonprofit institutions delivering social care services.[1] Annual negotiations were instituted between the Ministry of Social Affairs and third-sector representatives concerning the flat-rate subsidy paid by the state per user served by service providers that sign cooperation agreements with the state (*Acordos de Cooperação*).

From this point in time onward, there was considerable and sustained growth of the nonprofit sector. Due to its intricate relations with the state, many academics have labelled the nonprofit sector as a quasi-governmental sector. Others, more concerned about the impacts of the monopoly it holds over the case provision sector, have labelled this nonprofit sector as a frighteningly powerful quasi-market (Ferreira, 2010). From the roughly 1,500 of such institutions registered in 1983, we have grown to a total of 5,080 in 2015 (Social Security List of IPSS, http://www.seg-social.pt/publicacoes?bundleId=11899703).

Direct public care provision has also been made available as a cash benefit, initially known as "allowance for assistance by a third party"[2] and later renamed as Supplement for Dependency (*Complemento por Dependência*).[3] The overarching guiding principle is that the state needs to help individuals and their families compensate for the additional costs that come with dependence, but the task of caring should rest primarily and preferably on family exchanges. The cash benefit is paid to the dependent person together with his or her old-age pension, and there are no conditions on how it is used. At inception, the care allowance was universal and conditional to having dependency certified by social security officials and based on medical reports. In 2013,[4] a change was introduced with the shift to a means-tested approach: only pensioners that have a pension below a certain threshold (€600 in 2015) are eligible for the care allowance.

## 5.3 LTC in contemporary Portugal: provisions and providers

The mix of formal social care provision that has developed in Portugal combines public care allowances designed to help families shoulder the additional costs of performing their roles as primary care providers and a market of care servicing controlled by nonprofits subsidized by public funding. Informal care remains very high, and the private commercial sector has a very shy expression. In this section, we will briefly outline the contours of the different mechanisms of care provision in place.

62  *Alexandra Lopes*

Cash benefits for care have never allowed Portuguese families to outsource care provision – not to private commercial providers and not even to alternative informal carers such as migrant care workers. Migrant care workers have become a relevant category in several countries in Europe that offer relatively generous care allowances (Lamura et al., 2010). This was not the case in Portugal and the main reason is that, from their institution, cash benefits addressing care needs of the elderly have always been very meagre in terms of their monetary value. The care allowance is set as a proportion of the value of the social pension, and depending on the severity of the dependency it varied, in 2015, between €90 and €180 per month.[5] Amounts are calculated under a dual system: one for those who are in the contributory system and one for those who are not entitled to any pension and are therefore integrated in the social assistance system. The amounts are always more generous for those in the regular contributory system. For both systems, dependency level is taken into account but in a very standardized format that shows little to no capacity to differentiate care needs. There are two levels of dependency: the first level applies to those who have limitations for the activities of daily living (without specifying which ones) but are not bedridden; the second level is for those who are bedridden or have dementia problems. In any of the cases, incapacity is certified by medical reports and does not involve any assessment of specific needs within the broad group of activities of daily living. Table 5.1 summarizes the amount of money for care in place.

Provision of care in Portugal has been primarily secured by intrafamily exchanges, with families shouldering not only the provision but also the financial burden that comes with engaging in caring for a relative. There is no registry of family carers and no national survey collects information to estimate that number. Data from some international surveys such as SHARE (Survey on Health, Ageing and Retirement in Europe) suggest that the difference in patterns of engagement of family carers in elderly care may vary across countries more in terms of the intensity and the locus of caregiving rather than in global levels of engagement. Portugal shows a pattern of family care that involves, for the majority of carers, a high number of hours of care and co-residence with the looked-after relative,

*Table 5.1* Amounts available under the care allowance in Portugal, 2015

| Eligibility criteria | Level of dependency | |
| --- | --- | --- |
| | First level | Second level |
| Pensioners integrated in the social insurance system | 50% of the value of the social pension (in 2015 = €100.77) | 80% of the value of the social pension (in 2015 = €181.38) |
| Pensioners not included in the social insurance system | 45% of the value of the social pension (in 2015 = €90.69) | 75% of the value of the social pension (in 2015 = €171.30) |

Source: Social Protection Online, http://www.seg-social.pt/complemento-por-dependencia (accessed on January 31, 2016).

*Long-term care in Portugal* 63

which is the reason why it is often portrayed as a country where family care ranks high in the global system of care provision (Rodrigues, Huber and Lamura, 2012).

Just to illustrate this pattern of family care provision, the last estimates available drawing on data collected in 2010 indicate that roughly 16% of individuals aged 50 and older reported being informal carers, a figure that is more or less the same as one finds in the majority of other western European countries. However, when we look at the intensity of their involvement in care tasks, similarities disappear and differences become clearer: in Portugal, roughly 87% of informal carers do it on a daily basis (similar to what happens in Spain, Poland or Italy) while that figure hardly passes 50% in countries such as Sweden, Denmark, Germany or the Netherlands (OECD estimates based on SHARE survey, http://dx.doi.org/10.1787/health_glance-2013-en). Additionally, most of the times care takes place in a context of co-residence, even when the family carer is an adult child (Lopes, 2006).

The consequence of the clarification in the mid 1980s of the nature of the nonprofit sector and of the model of its articulation with the state has created the conditions for a very speedy development of a formal social care services market dominated by the third sector. These institutions are expected, according to a repeated official political discourse, to create a support system that helps families in their effort to assist their elderly. The nature of formal social care is therefore complementary or even subsidiary to family care.

Reliable data for this sector is only available from 1998 onward, but the trends in the growth of the social care servicing sector over the next 15 years leave us with a clear picture of the importance of this nonprofit sector in the country.

Services and facilities available to the elderly are diverse: day care centers, home-based services (home help), nursing homes, as well as residential care (protected flats) and family accommodation (*Acolhimento familiar*). However, from the first years of expansion of the social care sector, the last two forms of care have remained very poorly developed. We focus therefore on the three others.

The data displayed in Table 5.2 include only the facilities that are legally registered and licensed to operate. In Portugal there has always been a parallel illegal market of private commercial institutions of a size that remains unknown but that consecutive efforts of inspection by judicial authorities have been containing. Those institutions are not considered in this chapter. The data include all services provided by nonprofit and commercial institutions. There is no disaggregated data to establish the number of commercial facilities. What we know, according to official data, is that in nursing homes and home-help services, and in most parts of the country, the private commercial sector represents a share lower than 10%. However, it has also been experiencing some expansion, and in the big urban centers (around Lisbon and Porto) it is already responsible for a bit over 20% of the offer (GEP, 2014). As for day centers, they are all run by nonprofits.

More recently, there have been some initiatives from big corporations operating in the health and insurance sectors interested in investing in the senior care market. It is still to come up with any conclusion. The facilities that have been opening, mostly in Lisbon and in Porto, are focusing on sheltered accommodation

64  *Alexandra Lopes*

*Table 5.2* Trends in service provision to older people between 1998 and 2014: nursing homes, day centers and home-help care

| Type of care service | Number of available places nationwide (Usage rate in %) | | | | | Coverage rates per 100 persons nationwide | | | |
|---|---|---|---|---|---|---|---|---|---|
| | | | | | | 65+ | | 80+ | |
| | 1998 | 2000 | 2005 | 2010 | 2014 | 1998 | 2014 | 1998 | 2014 |
| Nursing homes | 49,059 (94.6) | 55,863 (95.3) | 60,884 (97.2) | 71,261 (95.3) | 89,666 (91.5) | 3.07 | 4.29 | 14.87 | 15.28 |
| Day centers | 46,273 (78.5) | 51,143 (80.5) | 60,352 (70.0) | 62,472 (69.0) | 64,705 (65.0) | 2.90 | 3.10 | 14.02 | 33.11 |
| Home help | 38,022 (87.4) | 48,734 (94.3) | 73,575 (85.4) | 90,570 (83.9) | 104,551 (73.9) | 2.38 | 5.01 | 11.52 | 17.82 |

Source: *Carta Social* data, available at http://www.cartasocial.pt and *Instituto Nacional de Estatística*, National Estimates on Population by age groups, 1998–2014, available at http://www.ine.pt (author's calculations).

and assisted living for high-income groups. There is still some resistance from the population toward a product that is new and, although popular in other parts of Europe, relatively odd for a culture that still acknowledges little importance of independence and individuality.

The data on changes in provision between 1998 and 2014 point to two main conclusions. First, the last two decades have been critical for the expansion of social care services and have succeeded in bringing Portugal close to the European average concerning coverage rates, and this is despite the cuts in social expenditure after the financial crisis of 2008. Between 1998 and 2014, the number of available places in nursing homes has increased by around 82% and in home-help services have increased around 175%. Although the increase in the absolute number of individuals in the older cohorts has not allowed for a proportional increase in coverage rates, the growth in the number of facilities has been faster than the potential increase on the demand side and allowed for some catching up. Coverage rates in home help services in particular have practically doubled between 1998 and 2014.

Second, the trends of evolution over time show the materialization of a preferred model of service provision that privileges home help and complementary services along the lines of the move toward aging in the community experienced in most other European countries. This corresponds to what many experts had been advocating as the preferred model for Portugal, one where social care is of a mixed nature, with flexible residential care flanking home care services and day care facilities. This approach has been argued to be the best in reconciling the pressures to alleviate families from the excessive effort required if taking exclusive responsibility for care provision without crowding them out of the global system of welfare provision (Lopes, 2013). Usage rates, however, call for some caution. If they are consistently high in nursing homes, they have been decreasing in day care centers and home-help services. This indicates a mismatch between the principles on which the architecture of the system rests and the actual uptake of services by potential users. No explanations for this have been found in the literature but tentative ones could be: it may be the result of lack of capacity or will to pay for the services, or it may be the consequence of a perceived poor quality of services provided.

## 5.4 The national network for long-term care: rehabilitation and integration of health and social care in the new millennium

The first time the expression long-term care appears in an official piece of legislation was in the mid-1990s and came in the form of a national programme – the Programme of Continuous Care (*Programa de Cuidados Continuados*) – that was established by the government for the period between 1995 and 1999 and that set the goal of providing a wide range of caregiving facilities for elderly persons with high levels of dependency. The main purpose was the establishment of hospitals for convalescence and temporary care of elderly persons as well as the improvement in the coordination of the different services supporting this group of the population. In practical terms, nothing significant changed in the existing LTC landscape, but the topic of LTC was definitely brought to light. The main novelty was the official recognition that provision of care for dependent elderly involves both social and health care, and therefore the way forward should involve the articulation of these two fields.

This shift in the approach to care for older people took place as the result of several factors. On one hand, it came in response to the calls from different international forums such as the OECD or the European Commission that had been raising awareness among national states for the topic of integration of health and social care. On the other hand, it happened as a response to domestic pressures of two kinds. One source of pressure originated in the tension between the social care sector and some professionals from the health care side. Licensed providers, especially in the domain of home-based services, were only funded and accredited to provide social care but were often confronted with demands from users that required help with a wide range of health-related issues (e.g., intake of medication and administration of injections, among others). Although care workers do not include any licensed nurses, they would often end up providing those services. This has triggered a vivid debate between representatives of the social care sector and the unions and representatives of nursing professionals in a fight to establish the borders between what falls under the definition of social care and what is exclusive of health care. One other source of pressure came from hospital administrators concerned with the inefficiencies of the existing LTC provision in tackling bed-blocking caused by prolonged stays in hospital beds of dependent elderly not needing acute hospital care. There was never any study carried out on this bed-blocking phenomenon and nobody knows how significant it was from a quantitative perspective. However, toward the middle of the 1990s it became relevant as a policy argument.

## 66   *Alexandra Lopes*

After some tentative initiatives along the next years, the National Network of Integrated Long-Term Care (*Rede Nacional de Cuidados Continuados Integrados – RNCCI*) was launched with the issuing of the Decree-Law No. 101/206 (June 6, 2006). The two years that would follow would be for experimentation with some pilot projects that were monitored and used for subsequent adjustments. The RNCCI would become a national reality in 2008.

RNCCI is officially defined as a system that articulates the services that fall under the hat of the Ministry of Social Security with those that are under the responsibility of the Ministry of Health, aiming at the implementation of an integrated model of LTC. It shows a design that generally follows the principles of the care continuum as defined by Evashwick (1989) and that rests on a new approach to the coordination of the provision of long-term care by bringing together teams operating on the social support and palliative care side with teams operating on the health care side (at hospitals and health centers). The goal was to implement an intermediate level of health and social care, between hospital care and community-based care, centered on the principle of rehabilitation. The approach is to invest in rehabilitation of functional capacities in order to achieve the maximum potential of autonomy of each individual after a debilitating episode of illness or functional deterioration in order to delay institutionalization and create the conditions for his or her reintegration in the community, even if the person needs some social care assistance.

More than the creation of new services and facilities, the new system launched a new structure of coordination aimed at making a better, more integrated and equitable use of the existing facilities and a better allocation of responsibilities among the different agents involved in long-term care. This coordination structure operates at the local level primarily, but it is also integrated at the regional and national levels. The entrance points are confined to the hospital (from where roughly 63% of referrals take place) (ACSS, 2015) and the local health center. Once referred to a local coordinating team (that operates in a relatively restricted territorial region, equivalent to the administrative division of the national territory for the purpose of health administration), each individual case is assessed in the context the person's own needs but also in the context of their own resources (including family resources) to (1) confirm the eligibility criteria for admittance in the LTC system; (2) define the type of intermediate level service required, considering the resources available within the personal support network of the individual; (3) locate vacancy in the local network of services; and (4) present proposal and get the patient's consent or, in case patient is not able to provide consent due to cognitive impairment, from legal representative. When there are no places available in the local area, the referred patient will be transferred to the regional coordinating team that operates at a broader geographical level and that will try to locate a vacancy across the country. This coordination structure is managed by officials operating under the Ministries of Social Affairs and Health.

This new branch of care provision though did not represent any major change in the fundamental principle of care privatization: the state acts primarily as coordinator and funder and hands the provision of services to private institutions (commercial and nonprofit). As in the traditional social care sector, nonprofits are the dominant providers here, with currently 76.2% of the provision. The commercial sector represents 19.7% of the places available and public facilities account for a very residual 4.1% of the total places available (ACSS, 2015).

The LTC system operates according to a typology of services that include in-patient care (convalescence units, middle duration and long-stay units), out-patient care (ambulatory care) and home-based services (long-term care integrated home teams and palliative care community teams).

In terms of implementation, there was not a considerable expansion in the number of providers; rather, existing ones that were operating in the social care sector and that, after some adaptation in both facilities and employed staff, became eligible to be relabelled and integrated into the RNCCI. There was some public investment over the first years of operations and until 2012 in building new infrastructures. With the cuts introduced in public expenditure as a result of austerity policies, funding for these services was interrupted after 2012 with hardly any new cooperation agreements being signed between the state and candidate providers. Currently there are facilities that third-sector organizations have built using European funds, but they are not running given the agreement with the state for provision of care has not been signed. Plans to resume LTC as a priority are on the table since the new left-wing government took office in late 2015, but to date no developments have been observed.

The expansion of the number of places available in the LTC network has brought coverage rates to levels that generally still fall below the targets set by the national authorities by roughly 50%.

The distributions displayed in Table 5.3 are further reinforced by territorial disparities that have been highlighted by several reports on the performance of the

*Table 5.3* Some figures on availability and coverage of the RNCII, 2014

| Type of service | No. beds/places | Coverage rate (per 1,000 residents) | | Target coverage rate for 65+ |
|---|---|---|---|---|
| | | *65+* | *80+* | |
| Convalescence units | 860 | 0.41 | 1.47 | 1.4 |
| Medium-stay units | 2,021 | 0.97 | 3.44 | 1.6 |
| Long-stay Units | 4,094 | 1.96 | 6.98 | 4.0 |
| Palliative care units | 185 | 0.09 | 0.32 | 0.2 |
| Out-patient and home-help teams | 6,766 | 3.24 | 11.53 | n/a |

Source: ACSS (2015) and *Instituto Nacional de Estatística*, National Estimates on Population by age groups, 2014, available at http://www.ine.pt.

68   *Alexandra Lopes*

RNCCI (Lopes, 2013). The main urban regions of Lisbon and Porto are particularly affected by access problems with coverage rates below the national averages. What the coverage rates suggest is that there has been an easier expansion in home-based services since these benefit from the capacity already in place from the institutions operating in the social care sector, and these can easily convert into the new category under the RNCCI just by adding health care staff to their teams (mostly nurses and geriatric staff). The investment required to convert nursing homes into in-patient LTC units is somehow more demanding in terms of the financial effort required and is less appealing for institutions that are historically more oriented to social care and deficient in capital of their own. It has been in less urbanized areas of the country, where health care services were already being provided by nonprofits managing local hospitals funded by the state, that more LTC in-patient care units have been implemented. But this raises another problem: the mismatch between the geographical location of the care units and the residential areas of potential users and their families.

### 5.5  The financials of care provision

The funding principle for the provision of care rests on a mixed model of public funding and private out-of-pocket payments for both social care services and provision under the RNCCI network. For each user, and depending on the type of service provided, the state will transfer a certain amount of money to the institution providing the service per user served. Copayments apply for the social care services and for the social care component of the LTC network. They are defined according to rules that are also regulated by the cooperation agreements. The responsibility for the copayments rests not only on the user of the service but also on his or her children, according to the general law that stipulates the duty of assistance from adult children to their parents. The health care component of services under the LTC network is tax-funded and is the responsibility of the Ministry of Health. For this component, user fees may apply at flat rates, but means-tested exemptions are possible.

Tax deductions for families engaged in care provision to dependent elders apply. These include situations where the family has to make payments of nursing home fees as well as situations where the dependent elder is in co-residence with descendants. These tax deductions are generally low (defined as a proportion of the national minimum wage, which was €500 in 2015) and only apply if the elder has a personal income below the minimum established for the contributory old-age pension (in 2015 this was €261.95).

The estimates on the share of GDP allocated to LTC are not consistent throughout the different sources, but Portugal has been taking a modest position across the last two decades in the comparative picture of the European Union countries. Although it is expected that the weight of LTC expenditure on the GDP will increase, the majority of the estimates do not put it above 1% of the GDP in the coming decades and place it currently at roughly 0.5% of GDP (EU, 2015).

More revealing is the analysis of the composition of the total expenditure on elderly care for what it reflects about structural policy options. We have selected data from the annual reports issued by the Ministry of Social Affairs on the financial performance of the public social security system. Figure 5.1 displays the evolution of total expenditure, in thousands of euros, over the last 5 years for which we have definitive data. We have grouped expenditure according to two main functions: care in cash and care in kind. Care in cash corresponds to the expenditure with the care allowance *Complemento por Dependência* across all categories of pensioners. Care in kind corresponds to the transfers from the Ministry of Social Affairs to nonprofits, under cooperation agreements, and for the provision of day care, home-based services and nursing homes. Care in kind also includes transfers made to institutions operating under the LTC integrated network (RNCCI) for the component of social care.

What is more striking about the trends displayed in the figure is the clear orientation toward care in kind that continues to expand even after the financial crisis, contrasting with the decrease in the provision of cash for care. In fact, it is in this specific benefit, and certainly as a result of the legislation published in 2013

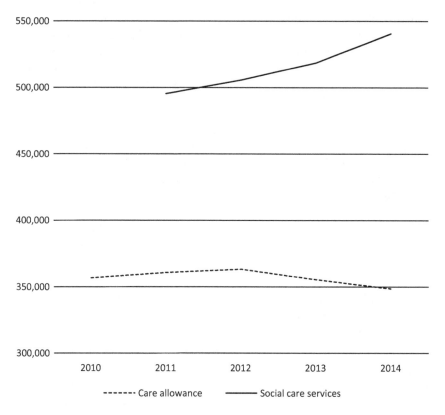

*Figure 5.1* Public expenditure in care provision in cash and in kind under the Social Affairs Ministry (in thousands of euros), 2010–2014

Source: Conta da Segurança Social, 2010–2014 (Annual Financial Performance Report of the Social Security) (author's calculations).

introducing means-tested conditional access to the care allowance, that we see a relatively sharp decline in the absolute amount of public expenditure. And here rests the most distinctive feature of the Portuguese care system. Choosing a path of service provision is not exclusive to Portugal. Neither is choosing a path of partnering with institutions from the civil society. But choosing service provision by nonprofits subsidized by a state that abdicates its role as a social regulator comes with some risks. The fact that citizens cannot themselves introduce some regulation, at least by means of choice, increases those risks.

Currently, nonprofits operate in a quasi-monopoly that, due to the funding model that comes directly from the state to the providers without users having any say, impedes any free markets to develop. The care allowance that has been slowly withdrawing from the policy arena is kept at such low amounts that it does not offer any possibility for alternatives to existing providers. The private commercial market has been kept underdeveloped also as a consequence of this monopoly of nonprofits. The preferential relationship they have with the state crowds out any proposals for cash benefits, which leaves little room for expansion for commercial providers apart from the segment of the well-off elderly.

Individuals and their families make decisions about outsourcing on the basis of not only the availability of services but also of fees and prices. Deprived of the possibility of choosing how to use the amount that is annually defined as the payment per elderly institutions get form the state, individuals and families are left with no other alternative than taking whatever is available in the existing nonprofits or continue to insource care.

Access to care provided by nonprofits rests often on discretionary routines, and persistent lack of transparency has been discussed in the literature (Hespanha et al., 2000). There is no legally recognized right to social care with access dependent on availability of services. Relationships of patronage that have historically characterized the Portuguese welfare system remain alive, with social capital (often aided by economic capital) being a determining factor to define access to services.

The impacts of all these leave reasons for very contained optimism, namely concerning issues of quality, staff qualification and labor conditions as well as innovation. We discuss these issues in the next section.

## 5.6 Critical challenges for formal care provision in Portugal: LTC staff shortage and absence of quality assessment mechanisms

Although we have been seeing some convergence toward the EU average in coverage rates for formal care provision, it should be noted that coverage rates alone do not necessarily correspond to appropriate coverage. This is particularly the case in Portugal, where there is a mismatch between coverage rates of services and coverage rates of LTC workers. According to estimates from the International Labor Organization (ILO), among the family of European countries, Portugal displays one the lowest coverage rates of LTC workers per 100 individuals aged

*Long-term care in Portugal*   71

65 years and older. In 2014, ILO's estimates put that figure for Portugal at 0.4. Taking as a reference the median population weighted number of formal LTC workers (FTE) in OECD countries, which amounts to 4.2 workers per 100 persons aged 65 years and older, one can grasp the dimension of the deficit in staff coverage currently affecting Portugal (Scheil-Adlung and ILO, 2015). Shortage of staff in a sector that shows coverage rates at the level of the EU average can only mean one thing for workers: excessive workloads and long working hours. For service users, it can only mean insufficient care.

Shortage of staff is further aggravated by the low wages paid to a work force that is predominantly female. In 2007, ILO data indicated that in Portugal the ISCO_513 group (personal care workers and related workers) is 93.5% female (EU, 2012). As for wages, the salary rates for the nonprofit sector place salaries of personal care workers between €505 and €600 per month.[6] These poor working conditions are coupled with high rotation of staff and ultimately make us raise an eyebrow as to the quality of the care that is provided.

Quality of care is a topic that has remained absent from the public debate on LCT in Portugal, and once more this can be a side effect of the chosen model of provision based on the quasi-monopoly of provision by the nonprofit sector.

In its path of privatization of care provision, the Portuguese state has been progressively relinquishing its role as social regulator (Ferreira, 2010). At present, the state acts primarily as a funding body and a licensing body for accreditation of providers. It has no interference in operational issues, and in its role as supervision agent it limits inspections to assessments of technical requirements of facilities to keep licenses active. The nonprofit sector itself, either because it operates as a monopoly or because of ideological orientations toward care, is still very much embedded in the Christian doctrine of charity and assistance and not in a culture of social rights, and it has shown little interest in implementing standard routines of quality control that can be disseminated and used to assist candidate users in their choice of providers.

This is in contrast with some routines of quality assessment that were introduced in the branch of the LTC system operating under the RNCCI. Here, most likely because of the integration of health care, routines of quality control typical of health care settings have been introduced and enforced by specific legislation. Among the dimensions of quality assessment in place we find assessment of admission times, assessment of care outcomes against envisaged care plan and regular surveys among users and their families. This, from our perspective, strengthens our argument about the importance of a strong regulation in quasi-monopoly markets as it shows it can be done only if the stakeholders involved are willing to do it.

Access to care rests often on discretionary routines, and persistent lack of transparency has been discussed in the literature (Ferreira, 2012). There is no legally recognized right to social care with access dependent on availability of services. Relationships of patronage that have historically characterized the Portuguese welfare system remain alive, with social capital being a determining factor to define access to services (Sousa Santos and Ferreira, 1998).

72   *Alexandra Lopes*

## 5.7 Conclusions

The last decades have been critical in the consolidation of formal LTC in Portugal, although today, as before, family remains the leading agent of care provision. Formal provision is primarily secured by the activities of nonprofit organizations, most of them with a religious background. Nonprofits are subsidized by the state, which has been progressively stepping out from its role as social regulator and inducing a quasi-privatization of care servicing.

Coverage rates of formal care provision have been increasing steadily since the mid-1990s, and the positive trend of growth remained throughout the period after the financial crisis of 2008. On this it is relevant to remember that when Portugal opened the public debate to the need of expanding care provision to older people, most European countries were already implementing reforms to reduce provision in response to adverse demographic, economic and fiscal conditions calling for welfare state retrenchment. One can argue that there is a time-lag dimension that has systematically characterized the welfare state and the policy debate in Portugal, and LTC is probably one of the domains where that is clearer to see. In that sense, rationalizing provisions and putting pressure on the family to insource rather than outsource care, as several other countries have been doing, was really not an option. Instead, the country pursued a path of consolidation of care provision in kind, negotiating the lowest possible rates of subsidizing and reducing even more the already meagre cash for care allowance.

The system in place displays features that give reason for reduced optimism. Nonprofits operate in a quasi-monopoly and users are not able to effectively exercise their legally recognized right to choose providers and provision. Private commercial providers struggle to offer costly services to families at affordable prices, but they are competing in an unfair way with a heavily protected nonprofit sector. From the standpoint of the labor force employed, the care sector survives on the basis of low wages and a lesser-qualified workforce with poor working conditions. Innovation is very shy, and incorporation of welfare technology is practically nonexistent. Discretion and patronage remain common features of how many institutions operate. Consolidating a culture based on social rights is probably the biggest challenge ahead. The result of that is likely to influence the development of care provision in Portugal in the decades to come.

## Notes

1 The piece of legislation – Decree-Law No. 119/83 (February 25, 1983) – defines the nature of the nonprofit institutions that would from then onward be eligible for signing provision contracts with the state. The legal diploma sets the requirements that institutions need to fulfill in order to be considered an IPSS.
2 This allowance was implemented by Decree Law No. 29/89 (January 23, 1989). It was first introduced in 1975, soon after the democratic revolution (*Portaria* No. 144/75, March 3, 1975) as a supplement for highly dependent invalids. This first form of care allowance did not specifically target older people but rather all individuals with impairments that would make them dependent of others for the normal activities of daily living.

## Long-term care in Portugal 73

3 The cash benefit known as *Complemento por Dependência* (complement for dependency) has replaced the Assistance by a Third Party Allowance for pensioners aged 65 years and older. The Decree Law No. 265/99 (July 14, 1999) defines the contents, eligibility criteria and amount of cash to be made available. It remains today as the main piece of legislation framing LTC cash benefits.
4 Decree Law No. 13/2013 (January 25, 2013).
5 Every year the Ministry of Social Security publishes the value of the social pension according to which a variety of other cash benefits are defined. This information is available for consultation at http://www.seg-social.pt/complemento-por-dependencia.
6 The Confederation of Non-Profits that provides social care issues an annual list with the salary rates applicable to all categories of workers employed by these institutions. The values indicated in the body of the text are the last available and were published for the year 2015 (http://www.novo.cnis.pt).

## References

ACSS (2015), *Monitorização da Rede Nacional de Cuidados Continuados Integrados*, Lisbon: ACSS Departamento de Gestão da Rede de Serviços e Recursos em Saúde (DRS).
EU (2012), *Long-Term Care for the Elderly: Provisions and Providers in 33 European Countries*, Luxembourg: Publications Office of the European Union.
EU (2015), *The 2015 Ageing Report: Economic and Budgetary Projections for the 28 EU Member States (2013–2060)*, Brussels: European Commission, Directorate-General for Economic and Financial Affairs.
Evashwick, C. (1989), Creating the continuum of care, *Health Matrix* 7(1): 30–39.
Ferreira, V. (2010), *Elderly care in Europe: Provisions and providers in Portugal*. External report commissioned by and presented to the EU Directorate-General Employment and Social Affairs, Unit G1 'Equality between women and men'.
Ferrera, M. (1996), The southern model of welfare in social Europe, *Journal of European Social Policy* 6(1): 17–37.
GEP (2014), *Carta Social*. Lisbon, Gabinete de Estratégia e Planeamento (GEP), *Ministério da Solidariedade*, Emprego e Segurança Social (MSESS).
Hespanha, P., Monteiro, A., Ferreira, A.C., Rodrigues, F., Nunes, M.H., Hespanha, M.J., Madeira, R., van den Hoven, R. and Portugal, S.(2000) *Entre o Estado e o Mercado: As Fragilidades das Instituições de Protecção Social em Portugal*, Coimbra: Quarteto.
Lamura, G., Chiatti, C., Di Rosa, M., Melchiore, M.G., Barbabella, F., Greco, C., Principi, A. and Santini, S. (2010), Migrant care workers in the long-term care sector: Lessons from Italy, *Health and Ageing* 4(22): 8–12.
Lopes, A. (2006), *Welfare arrangements, safety nets and familial support for the elderly in Portugal*. PhD thesis, The London School of Economics and Political Science (LSE).
Lopes, A. (2013), New approaches to familism in the management of social policy for old age. In J. Troisi and H.J. Kondratopwitz (eds) *Ageing in the Mediterranean*, Bristol: Policy Press, pp. 215–233.
Naldini, M. (2003), *The Family in the Mediterranean Welfare States*, London: Portland, Frank Cass.
Rhodes, M. (ed) (1997), *Southern European Welfare States: Between Crisis and Reform*, London: Frank Cass.
Rodrigues, R., Huber, M. and Lamura, G. (eds) (2012), *Facts and Figures on Healthy Ageing and Long-term Care*, Vienna: European Centre for Social Welfare Policy and Research.

74 *Alexandra Lopes*

Scheil-Adlung, X. and ILO (2015), *Long-term care protection for older persons: A review of coverage deficits in 46 countries*. ESS – Working Paper No. 50. Geneva: International Labour Office.

Sousa Santos, B. and Ferreira, S. (1998), Para uma Reforma Solidária da Segurança Social. In Ministério do Trabalho e da Solidariedade, *Sociedade e Trabalho*, Lisboa: MTS, pp. 50–57.

# 6 Long-term care in Italy

*Emmanuele Pavolini, Costanzo Ranci
and Giovanni Lamura*

## 6.1 Introduction

Elderly care has become a relevant issue in social policy for a number of reasons (Antonnen and Sipila, 2003): population ageing, increasing LTC costs and families' decreasing caring capacities. The analysis of the way in which care regimes tackle the growing care needs of older people is therefore important in order to measure the capacity for innovation of contemporary welfare systems (Bonoli and Natali, 2011; Ranci and Pavolini, 2012, 2015). In Italy, the supply of LTC has been traditionally characterised by a low level of public provision and funding when compared with Northern European countries. A highly selective public system has been set against the considerable capacity of family and kinship networks to internalise caring functions. For a long time, these two elements have constituted the principal traits of what has been termed the Italian *familistic model*, a model traditionally shared with other Southern European countries (Naldini and Saraceno, 2008).

For many decades, the poor extension of long-term care services did not constitute an urgent public policy problem as the strength of family-based intergenerational ties made it possible to absorb a large part of the emerging demand for care. It was only in the 1990s that the traditional familistic configuration of care arrangements began to be put under pressure by the emergence of two new trends: the ageing of the population and an increase in female participation in the labour market.

The main hypothesis of this chapter is that, after decades, recent years show quite a new feature: the LTC public system has reached a level of needs coverage (at least in terms of the population aged 65 years and older) similar to Continental European countries (like France and Germany). However, there are two peculiarities about this transformation. First, it was politically unintentional and driven by inertia, also due to processes of institutional "conversion" and "layering", to use the terminology from Streeck and Thelen (2005). Second, the needs coverage extension came about 'the Italian way', in other words, broader universalism in financing going along with more privatisation in delivery and organisation of the LTC services, with little attention to quality of care.

## 76  *Emmanuele Pavolini et al.*

In order to understand which factors have affected this transformation, a causal sequence structured in four steps is given below:

1   Since the 1990s, the familistic care model, historically dominant in Italy, has entered a deep crisis (Pavolini, 2004). This fact is not only the result of an increase in the number of older people with disabilities as might be expected, but also the effect of profound labour market transformations following a consistent growth in women's employment; therefore, it is also the increasing difficulty of conciliating working and caring, in a context of unchanged family organisation, that has weakened the traditional intergenerational solidarity on which the familistic system was historically grounded.

2   The national public welfare system has formally reacted to this crisis with institutional inertia as opposed to the reforms introduced in this field in most other European countries (Ranci and Pavolini, 2012). Given a dual LTC public system, based on highly residual in-kind services and a nationwide cash programme, the institutional inertia has meant that more and more dependent older people started requesting cash measures; as a consequence, the Italian public care system has strongly radicalised the cash-based character of its long-term care provision, reaching a level of coverage similar to that of other continental countries.

3   The reduction in families' caring capacities, both in relative and absolute terms, has been counterbalanced by the dramatic growth in private care provision. This growth has been largely favoured not only by the migration policy tolerating the entry of high numbers of (female) undeclared immigrants, but also by the availability of public transfers; therefore, the inertia of public policy related to LTC services, tied to an automatic increase in the beneficiaries of universalistic cash-based programmes, has driven the Italian dependent population and their families towards a new market-oriented, but publicly financed, solution.

4   The growth of this private care market cannot be simply interpreted in terms of the marketization of the Italian care system and of the end of the traditional care regime; indeed, there is complementarity between private paid care and family care; therefore, the huge reliance on 'family assistants' is also to be considered as a reaction of the traditional familistic system to an increased female employment rate and the subsequent increased reconciliation difficulties. The growth of a private care market in Italy can be understood as a consequence of changes occurring in the domestic labour market, requiring a reorganisation of family care arrangements that can combine working and caring responsibilities more easily than in the past. The inertia of public policy has paradoxically facilitated a solution that makes it possible to adapt the traditional care regime under new labour market and social conditions.

The economic crisis and the ensuing austerity measures have, on the one hand, made this model stronger in that public services have been cut, although it has been more difficult to curtail the access to cash allowances, given their universalistic nature. On the other hand, it has been weakened because households find

Long-term care in Italy   77

it more difficult to pay private carers now that unemployment and economic difficulties have hit a large part of Italian society.

The chapter supports this interpretation by analysing the characteristics and reactions of the public system and illustrating the main social changes causing the crisis of the traditional familistic model. It goes on to focus on the coping strategies adopted by families, giving specific attention to the growing role of private care providers. Finally, it identifies the central challenges facing Italian public policy makers, including the issues of lack of quality and of technology-based solutions in the care system.

## 6.2 Developments in long-term care policies for older people

The structure of the Italian public LTC system has been traditionally characterised by the presence of two parallel models of intervention based on heterogeneous criteria for eligibility. The first and most important track consists of a cash-for-care programme, the *Indennità di accompagnamento* (attendance allowance – IA). The second more residual track is based on local welfare programmes, which include the provision of residential and domiciliary services offered either by the National Health Care System (NHS) or the social services departments of Local Authorities (LAs).

Table 6.1 reports the amount of LTC public expenditure by type of provision (allowances or services) in 2014 compared to previous years. Around €20 billion (equal to 1.28 of the GDP) were spent by the Italian state in 2014 for LTC provision, specifically addressing the needs of the elderly. Half of this expenditure came through cash allowances (IA), and the other half was delivered through services (mostly home and residential care).

IA (*Indennità accompagnamento*) is a nationwide universalistic non-means-tested allowance of up to around €500 per month accessible to all citizens certified as totally dependent. The right to this benefit is officially ensured to those who

*Table 6.1* LTC public expenditure for older people (65 and older) by type of provision, 2014

| | Expenditure in 2014 | | Expenditure by source (%) | | Variation of expenditure in real terms over time (%) | | |
|---|---|---|---|---|---|---|---|
| Type | billion euros | as a % of GDP | 2005 | 2014 | 2005–2014 | 2005–2008 | 2008–2014 |
| Services (NHS and LAs) | 10.2 | 0.63 | 53.9% | 49.8% | +0.4% | +10.0% | −8.7% |
| Cash allowances (IA) | 10.3 | 0.64 | 46.1% | 50.2% | +19.2% | +15.7% | +3.1% |
| Total | 20.5 | 1.28 | 100.0% | 100.0% | +9.2% | +12.6% | −3.0% |

Source: Author's elaboration on Barbabella et al. (2015).

are "100% unable to walk and to perform everyday tasks and require continuous care". The National Institute for Social Security (INPS) manages the programme without any substantial coordination with local authority care provision.

Although this measure was introduced in the 1980s primarily to provide disabled adults with benefits (it was extended to the older population only in 1988), over the last 25 years there has been an exponential growth of its use by dependent older people. While the coverage level among those aged 65 and older was inferior to 3% in 1989, it reached 12% in 2012. Older people represented around 20% of all beneficiaries in 1989, to become 78% in 2012. The way IA has functioned and evolved in 35 years seems to be what Streeck and Thelen (2005) define as a "gradual but transformative" institutional change. The institution of IA has changed its objective; in qualitative terms it has gone from being a measure for disabilities of young people and adults to a measure for dependent older people, whereas in quantitative terms it has shifted from a measure designed for a relatively contained and stable number of potential beneficiaries to a measure expected to cover a rapidly growing target group. These processes of institutional transformation have taken place in a context of institutional inertia since no major reforms concerning LTC have been passed in the last decades (discussed later). Moreover, they were the results of the 'by default' functioning of tools such as the IA.

IA guarantees a coverage level that is comparable to the benefits provided by national programmes in France and in Germany. However, it is less generous towards the most severely dependent, as the amount offered is not related to the degree of dependency, whereas in the two continental countries there is a diversification of provision by the beneficiaries' level of dependency (three levels in Germany, six in France). Second, IA consists solely of monetary transfers, while the scheme adopted in Germany allows a choice between money transfers and services and a combination of cash and care. The French APA is a voucher which the beneficiary can only spend by purchasing services in kind. Furthermore, IA does not involve any form of *ex ante* definition (or *ex post* control) on how the cash granted is actually used. Once the right of a citizen to the benefit is recognised, it is given without any restriction placed on its use. IA can consequently be used to purchase services on the private market without restrictions and may thus indirectly encourage the growth of a grey care market.

This means that despite representing a fundamental resource for dependent people, IA runs the risk of constituting more of an income supplement than a cash-for-care measure designed to guarantee and support the provision of care services. Indeed, the amount of IA is relatively low given the average high disability level of beneficiaries. This means that although it does not provide the dependent older people with adequate support, it does paradoxically limit the risk of entrapment for their caregivers since, if caregivers work, the amount of resources provided by the IA is not high enough to become a functional equivalent of the caregiver's salary. The monetary incentive to leave work is simply too weak to have an effective impact on labour strategies of most caregivers, but it is high enough to drive

Long-term care in Italy   79

families to adopt another type of strategy – namely to rely on a peculiar private care market often characterised by irregular labour contracts (Naldini et al., 2016).

The second track of the public LTC system consists of local and regional welfare programmes, including the provision of residential and domiciliary services. The very fragmented provision of such LTC services is the result of the clear-cut division of responsibilities between local and health authorities in this respect. Health services (geriatric departments in hospitals, health home care etc.) are distributed on a universalistic basis and almost free of charge, but they are strictly limited to medical and nursing services, while social services are provided by local authorities on the basis of highly selective and extremely territorially varied criteria of access.

As a consequence of this lack of coordination, not only is the provision of these services subjected to great geographical variation, but intervention is limited to a very small number of people if compared with most of the other continental or Northern European countries (Pavolini and Ranci, 2012). In 2013, around 5% of the older population benefited from public home care programmes and only 2% from residential and nursing care (Chiatti et al., 2015). The difference in data for other European countries is as follows: around 7–8% receive home care in Germany and France and around 5–6% receive residential care in Germany, France and the UK (Pavolini and Ranci, 2012).

If we look at what happened in more recent years (see Table 6.1), the LTC public expenditure for services remained practically steady in real terms between 2005 and 2014. A robust growth (+10% between 2005 and 2008) had taken place before the crisis, but thereafter cuts were clearly implemented (–8.7% between 2008 and 2014) as a result of austerity measures. In the same years 2005 to 2014, the cash allowance programme (IA) increased by 19%. This growth was particularly strong before the crisis (+15.7%), but continued at a slower pace even after its onset and the implementation of austerity plans (+3.1%).

These changes in expenditure took place in a country which, unlike others, has not introduced any significant reform in the LTC field (Ranci and Pavolini, 2015). The increase in the demand for LTC by households (see the next section) and the need to contain costs (especially after the onset of the crisis) has produced a substantial inertia at national level in terms of institutional change and only cuts.

Although the issue has been debated in the public arena since the mid-1990s and has at times seen declarations of commitment by governments in office, no reform project has actually been launched so far. Three basic reasons can be found to explain this governmental inertia. First, there has been the difficulty in finding the necessary funds to build a new national programme to protect against the risk of dependency in a historical period when there has been strong pressure to avoid increases in welfare spending and to levy new taxes on citizens. Second, paradoxically, the availability and possibility to access a universal cash programme such as the IA, even if providing a limited amount of resources to beneficiaries (around €480 per month), was a buffer to social demand. Third, a constitutional reform in 2001 has made it more difficult for national governments since then to introduce

80   *Emmanuele Pavolini et al.*

overarching reforms in the field of social services, including LTC, as these competences are now allocated at regional level (Ascoli and Pavolini, 2015).

The inertia of national governments has been met with a certain dynamism by local and regional governments (Leon and Pavolini, 2014). However, innovations introduced at the local level have not produced a bottom-up development of LTC policy. The reasons for the absence of such bottom-up development are related to the particular relationship between national and local welfare in Italy. First, local assistance schemes are very limited quantitatively, accounting for not more than 15% of total public spending in social assistance. Second, local programmes have never been addressed by national policies. National social assistance schemes, such as IA, have been regulated by central government without introducing any joint responsibility with regional and local government in the management of the intervention. Therefore, the development of both municipal and regional LTC policies has always suffered because of the absence of central government regulation and adequate funding. The absence of a clear regulatory framework and the lack of enough national funding have inevitably driven most local programmes towards intervention characterised by discretion and residualism.

Contrary to local LTC services, IA beneficiaries increased dramatically: 6% of older people received it in 2002 versus 12% in 2013. In the same time span, home care increased from around 3–4% to 5%, and residential care remained substantially stable. There are at least two reasons behind this increase in coverage. First, the change in the nature of dependency needs with a relative shift from less to more severe forms of disability (see section 6.4) had a significant impact on the growth of those eligible to access the programme. However, this shift in needs can only partially explain what has happened. A second explanation seems more important, namely that the absence of services put greater pressure on both the families and the commissions evaluating the eligibility of frail older people for a universalistic programme such as IA, thus promoting a less tight approach to this evaluation.

### 6.3  The role of civil society in LTC delivery

There is limited space for service provision in a public LTC system where a large part of the economic resources and beneficiaries is covered through a cash allowance programme without any accountability requirement on how the money is spent. As shown in the previous section, only around 2% of older people receive residential care and around 5% receive home care. Moreover, the principal provider of home care is the NHS, and in 2012 it covered 4.3% of older people, offering to each beneficiary on average 21 hours of care *per year* (Health Ministry, 2014). Therefore, not only is the coverage limited, but the intensity of such coverage is also very low.

Private care provision is increasingly important in Italy, but so far it has not taken the facets of delivery based on organisations, but rather that of a market of individual (migrant) care workers (see section 6.5).

Long-term care in Italy 81

In this system of limited public service provision, the nonprofit sector plays a significant role mainly in partnership with local authorities. Most of the state-funded care services are actually provided by nonprofit organisations. In 2013, around 45% of residential care beds (including in nursing homes) were run by nonprofit institutions, and another 25% were run by private for-profit organisations. Only 29% of beds were in publicly owned institutions (ISTAT, 2015). For home care, the estimation is more complicated, given the absence of recent data. For 2005, Istat indicated that "social cooperatives" with their home care services covered around 3.3% of the older population (ISTAT, 2007). It should be noted that social cooperatives are the main type of nonprofit organisations running complex services contracted out by local authorities and the NHS. In the same year, the coverage rate of local authorities (LAs) and the National Health Service (NHS) home care was around 4%; therefore, it is evident that the vast majority of public home care users (approximately around 80%) were receiving services through nonprofit organisations. This phenomena was already underway during the 1990s and early 2000s, when nonprofit organisations had increasingly taken over the delivery of publicly funded social services in Italy through contracting-out mechanisms (Ascoli and Ranci, 2002). A more recent analysis on the nonprofit sector as a whole shows that this process has continued and probably become even stronger (Lori and Pavolini, 2016; Ranci, 2015) since there is no reason to think that these general trends have not applied also to home care provision for older people.

## 6.4 Long-term care amid increasing individual needs and diminishing family capacity

Another crucial phenomenon to be kept in mind is that Italy has the highest share of older population in Europe. The percentage of individuals aged 65 and older (21.4% in 2014) is 3% higher than the figure for the whole EU-28 (18.5%) (Eurostat, 2015). In comparison with 1990, the incidence has increased from 14.7% to 21.4%. In absolute terms, this means an increase of around 4.7 million people aged 65 years and older in just a quarter of a century.

This progressive growth in the older population has not translated into a parallel relative increase in the dependent population. According to official estimates (ISTAT, 2014), in 2013 there were approximately 2 million dependent people over age 65, which is equal to around 20% of the older people. In comparison with the mid-1990s, the relative spread of disability among the older population declined slightly (it was 21.7% in 1995).

However, while the relative weight of dependency did not increase in the last decade, the degree of disability changed enormously. If we consider the severity of disability, the most severe cases (confined at home) increased dramatically in the last 20 years both in absolute (around +500,000 older people) and relative terms (the severe disability rate increased from 8.8% in 1992–1993 to 9.4% in 2012–2013), whereas the less severe cases remained stable in absolute terms and decreased in relative terms (own elaboration on ISTAT, 2014).

82  *Emmanuele Pavolini et al.*

Therefore the hypothesis of a compression of morbidity (Baltes and Smith, 2003), countering the increase in the overall older population and limiting the growth in terms of caring needs, holds only partially true for Italy. The speed and relevance in quantitative terms of the ageing process and the relative shift from less to more severe forms of disability had a significant, albeit not dramatic, impact on the growth of the demand for protection.

The other fundamental factor to consider in order to understand the emergence of the need for broader public intervention for LTC in Italy is the crisis of the traditional system of care provided by families.

Over the last decades, there have been partial changes in the structures of households with older people: 27.9% of the older people lived alone in 1993 and 29.5% did so in 2012. However, living alone in Italy does not necessarily imply lack of family assistance. A large majority of older people living alone can rely on a support network of relatives, while only around 20% of them are childless or have children living in other towns (Costa, 2012). Due to a high level of geographical proximity, help and assistance provided by the family network are still very diffuse: 93% of frail older people receive informal help from their relatives, and 88% can also count on at least a weekly meeting with a child.

Changes in living arrangements have taken place only partially, which has led to two specific phenomena: the absolute numbers and the resilience of family support networks. The simple ageing structure of the population has created a much more marked phenomena in the single elderly. In 1993, 27.9% of single older people living alone meant 2.4 million people. Whereas 29.5% in 2012 meant 3.8 million elderly. This is an increase in real terms of 1.4 million people in two decades.

Moreover, a dramatic decrease in the caring capacity of families, both in absolute and relative terms, is visible. Most providers of informal care are increasingly middle-aged women – the daughters and daughters-in-law of older parents (Perrig-Chiello and Hopflinger, 2005). The female cohorts who enter this age have higher activity rates than the previous generation. The female activity rate for 45- to 54-year-olds and 55- to 64-year-olds increased from 45.6% in 1993 to 64.2% in 2014 and from 16.4% to 38.3%, respectively (own elaboration from Istat online database). In real terms, the total number of women aged 45 to 64 who are inactive on the labour market (therefore being potentially more available for informal caring activities) decreased by around 0.7 million between 1993 and 2014 (–15.6%).

To sum up, in the last 20 years there have been limited changes in the patterns of household behaviour concerning older people (single household formation) and in the diffusion of rates of disability. The new and increasing social demands for care have come from three different sources: the magnitude of the growth in the older population; the increase in the most dependent part of this population; and a considerable decrease in the caring capacity of families due to increasing difficulty in work-care arrangements, mainly related to rising female labour market participation. In absolute numbers, the third phenomenon is a very significant one: in two decades, the ratio between the number of dependent older people for each inactive woman (45–64 years old) increased from 1.9 to 3.2.

*Long-term care in Italy* 83

The growing need for care is therefore to be understood also as a consequence of profound changes in the work/care arrangements of Italian families who are less and less able to cope with LTC needs, rather than as simply driven by demographic trends.

## 6.5 A peculiar marketization: migrant care workers as the new cornerstones of the Italian LTC system

Given the growing difficulty of directly providing care and the weakness of public provision, in the last two decades a substantial proportion of households with frail elderly have turned to a peculiar type of private market: (migrant) care workers. The phenomenon grew fast because even though care work is increasingly provided by ethnic minorities in many European countries (Pfau-Effinger et al., 2006, Williams, 2013), this phenomenon is particularly notable in Italy. In 2013, a presence of 830,000 paid care workers was estimated nation-wide, 90% of them migrants, mostly working on an individual basis in frail elderly people's homes and very often without any specific formal training in LTC activities (Pasquinelli e Rusmini, 2013). The same estimate for 2008 was around 700,000 (Pasquinelli and Rusmini, 2008). Although unemployment increased remarkably during the recent crisis (the female unemployment rate went from 8.5% in 2008 to 13.8% in 2013), the LTC market was one of the few sectors in the labour market where employment kept on growing.

The widespread use of private individual caregivers is encouraged not only by the desire to keep elderly people living at home, but also by the substantial savings which this solution allows. While the average fee in a (basic) residence home is at least €1,500 per month, the monthly cost of a care assistant employed on the grey market, working 24 hours for six days a week (but cohabiting full time) is about €1,000 to €1,200 (Pasquinelli and Rusmini, 2008).

Furthermore, the recourse to individual care assistants is highly competitive in terms not only of costs but also of flexibility of working hours and services. Families do not seem to place excessive importance on the workers' professional qualities (Costa, 2012); they mostly value the discretionary use they can make of these assistants and the absence of specific contract rules. The practical absence of administrative controls contributes to the high amount of irregular work in this field. The rate of irregular jobs in the 'domestic services' sector is estimated at 64% (ISTAT, 2015). Furthermore, the existing regulation on immigration flows, strictly conditioning the legalisation of new migrants to a job contract and to the declared availability of housing accommodation, has increased the propensity of migrant women to accept, as a first job, work as an individual care assistant living with the employer.

However, the fact that the cash allowance (IA) provides €508 monthly for each beneficiary means that these resources are enough to pay a salary to a migrant care worker only if household incomes are adequate. Otherwise, it is not enough for low-income households to access the market by themselves. The result is that informal care (when present and available) is the main source of LTC for

## 84    *Emmanuele Pavolini et al.*

low-income households with frail elderly, given the difficulty to access formal public services (especially residential ones). Albertini and Pavolini (2015), analysing four European LTC systems (Denmark, France, Germany and Italy), showed that care systems based on service provision grant higher access to formal care and demonstrate lower inequalities. Moreover, countries where cash-for-care programmes and family responsibilities are more important register inequalities in access to formal care. Given its institutional design based more on cash allowances (IA) than services, Italy is the one country of the four considered in the study that shows the highest level of inequalities among frail elderly individuals in accessing formal care.

The interplay between health care and LTC must also be considered. The elderly population has been severely hit during recent years by the austerity measures adopted in health care.

Table 6.2 reports the same type of data about self-reported unmet needs for medical examination for reasons related to costs, distance or waiting times by income quintile, focusing only on individuals aged 65 years and older. The Italian (negative) specificities in relation to the access to health care services (including probably also some LTC services, e.g. nursing care) become amplified among the elderly population: in 2013, 9% of individuals 65 and older reported unmet needs and, respectively, almost 18% and 12.5% of those in the lowest and second-lowest income quintiles declared access problems. These percentages are more than twice as high as those registered in the EU-27. The situation worsened dramatically before and after the onset of the crisis and the implementation of austerity plans.

Considering the growth of the private market in combination with the stagnation of the public supply of services, some authors have concluded that Italy is experiencing a progressive commodification of the traditional familistic model,

*Table 6.2* Self-reported unmet needs in Italy for medical examination for reasons related to costs, distance or waiting times by income quintile for individuals aged 65 years and older

|  |  | *2007* | *2013* |
| --- | --- | --- | --- |
| Total | EU-27 | 4.4 | 4.8 |
|  | Italy | 5.7 | 9.0 |
| First income quintile | EU-27 | 6.4 | 7.4 |
|  | Italy | 9.6 | 17.9 |
| Second income quintile | EU-27 | 4.8 | 5.5 |
|  | Italy | 7.0 | 12.5 |
| Third income quintile | EU-27 | 3.6 | 4.3 |
|  | Italy | 3.7 | 6.9 |
| Fourth income quintile | EU-27 | 3.4 | 3.7 |
|  | Italy | 3.9 | 5.0 |
| Fifth income quintile | EU-27 | 1.7 | 2.0 |
|  | Italy | 1.7 | 2.2 |

Source: Based on Eurostat EU-Silc online database (2016).

quickly moving to an American-type model (Da Roit, 2007). This new model is characterised by the access to low-cost private services in which the traditional problem of 'cost disease' afflicting private markets is solved by recruiting migrant workers who receive little recognition in terms of basic citizenship rights and must accept particularly poor working conditions as a consequence. The recourse to the private care market basically depends not only on the lack of care alternatives, but also on the fact that family caregivers are present but are not able or no longer wish to provide care for all the time needed.

However, the phenomenon taking place in Italy is not only a marketization of care, but rather an adaptation and an extension of the informal family-based model to critically changing conditions in family arrangements, and it is facilitated by the presence of public policies that indirectly continue to foster a familistic model through cash measures. In-house care work provided by migrant care workers often complements family-based informal caregiving and seems to be consistent with the strong attitude of Italian families to privilege an 'ageing in place' strategy when dealing with a dependent person. Italy faces therefore a transition towards an 'Italian way' of privatisation of care, which is based on (1) a high incidence of paid carers who live together with the frail older people, introducing elements to the work relationship that are not typical of work contracts (co-residence); (2) a very high level of irregular working contracts (grey market); and (3) often strong complementarities between the use of private paid carers and the informal care supply.

## 6.6 Use of rehabilitation and welfare technology

The features of the Italian LTC system illustrated previously are related also to an overall limited investment in new technologies as a possible solution to LTC challenges. The analysis of how the Italian welfare state is using new technologies – as a tool to support and improve LTC provision or to mitigate the demand for it – shows three main characteristics of the Italian context: (1) a comparative backwardness compared to most Western European countries; (2) a high level of regional inequality; and (3) a still perceptible, mainly user-driven move towards a broader use of such technologies, despite the inertia of the public sector in this respect.

When we look at data showing the demand side, we should consider that older Italians are among the least digitally skilled in Europe, this being especially true for women and the least educated, so that only 1 out of 10 people aged 65 to 74 years uses the Internet to interact with public services, compared to 24% on average across Europe (Eurostat, 2015). Actually, at the end of 2014, the use of the Internet to search for health-related information at least a few times per year was reported by 59% of Italians, which is in line with the EU-average (European Commission, 2014). However, a relatively higher share of Italians valued this Internet-based information as not reliable (60% compared to an EU-average of 50%), and relatively few found it useful (60% vs. 80%). This seems to suggest that digital health literacy is lower among Italians compared to their European

## 86 Emmanuele Pavolini et al.

counterparts, so they experience more difficulty in using the Internet as a tool to tackle everyday long-term care issues.

As for the supply side, data show that the implementation of e-health tools within current programmes addressing the chronic care of older people is rather limited (Melchiorre et al., 2015). One of the reasons explaining this situation might be identified in the recent economic crisis, which may have slowed down the process of introducing new technologies in everyday long-term care provision. As a matter of fact, public expenditure for digital investments in the Italian health care sector dropped in 2013 by a further 5% after a remarkable decrease already in the previous year (Osservatorio ICT in Sanità, 2014). Other in-depth analyses, however, show that the cause of the current backwardness in this area might be more structural and lie even further back in time, as the level of investments in ICT in Italy has been lagging behind since the mid-1990s (Hassan and Ottaviano, 2013), thus affecting the overall development and use of new technologies in the country, including in the long-term care sector.

Another indicator in this respect is the limited linking and use of electronic data records in Italy's long-term care system (OECD, 2014). This structural weakness jeopardises the possibility for both national and regional governments to pull together data from different sources for reporting purposes and integrate them into more coordinated efforts to provide long-term care for chronic diseases. This flaw, along with a very limited support from ICT-based solutions, which represent only 16% of all the country's diagnostic and therapeutic pathways (FIASO, 2014), perpetuates the traditional focus on hospital acute care. This is confirmed by the high share of such investments absorbed by the digitalisation of medical records within the hospital care sector, while only marginal resources are dedicated to developing ICT-based supports for home and community care (Osservatorio ICT in Sanità, 2014).

Another structural characteristic of the Italian long-term care system is the high level of regional inequalities, this being true also in the area of new technologies. On the whole, digital-based services in the health care sector are much more frequent in the northern regions of the country (Osservatorio ICT in Sanità, 2014). Paradoxically, the availability of high-tech machineries such as echotomographies, computerised axial tomographies and nuclear magnetic resonance scanners is actually remarkably higher in terms of number of machines per inhabitants in the southern part of the country (ISTAT, 2015). This area, however, is the one traditionally reporting the lowest per capita health spending levels and the highest inequalities in terms of public health care spending (Spandonaro, 2015), thus reflecting an overall inappropriate or inefficient use of such technologies within the local care system.

The situation described is already improving slightly, since the share of citizens who book a medical check via Internet has increased from 3.9% in 2011 to 9.7% in 2013 (Censis, 2013). In addition, the use of smartphones and tablets for professional purposes by family doctors is rapidly increasing, as these devices are currently used by 51% and 38% of family doctors, respectively (Osservatorio ICT in Sanità, 2014).

Besides quantitative data, which are still lacking in this sector, several recent promising initiatives are being reported that might have an important impact in the years to come. Among these initiatives, some have been undertaken by the Italian Association of Italian Municipalities to improve the understanding of the role new technologies (particularly digital ones) can play in providing health and social care services by identifying the most appropriate solutions to the specific local needs and to best introduce them into everyday care provision (Federsanità ANCI, 2015). Furthermore, in a country characterised by widespread employment of private care workers hired by households to provide hands-on care for frail older people, it is no surprise that apps have been developed and made available for tablets and smartphones to support family carers in managing the care work provided by this staff (Stefani, 2015). So far, however, no data are available with regard to the number of users resorting to these kinds of tools. Telecare – that is, the use of electronic devices combined with ICTs and professional practices to care for people from a distance – is another field of widespread application. This concerns especially the tele-alarm and tele-monitoring services activated by many local municipalities and some private providers, but it also includes some important experiments in telecare with clinical content, such as those offering tele-rehabilitation (Dallolio et al., 2008) or tele-cardiology assistance (Brunetti et al., 2014).

Although attempts to implement ambient assisted living technologies on a routine basis are rare, a recent, remarkable exception is the up-tech intervention that was implemented in a Central Italian region to support Alzheimer patients and their family caregivers (Chiatti et al., 2014). As a result of this initiative, over 400 households in this area can benefit from a set of home-based domotic supports over a two-year period, which in some districts will even become a permanent component of the local long-term care service provision. Currently, an extension of this initiative to other Italian regions and even other European countries is being planned, thanks to funding granted by the European Union (EU).

And indeed, several of the most promising initiatives in this area have been benefiting from EU grants. One of them is the SmartCare project, which has recently validated the socioeconomic impact deriving from the implementation of an integrated range of e-health and social care services for older people living in some areas of Friuli-Venezia Giulia, a Northern Italian region. The support of tele-monitoring and other ICT-supported solutions is enhancing patients' and caregivers' quality of life, thus preventing duplication and/or fragmentation of services and promoting care integration and sustainability (SmartCare, 2014). Robotics is another area in which the experimental application of service robots in real-life, long-term care settings is coming into effect in Italy as a consequence of large EU-funded projects such as Robot-Era (Lezza, 2015). Recently, a platform of web-based services to support informal carers of older people has been developed under the coordination of Italian researchers and made available in local languages for all EU-countries (http://eurocarers.org/InformCare). Although similar internet-based solutions that provide both static information and interactive opportunities for informal carers are becoming more and increasingly common

## 88 *Emmanuele Pavolini et al.*

in Italy (for another innovative example, refer to http://www.anzianienonsolo.it/corsi-di-formazione/), it can however be safely stated that the total number of informal carers using these tools is still a minority of the total population. A more systematic approach to intensify and coordinate efforts in this and other technology-related areas is needed in order to make new technologies a substantial pillar of Italian LTC, as is already the case in other countries (Lattanzio et al., 2014).

### 6.7 Quality measures and the quality of the Italian LTC system

It is difficult to assess the performance and quality of the Italian LTC system due to the fact that the system is strongly based on informal care by relatives and care provided by migrant care workers who often do not have regular contracts and adequate training for the care functions they have to perform (see sections 6.2 and 6.5).

As shown previously, the importance of informal care and care provided by migrant carers is the result of the limited provision of public services. Italian households therefore have to rely on informal help and the market, because there are often no real alternatives. The issue of quality of LTC provision is closely related to the poor working conditions in this policy field (Pavolini, 2004; Rusmini and Pasquinelli, 2015). Many workers have irregular contracts, no specific training, report long hours of work (frequently living with the frail older people and being available for help during the day and also at night), have no supervision and support in a very stressful and demanding work environment, and are subject to risks of job-related injuries and, sometimes, abuse. Both the type of care and the quality are negatively influenced by such conditions. At the same time, families have limited alternatives since public service coverage is low both in terms of the number of beneficiaries and intensity (hours of care), and in many cases the economic resources available to households are enough to pay a migrant care worker in the grey market but not to question quality issues. The recent economic crisis has made this type of problem even more dramatic as resources held by households have decreased, whereas the complexity of care needs has increased due to the growing share of very old people among those with LTC needs.

It is also difficult to assess the quality of the formal LTC service provision because, as stated, the bulk of home care offered by the NHS is extremely scant and poor in terms of hours provided to each beneficiary. An average of 21 hours per year means that the service is often mainly nursing home care, without any other type of social care provision, and is offered for a relatively short time (after a hospital discharge or in case of very severe need, e.g. in end-of-life situations).

The main sector where there is a stronger focus on quality is residential care, with a very broad regulation of how delivery should work and prerequisites requested for the accreditation of the residential institutions (Pesaresi, 2013). However, in this case it should not be overlooked that the diffusion of this service is quite limited, reaching only slightly more than 2% of the population aged 65 years and older. Moreover, LAs sometimes tend to assess LTC beneficiaries as not dependent (instead of as dependent) in order to offer them a type of residential care service that has less stringent personnel and organisational requirements and thus lower costs (Pavolini, 2004; Ranci, 2008).

## 6.8 Conclusions

In the last few decades, Western European countries have been facing tensions caused by the growing gap between the emerging needs of a dependent population and the capacity of the existing public care systems to meet them. Many countries have introduced far-reaching reforms of their care systems.

Italy inherited a very poorly developed public care system from the past that concentrated almost exclusively on monetary transfers and delegating care responsibility to family networks. The structural conditions which favoured the limited development of public LTC programmes in the past – social solidarity supported by the persistence of a strong family model characterised by close intergenerational ties – have been declining in the last two decades, making the growing population of dependent people increasingly vulnerable. A large set of changes, ranging from demographic trends (ageing of the population) to higher female participation in the labour market, have placed the Italian care system under great pressure, calling for new strategies and solutions.

The persistent institutional inertia permeating care policies and the parallel growth of the traditional cash transfer-based benefits (IA), while neglecting investments in new technologies, have favoured the creation of a private market response to the problems of dependency. The disadvantaged conditions in which the new supply of migrant care workers operates has enabled many dependent people to find autonomous answers to their care needs without converting their need into demand for direct public assistance. The employment of migrant home care workers has allowed Italian families to devise new solutions to the problem of care that are both affordable, given the low cost of these workers, and feasible on a practical level because they guarantee the necessary flexibility to integrate care found on the market with care that is still provided by the network of family solidarity, but without questioning the quality of provision. In this sense, the recourse to the market constitutes a new organisational formula within which the old familistic model is reproduced, based on the self-determination of families and on the still residual role of public services.

Public care policies have played a paradoxical role in this transformation. Contrary to what has happened in many other Western European countries, national LTC policies have been passive and stagnant. Moreover, the increased activism of local and regional authorities has only marginally changed the situation due to the limited amount of their financial and organisational resources. Generally speaking, therefore, institutional inertia has dominated in the care policy agenda in the last decades. Through this inertia, however, the traditional model has gradually shifted to a new pattern, still strongly driven by the self-sufficient capacity of families and characterised by a new mix of familism and marketization.

Quite paradoxically, the inaction and passivity of public policy has contributed to a great transformation in the Italian care regime, which has followed a path of incremental institutional change and has ultimately resulted in a largely

90 *Emmanuele Pavolini et al.*

unintended extension of the public LTC provision. This transformation in Italian society in the last decade unexpectedly changed the use of the main cash allowance programme (IA). From a cash benefit largely used to cover the supplementary income needs of the adult dependent, IA has become a financial resource allowing dependent older people to buy the low-cost care services offered in the private market. The relatively low amount of this benefit has been compensated by the availability of a large number of migrant care workers who are willing to accept low salaries. Institutional inertia, therefore, combined with recurrent institutional measures allowing the regularisation of migrant workers plus a large administrative and political tolerance of illegality has paved the way for the creation of a new publicly supported private care market.

However, while the recourse to the private care market has responded to emerging needs, it has also created new problems. There are great inequalities in the care market, as private care is clearly more accessible to the middle and upper classes. Furthermore, the ability of citizens to act as employers often seems very fragile, exposing people to the risk of manipulation and economic damage. The ambiguity of public regulation of migration fuels an illegal labour market. Moreover, the growth of IA beneficiaries risks further stimulating this irregular market, as cash benefits are distributed without any obligations on the part of recipients. The lack of adequate resources paid to the heavily dependent leaves these people in very severe and fragile situations due to the fact that IA is not graduated according to the level of dependency. Furthermore, there is little debate on the impact of this approach at a micro level, in other words, on the migrant care workers themselves and on their own (often transnational) families or, at a macro level, on the LTC provision of the migrants' source countries (Chiatti et al., 2013). Finally, the market solution does not necessarily appear to be definitive, since it is dependent on a constant flow of migrant women, a fact on which experts and policy makers can make no reliable future predictions. If this flow should decrease in the future, Italy will face a real policy crisis since the LTC public system has remained quite similar to that developed up until the 1990s. It is still technologically backward and highly undersized – for instance, in terms of the very low level of institutional care provision – especially when compared to those of the many EU countries that have reformed LTC programmes in the last two decades.

## References

Albertini, M. and Pavolini, E. (2015), Unequal inequalities: The stratification of the use of formal care among older Europeans, *Journals of Gerontology: Social Sciences* 1–10, doi:10.1093/geronb/gbv038, Advance Access publication 29 July 2015.

Antonnen, A. and Sipila, J. (2003), *The Young, the Old and Social Care in Five Industrial Societies*, paper presented at the ESA Conference, Helsinki.

Ascoli, U. and Pavolini, E. (eds) (2015), *The Italian Welfare State in European Perspective: A Comparative Analysis*, Bristol: Policy Press.

Ascoli, U. and C. Ranci (eds) (2002), *Dilemmas of the welfare mix*, New York: Springer.

Baltes, P.B. and Smith, J. (2003), New frontiers in the future of aging: From successful aging of the young old to the dilemmas of the fourth age, *Gerontology* 49: 123–135.

## Long-term care in Italy 91

Barbabella, F., Chiatti, C. and Di Rosa, M. (2015), 'La bussola di NNA: lo stato dell'arte basato sui dati', in NNA (eds) *L'assistenza agli anziani non autosufficienti in Italia V Rapporto*, Sant'Arcangelo di Romagna: Maggioli Editore, pp. 33–37.

Bolin, K., Lindgren, B. and Lundborg, P. (2008), Your next of kin or your own career? *Journal of Health Economics* 27: 718–738.

Brunetti, N. D., Amoruso D., De Gennaro L., Dellegrottaglie G., Di Giuseppe G., Antonelli G. and Di Biase M. (2014), Hot spot: impact of july 2011 heat wave in southern Italy (Apulia) on cardiovascular disease assessed by emergency medical service and telemedicine support, *Telemedicine and E-Health* 20(3): 272–281.

Censis (2013), *L'evoluzione digitale della specie. Undicesimo rapporto CENSIS/UCSI sulla comunicazione*, Rome: CENSIS.

Chiatti C., Bonfranceschi F. and Rimland J. (2014) *Report finale del progetto Up-Tech – 3 anni di sperimentazione per la domiciliarietà nell'area dell'Alzheimer*, Ancona: INRCA.

Chiatti, C., Di Rosa, M., Barbabella, F., Greco, C., Melchiorre, M.G., Principi, A., Santini, S. and Lamura, G. (2013), Migrant care work for elderly households in Italy. In J. Troisi and H.-J. von Kondratowitz, *Ageing in the Mediterranean*, Bristol: Policy Press, pp. 235–256.

Costa, G. (2012), Long-term care policies in Italy, In C. Ranci, and E. Pavolini (eds) *Reforms in Long-Term Care in Europe: Investigating Institutional Change and Social Impacts*, New York: Springer, pp. 221–241.

Dallolio, L., Menarini, M., China, S., Ventura, M. and Stainthorpe, A. (2008), Functional and clinical outcomes of telemedicine in patients with spinal cord injury, *Archives of Physical Medicine and Rehabilitation* 89(1): 2332–2341.

Da Roit, B. (2007), Elderly care in Italy, *Current Sociology* 55: 251–273.

Eurostat (2015), *Individuals using the internet for interacting with public authorities*, Brussels, http://appsso.eurostat.ec.europa.eu/nui/show.do.

Federsanità ANCI (2015), I modelli innovativi di Integrated Care assistiti dalle tecnologie digitali, *Quaderni di Innovazione e Salute* 1, Rome.

Hassan, F. and Ottaviano, G.I.P. (2013), Così l'Italia ha disimparato a produrre, *La Voce*, http://www.lavoce.info/archives/15656/cosi-litalia-ha-disimparato-a-produrre.

Health Ministry (2014), *Rapporto annuale sulle attività. Anno 2012*, Rome: Health Ministry.

ISTAT (2014), *L'assistenza residenziale in Italia (Anno 2011)*, Rome: ISTAT.

ISTAT (2015), *I servizi sociali dei Comuni (Anno 2011)*, Rome: ISTAT.

Lattanzio, F., Abbatecola, A.M., Bevilacqua, R., Chiatti, C., Corsonello, A., Rossi, L., Bustacchini, S. and Bernabei, R. (2014), Advanced technology care innovation for older people in Italy: Necessity and opportunity to promote health and wellbeing, *Journal of the American Medical Directors Association* 15(7): 457–466.

Leon, M. and Pavolini, E. (2014), ' Social Investment' or back to 'familism': The impact of the economic crisis on Family and Care Policies in Italy and Spain, *South European Society and Politics* 19(3): 353–369.

Lezza, L. (2015), Robot looks after residents at Italian care homes, *The Guardian*, 21 December, http://www.theguardian.com/technology/gallery/2015/dec/21/robot-looks-after-residents-at-italian-care-home-in-pictures.

Lori, M. and Pavolini, E. (2016), Cambiamenti organizzativi e ruolo societario delle organizzazioni di Terzo settore, *Politiche Sociali* 3(1): 41–64.

Melchiorre, M. G., Quattrini, S., Papa, R., Barbabella, F., Zanetti, E. and Lamura, G. (2015), Caring for People with Multiple Chronic Conditions in Italy: Policy and Practices, Ancona, http://www.icare4eu.org/pdf/Country_Factsheet_Italy_ICARE4EU.pdf.

## 92 Emmanuele Pavolini et al.

Naldini, M., Pavolini, E. and Solera, C. (2016), Female employment and elderly care: The role of care policies and culture in 21 European countries, *Work, Employment and Society*, doi: 0.1177/0950017015625602.

Naldini, M. and Saraceno, C. (2008), Social and family policies in Italy: Not totally Frozen but far from structural reforms, *Social Policy & Administration* 42(7): 733–748.

Osservatorio ICT in Sanità (2014), *Innovazione digitale in sanità*, Milan: Politecnico di Milano.

Pasquinelli, S. and Rusmini, G. (2008), *Badanti: la nuova generazione.* www.qualificare. info.

Pasquinelli, S. and Rusmini, G. (2013), *Badare non basta. Il lavoro di cura: attori, progetti, politiche*, Rome: Ediesse.

Pavolini, E. (2004), *Regioni e politiche sociali per gli anziani: le sfide della non autosufficienza*, Rome: Carocci.

Perrig-Chiello, P. and Hopflinger, F. (2005), Aging parents and their middle-aged children: Demographic and psychosocial challenges, *European Journal of Ageing* 2: 183–191.

Pesaresi, F. (2013), *RSA. Residenze sanitarie assistenziali: costi, tariffe e compartecipazione dell'utenza*, Sant'Arcangelo di Romagna: Maggioli.

Pfau-Effinger, B., Schüttpelz, A. and Sakac-Magdalenic S. (2006), *The Hidden Work Regime: Formal and Informal Work in Europe*, Hamburg: University of Hamburg, February.

Ranci, C. (ed) (2008), *Tutelare la non autosufficienza*, Rome: Carocci.

Ranci, C. (2015), The long-term evolution of the government–third sector partnership in Italy: Old wine in a new bottle?, *Voluntas* 26: 2311–2329.

Ranci, C. and Pavolini, E. (eds) (2012), *Reforms in Long-term Care Policies in Europe*, New York: Springer.

Ranci, C. and Pavolini, E. (eds) (2015), Not all that glitters is gold: Long-term care reforms in the last two decades in Europe, *Journal of European Social Policy* 25(3): 270–285.

Rusmini, G. and Pasquinelli, S. (2015), Lavoratori stranieri nel lavoro domestico e di cura. In Idos (ed.) *Dossier Statistico Immigrazione 2015*, Roma: Idos Edizioni, pp. 287–292.

Spandonaro, F. (2015), *L'universalismo diseguale (o imperfetto)*, Rome: CREA.

Stefani, S. (2015), BadaPlus, la nuova applicazione per tablet e smartphone per la gestione del lavoro domestico di assistenza, *Sociale.it*, http://www.sociale.it/2015/08/05/badaplus-la-nuova-applicazione-per-tablet-e-smartphone-per-la-gestione-del-lavoro-domestico-di-assistenza.

Streeck, W. and Thelen, K. (eds) (2005), *Beyond Continuity: Institutional Change in Advanced Political Economies*, Oxford: Oxford University Press.

# 7 Greece

## Forced transformation in a deep crisis

*Platon Tinios*

## 7.1 Introduction

The Greek welfare state is possibly an extreme example of the Mediterranean welfare state (Ferrera, 1996). In the 1990s, a time when other welfare systems were trying to cope with ageing and with the challenge of globalisation, the EU countries of the Mediterranean were struggling to modernize their welfare arrangements in a process of 'recalibration of the Welfare state' (Ferrera, 2010). The transformation was underway from the early 1990s and had at its core the dilution of the familial character of welfare arrangements and their replacement by more formal models that were largely based on European patterns. This process entailed taking over roles previously served by the family and assigning them to formal structures; it also meant filling many gaps left behind by the late development of Bismarckian social insurance (Bettio and Plantenga, 2004). These gaps could be found on the occupational level, where some occupations were typically better covered than others; they were also common on the *content* of social protection, where old age and health secured the greatest share of funding, leaving other needs to compete for what was left.

In such a process, personal services and long-term care were likely to be amongst the last to be affected. Current needs were being met by family and other informal arrangements; this would make other areas seem more pressing. Ageing in the 1990s appeared more as a future rather than a current threat. The arrival of foreign migrants as informal carers in large numbers also took some pressure off informal mechanisms (Lyberaki, 2011).

The process of recalibration in Greece remained largely on a rhetorical level (Matsaganis, 1999). Policy focussed on pensions and health care. Pension reform stalled even as pension expenditure was rising unchecked and was being financed by government grants. Health care costs were also rising fast.[1] As a result, there was little inclination and, certainly, less finance to start large new programmes. Though a transformative process had theoretically started at the beginning of the crisis, it was still at an early phase. The country faced the crisis equipped essentially with the very structures that had caused the crisis (Lyberaki and Tinios, 2014).

Long-term care was a case where this transformation was less advanced than elsewhere. So, the start of the crisis proved the arrangements for formal care unsustainable, necessitating that a solution be found quickly and with little preparation. In the meantime, the exceptionally deep and lengthy crisis was affecting all societal players involved in the provision of residual care – the family and carers,

94 *Platon Tinios*

both formal and informal. This chapter describes this process. We try to understand the kind of arrangements that apply to the long-term care sector in Greece
currently and to predict their likely development.

## 7.2 The mixed system before the crisis

The final arbiters of what kind of care is selected for an individual are those who
have both the interest and the information to judge what is best for the person's
welfare. This, even in systems with near complete formal coverage, is almost
always the family. Because they are most closely associated with the person who
needs the care, close family members are best placed to judge the need and extent
for care at the individual level.[2] On a micro level, the family finds itself in the role
of 'carer of last resort'. If adequate provision is, for whatever reason, lacking, it is
the family that must decide how to fill gaps given the available alternatives.

When formal alternatives are insufficient, the position of the family as the
arbiter is enhanced. Table 7.1 shows in schematic form the landscape that Greek

*Table 7.1* The pre-crisis uncoordinated mixed system for care (default shaded)

|  | State/formal | Paid for/private | Unpaid/family |
|---|---|---|---|
| **Who decides? Decisions and finance** | | | |
| **Residential** | Health care budgets Charitable trusts | Families on *ex post* basis (limited reimbursement from health insurance) | |
| **Nonresidential** | **Municipalities** EU structural funds (Pension funds post 2012) | Family budgets Some reimbursement for recognised conditions | **Families** |
| **Who supplies? Institutions and supply arrangements** | | | |
| **Residential** | Hospitals (medicalisation) charity homes | Hospitals Οίκοι Ευγηρίας (often converted hotels) | Co-habitation Family apartments |
| **Nonresidential** | KAPI ('Friendship clubs') **Help at Home** Day care centres (KIFI) | Unregulated market | Informal care by others Informal care by family member |
| **Who cares? How caring is staffed** | | | |
| **Residential** | Some trained full time personnel (Social workers. nurses) | Some trained full time personnel Limited professionalisation | Family members with no support Unqualified staff |
| **Nonresidential** | Voluntary workers Contract workers by municipalities **Professional carers** | Unregulated market (word of mouth/ classifieds) Female immigrants | |

*Greece: forced transformation* 95

families had to navigate through in the years before the crisis. Preferable options are shown in bold; the default option that was in practice that was chosen if the other provision was unavailable is shaded.

The type of help available can be of three kinds: *formal*, run by state bodies, including by local authorities; *unpaid*, usually meaning family; and *paid*, run by regulated or unregulated private sectors.[3] Private carers can be called for to help out informal arrangements if the family for some reasons is unable to cope on its own. A key distinction is between residential and nonresidential care. Residential institutions are often selected if no other means of care exists; medicalising needs could solve pressing social problems when other facilities were either unavailable or the families could not cope. The existence of spare capacity in hospitals, especially in areas away from the major urban centres, made this choice easier to implement.[4]

In terms of finance, the default option was once again the family, even though formal help, if available, would have been preferred. In terms of institutional arrangements, most people would prefer professional help organised locally, that is, what is commonly understood as long-term care services in European countries. When that was lower than total demand, which was almost always the case, the choice available was to use informal help. This could be helped by cohabitation, including living close to needy relatives in small owner-occupied apartment houses in the big cities (Lyberaki, 2009). Alternatively, it would have to be done by informal help, sometimes supplemented by brought-in home help services. Even though the preferred solution may be a professional carer, in practice, family members would have to do, although they were aided sometimes by untrained staff.

Limits in the supply of formal care meant that its allocation was sought and dispersed as a kind of privilege, making access to care an important determinant of household welfare. In a highly fragmented system where few general rules or norms were applied, inequality depended on location (some municipalities placed greater emphasis on social services than others and/or were better financed), occupation (social insurance funds of some occupations were better funded or more sensitive to LTC needs than others) or even political connections (which could determine how scarce places were allocated). Formal care provision was coordinated by the welfare ministry and was mostly provided by trained social workers; that type of care was of a high quality, but it was grossly inadequate in quantity and hence difficult to access. The ministry saw its role as maintaining high standards for its *own* providers. It did little to define and monitor quality standards in private care provision, even though that would affect a larger share of the population. Private provision was left to operate informally, by word of mouth or through the classified advertisements in the newspapers. Family carers received no official recognition or help. The situation was thus characterised by a very marked dualism between the formal quality provision, on the one hand, and an anarchic private system with little quality monitoring, on the other. The family was left in the middle, mixing and matching what it could.

So, bringing long-term care into formal social protection could have exercised important social leverage. An overall care system was an idea first mooted in the 1990s. Social protection in Greece consists of a highly developed pension system based on social insurance; that was supplemented in 1983 by a National Health

96 *Platon Tinios*

System on universalistic criteria. In 1992, Law 2082 saw long-term care as part of a separate National Welfare System distinct from either but linked to local government. (Amitsis, 2011). The same law defined Help at Home (HaH) as the main type of nonresidential help provided at beneficiaries' homes. This was to supplement some personal care services which had been offered by some hospitals, KAPI (voluntary Friendship Clubs, which spread in the 1980s) or by some NGOs such as the Red Cross.

The formal blueprint of a National System of Social Care was provided in 1998 (L2646/98). That was divided into primary care (mostly provided by local authorities), secondary care (provided mostly on a residential basis by regions) and tertiary care dealing with specialised cases. Subsequent legislation assigned telematics and a new network of free day care centres (KIFI). These were set up in selected locations and could cover only a fraction of total needs, even on a local basis; the time when they could cover all potential demands was far in the future. All bodies would come under the strategic coordination of the Social Welfare Ministry, a part of the Health Ministry and distinct from social insurance, which was supervised by the Employment Ministry.

All legislation treated HaH as the main instrument and virtually exclusive instrument for public intervention in the care area (OECD, 2000, p. 67). Indeed, the two first National Action Plans for Inclusion (Ministry of Labour, 2001, 2003) mentioned its development as a key priority; the second in 2003 even highlighted it as an instance of good practice. The expectation at the time was clearly that the programme would be expanded quickly to meet outstanding needs as a major social protection initiative. Key features of the programme were (Amitsis, 2013) the following:

- Municipalities were the main unit for delivery and planning.
- Beneficiaries were all individuals with difficulty to meet daily needs (ADLs) who were living alone and had insufficient means. The system thus was squarely within the social welfare, rather than the social insurance, logic.
- Services offered would be matched to needs and could include medical services, personal care and help with meeting personal obligations (e.g. dealing with bureaucracy).

NAPIncl (2003) describes how HaH functions:

> Each service provision unit in the programme consists of a social worker, who is responsible for coordinating the programme, one or two nurses and one to three home helps or community carers. These people apply team work and community planning. . .. The members of the team must keep a daily record . . . to update the monitoring system.
>
> (p. 47)

It was envisaged that the delivery of social services would gradually expand to become a core service that municipalities would deliver to their citizens. Initially, 102 municipalities (approximately 1 in 10) signed five-year agreements to supply

*Greece: forced transformation* 97

services. The early emphasis given to the programme justified the finance of HaH structures as pilot actions that were financed for a strictly limited time by EU structural funds. It was hoped that a successful programme would encourage municipalities to provide these services on a larger scale and, crucially, finance them out of their own resources.

The expectation of rapid organic growth proved optimistic. Key to this was how municipalities understood their own roles. The monitoring of needs, whether at a local or national level, was never attempted. As there was no clear picture of what needed to be done, municipalities, with very few exceptions, did not feel under pressure to deliver services to meet needs. They saw their social policy role not as an obligation to citizens but as an imposition to their core duties. As the fulfilment of needs was not monitored, commentary was thus quickly dominated by supply-side considerations, notably by the employment status of the workforce hired to staff the programme.[5]

As the pilot phase financed by the EU structural funds approached its end, discussion of HaH centred not on how to define and serve unmet needs but on how to secure the continued employment of the temporary staff used; these had speedily formed an effective pressure group. Municipalities threatened that unless other funds were given them, they would stop the programme and leave thousands of employees jobless. Finance to keep the programme going was extended two times. This allowed things to tick over for four more years, but it did not answer who would finance it on an ongoing basis. As the question was how to finance existing actions; the question of how to move beyond a pilot phase towards universal provision was never raised.

In 2007, another equally temporary solution to tap the structural funds was found. This time HaH was characterised as a measure intended to promote the employment of staff rather than supplying services to beneficiaries. As such, it was included in the National Strategic Reference Fund (NSRF) 2007–2013 as a human resource development project. As a secondary target, it cited the employability of people who were caring informally for needy relatives. This had the highly paradoxical result of *excluding* from HaH those who did not live with a close relative, help to whom could not lead to anyone entering employment. In this way, in theory, it excluded those most in need of care. In *practice*, there have been no instances of care being withdrawn from individuals who have lost eligibility, though it is unclear what happened to the flow of new demands.

The official sense of unease about the situation in long-term care in Greece can be tracked through the country's participation in relevant OECD publications. In a questionnaire (OECD, 2000) addressed to all member states, the progress and extension of the HaH programme is confidently trumpeted as a major ageing reform. Greece is nowhere to be found either in some OECD publications (OECD, 2005, 2011a), presumably due to dearth of data and difficulty to justify and explain the current situation and its prospects.

The situation of long-term care was, in a way, typical of the mechanisms which led to the crisis in 2009. Finding a permanent funding solution would have necessitated some painful decisions, either by finding new sources of revenue (tax or user charges) or by rerouting expenditures from other uses. Faced with that dilemma, Greek authorities reacted in two ways, both of which had problems for the future. They either provided central grants financed by borrowing, or they rerouted investment funds towards what was essentially consumption. These recourses would either increase borrowing or limit potential growth, or both.

So, at the outset of the crisis in 2009, long-term care was still in a transitionary situation. In principle, formal provision should have expanded to fill needs, using the Help at Home programme as its main vehicle. In practice, the extension and development of that programme were hampered, if not completely halted, so long as no permanent source of finance was found. So long as HaH was paid by a series of temporary stop-gaps, formal provision remained far below needs, and informal provision managed by the family had no choice but to play the dominant role in long-term care.

The 1998 law clearly foresaw a decentralised system gradually expanding to cover needs. The ultimate objective would have been a unified system. Such a system would have been in a position to see where informal provision was insufficient and direct formal resources there. Such a course of action would have necessitated monitoring of the needs for care, on the one hand, and what was being done to meet it, on the other. Monitoring was never implemented or even ever planned. As questions of how such a care system would be financed were dodged, the existence of a monitoring system would have only added to political problems by bringing into the open gaps in protection, which the family was called to fill. Statistical invisibility, in this way, is not simply a by-product of decentralised provision, but allowed policy to proceed at a more leisurely pace. The absence of monitoring, by obscuring the existence of care gaps, allowed policy makers to claim credit for what was being done without accepting responsibility for gaps in provision. Policy was rewarded for effort without being judged according to results.

As a consequence, the dearth of statistics covering needs but also the supply of care is not surprising. In the EU Ageing Working Group's age-related projections (AWG, 2015), there are estimates of public LTC expenditure of 0.5 per cent of GDP, which places it at the extreme low end of EU-28 expenditure. However, the source and coverage of the data are not noted. Given that the greatest share is supposed to be composed of cash benefits which are not related to ADLs, we must conclude that this figure's link with LTC is tangential at best. With regard to the need for care, the only information available comes from sample surveys. The Survey of Health, Ageing and Retirement in Europe, which surveyed a representative sample of people aged 50 years and older, was conducted for the first time. The questionnaire had questions on the needs of care and also how these were met. Lyberaki (2009) presents data drawn from the first wave. This interdisciplinary panel survey would have shown how the crisis has affected both the demand and the supply of long-term care. However, Greece did not participate in the 2011 and 2013 waves; the effect of the crisis will have to wait for the data of the 2015, which will become available in late 2016.

The reliance on the family is portrayed vividly in Figure 7.1, which charts what type of help a group with clear care needs – individuals 75 years of age and older

*Greece: forced transformation* 99

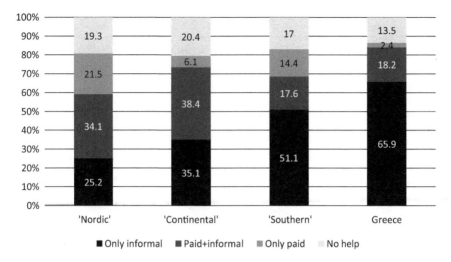

*Figure 7.1* Type of care received by people aged 75 years and older with serious health limitations, 2004

Source: Lyberaki (2009) from Survey of Health Ageing and Retirement in Europe (SHARE) data.

with serious health limitations – could access. Greek individuals had to use only informal care by 66 per cent, whereas even other southern countries (IT and ES) were only 51 per cent; at the other extreme, Nordic countries only had half that. The family was acting as the long-term care provider of last resort.

In this respect, the family was aided by the existence of female immigrant carers; their arrival in large numbers after 1992 from Albania and Eastern Europe enabled many women who previously had to stay at home to look after relatives to leave the home and join paid employment. Lyberaki (2011) makes a direct connection between the supply of female immigrant carers and the rise in female labour participation after 1995.

This attitude was internalised by the population in the sense that the state was also not *trusted* to deliver care services. Table 7.2, from the same survey, notes that Greece is a clear outlier in keeping the family in place for the role of looking after close relatives.

## 7.3 The crisis and the care economy

The financial crisis in Greece has two unique features (OECD, 2011, 2013, 2016). First, it is exceptionally deep. Between 2007 and 2014, GDP per capita lost a quarter (26.3 per cent) of its value. The impact of the crisis was pervasive and went far beyond the direct impact of austerity. Second, it was uniquely long. Seven years after its start in 2009, it was still showing no signs of abating. The

100  *Platon Tinios*

*Table 7.2* Attitudes about the role of the family and the state in long-term care

*Personal care for aged people in need: should the family or the state have responsibility?*

| | Exclusively family | Mainly family | Both equally | Mainly the state | Exclusively the state |
|---|---|---|---|---|---|
| **Nordic** | **1.6** | **4.5** | **25.3** | **49.7** | **19.0** |
| Sweden | 2.7 | 7.1 | 23.3 | 50.2 | 16.7 |
| Denmark | 0.8 | 1.6 | 8.9 | 50.7 | 38.1 |
| Netherlands | 1.3 | 3.9 | 32.4 | 49.0 | 13.5 |
| **Continental** | **3.3** | **19.0** | **51.0** | **20.8** | **5.9** |
| Germany | 4.0 | 23.9 | 55.4 | 12.4 | 4.4 |
| Belgium | 3.6 | 14.1 | 39.6 | 35.7 | 7.0 |
| France | 1.9 | 7.7 | 40.9 | 39.2 | 10.2 |
| Switzerland | 2.7 | 19.4 | 53.2 | 21.4 | 3.2 |
| Austria | 2.4 | 18.3 | 55.3 | 18.3 | 5.7 |
| **Southern** | **7.1** | **26.7** | **45.0** | **15.4** | **5.8** |
| Italy | 5.2 | 23.0 | 50.0 | 17.6 | 4.2 |
| Spain | 4.5 | 27.4 | 44.1 | 15.3 | 8.6 |
| Greece | 24.9 | 40.7 | 25.3 | 5.7 | 3.5 |
| **All countries** | **4.6** | **20.3** | **45.8** | **22.0** | **7.3** |

Source: Lyberaki (2009), based on SHARE, 2004.

third consecutive adjustment programme (and its accompanying bailout) was due to run to 2018, meaning that the country would be under externally supervised economic programmes for nine years at least.[6]

Crucially, that period coincided with important changes in two other areas. First, in the process of ageing: dependency ratios had long been expected to deteriorate in the middle of the decade as the Greek baby boom was entering retirement. Some of the changes experienced during the crisis might well have been to longer-term trends, which would complicate dealing with the crisis considerably. Second, there was administrative reform, including in local government. Under the Kallikratis programme in 2010, more than 1,000 local authorities were consolidated into 325 municipalities, prefectures were abolished and their functions were assigned to 13 regions. Under the new arrangements, the new municipalities would be responsible for all local social services and regions would assume planning roles.

The crisis affected the environment surrounding formal and informal care provision in a number of ways:

1   The public finance consequences of adjustment affected the size and direction of public expenditure flows. Fiscal adjustment was large and rapid (Matsaganis, 2011). However, most of it took place from the side of tax revenue rather than expenditure. Expenditure restraint sped up after 2013 (four years into the crisis) chiefly as a result of public sector pay cuts. Throughout the crisis, the authorities tried to protect long-term public commitments, chiefly

*Greece: forced transformation* 101

those towards the permanent public sector workforce. This meant heightened insecurity for those not in the front line of protection, such as the temporary staff employed at the HaH programme. Similarly, new and less entrenched programmes were in greater danger. This relative protection for (parts of) the public translated to even greater vulnerability for the private sector. Unemployment increased above 30 per cent. While GDP per head collapsed by a quarter between 2008 and 2013, private earnings fell earlier and by more than in the public sector (OECD 2016). Cuts were deeper on an after-tax basis. The informal care economy thus faced an attack from two directions: demand rose at the same time as fiscal pressures increased tax demands on households (Lyberaki and Tinios, 2014).

2    The political economy during the crisis was monopolised by the interplay between the troika and the authorities. Arguments between them overshadowed discussion of long-term issues; it was always easier to blame the crisis, or the troika, or both. The question of finding viable long-term finance to expand long-term care was never raised. The little discussion of the future of long-term care that took place centred around safeguarding the jobs of the HaH staff. The absence of any data on needs, or even in the outcomes of the programme, helped limit discussion.

3    Structural reform in social protection was overshadowed, as before, by pensions. Despite repeated pension reform initiatives (Börsch-Supan and Tinios, 2001; OECD 2011b), the pension issue was not put to rest. The third adjustment programme was preceded by action to curb early retirements, while pension reform was back in the agenda in 2016. While the pension scene remained fluid, there was little possibility of new long-term commitments in related areas. On the revenue side, there was constant pressure for extraordinary revenues to cover programme overruns, a fact which left little possibility to discuss expanding revenue in *new* directions. Similarly, though there was some awareness of looming needs in the long term, there were more pressing immediate needs. The troika had signalled the urgent need for a social safety net; a requirement to submit proposals by September 2010 had been ignored by the authorities. Partly as a result, the memorandum of understanding accompanying the third bailout set the unrolling of a safety net as a priority for 2016, preceded by a social spending review that should pinpoint opportunities to redirect expenditure to new directions (Tinios, 2015).[7]

This climate was not propitious for the Help-at-Home programme. Though there was a clear need and no alternative existed, longstanding issues were still unresolved. Since 2003, it had been kept going by temporary stop-gaps, mainly through the EU structural funds. These funds can be used to initiate a new programme but cannot be expected to finance it on a continuous basis.

The conundrum facing the HaH during the crisis was to find a way to continue the programme without relying on structural funds. More radical alternatives, such as user charges or the state withdrawing its direct involvement by instituting coupon programmes, were not considered, presumably on ideological grounds or

102   *Platon Tinios*

simply because no one suggested them. Given that non-wage costs were already considered too high, the solution of moving long-term care to an explicitly social insurance direction was also ruled out. That left open the possibility of tapping some other central financing source, even if that mean altering some of the design features of the programme.

The solution finally promulgated in Law 4052/2012 was to rely for finance on the pension social insurance system (Amitsis, 2013). Pension providers, even if massively in deficit, had a steady stream of revenue from which relatively small amounts could be tapped. This meant, however, that the beneficiaries of the programme had to be redefined, changing from the general population to the pensioners only. Given that pensions in Greece are based on social insurance, there is a very large number of old people, chiefly women, who do not have pensions (Betti et al., 2015). Given that the needs for pension finance were, if anything, growing, this solution could only be used if the finance was so small that it would not be missed by pensions. Major increases were thus effectively ruled out.

As a consequence, the programme was renamed as the Help-at-Home Programme for Pensioners. Planning responsibility also had to move from the Ministry of Health and Welfare to the Ministry of Employment. Paradoxically, the law mentioned that the programme can also cover those in receipt of the (means-tested) welfare benefit for uninsured old people (who, having paid no contributions, could have laid no claim for a pension).[8] This would, nonetheless, theoretically exclude a good number of people who were previously eligible under HaH. It is unclear to what extent these restrictions are actually being implemented; there have been no reports of care that was given being discontinued under the new arrangements.

Regarding finance, the law shied away from instituting long-term care as a separate insurance risk to be covered. Hypothecating 0.2 per cent of total contribution revenue was legislated in 2012 and repealed in 2013 without ever having been collected. Finance for the programme is derived by subtracting specific *ad hoc* amounts from the proceeds of some of the pension cuts imposed during the crisis. These are levied for specified periods of time, typically for no more than two years. The expiry of the last such period in December 2015 led to protests by the staff and to new *ad hoc* finance to last until the end of 2016. It is unclear what is to happen after the new deadline is reached.

The reformulation of HaH as a pensioner's benefit was accompanied by a number of other provision altering design features (Amitsis, 2013).

- Pension providers can, theoretically, buy services from a number of suppliers of HaH services. These can be local authorities, municipal enterprises, social enterprises and even private for-profit companies. However, this widening of scope has yet to be implemented in practice.[9]
- Beneficiaries can, in principle, chose providers from a local list provided by the pension provider, with whom an agreement is signed and is reimbursed by the pension provider. This agreement can be terminated at will.
- Service providers must supply services of social support (dealing with bureaucracy, mobility), nursing support (monitoring, simple medical practices) and

home help (shopping, cleaning, meal preparation etc.). Services must be provided twice a week and last no less than 30 minutes. Reimbursement is set at €100 per person per year. Copayments from the beneficiary are explicitly ruled out.

The ministerial decision that implemented the new arrangements introduced new, exceptionally restrictive eligibility conditions to access the programme (Amitsis, 2013, pp. 248–250): a minimum age of 78 *or* to have been judged disabled by 67 per cent. However, disability in the social insurance sense signals inability to work at the time when the pension was awarded and signifies nothing as to self-help. Thus, this requirement is simultaneously too restrictive (regarding age) and too lax (regarding disability). A further requirement is income well below that drawn by the minimum pension (below €7,700 per year). These requirements, taken together, would exclude many of those whose need for personal care could be not be met by any other way.

## 7.4 Conclusions: long-term care towards the end of the crisis

In conclusion, the formal long-term care system during the crisis did not correct any of the problems of the preceding period. It was still financed through a succession of stop-gaps and never managed to put to rest insecurity about its continued existence; if anything, in the stretched post crisis fiscal environment, insecurity was heightened further. Formal care focused narrowly on a small group of beneficiaries whose selection had more to do with legal issues in justifying the type of finance employed rather than any urgency of need.

Given the previous comments, the deterioration in perceived ability to afford long-term care in the early part of the crisis should come as no surprise. Figure 7.2, from Eurobarometer data, shows Greece as an outlier both in having high levels of insecurity and in the deterioration between 2010 and 2011.

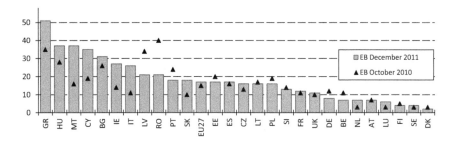

*Figure 7.2* Changes in ability to afford long-term care: October 2010 to December 2011
Source: Lyberaki and Tinios (2014).
Note: Eurobarometer 338 fieldwork conducted in December 2011 and published in April 2012. Eurobarometer 311 fieldwork conducted in October 2010 and published in February 2011.

104   *Platon Tinios*

So, by concentrating almost exclusively on HaH, Greece left completely open the arrangements for those not covered. Those left out are probably the majority of those who need long-term care; they would be excluded either *de jure* through the exclusion criteria or *de facto* through the limited places available. It is indicative of how the system is run that no statistics are available (in either published or unpublished form), either for those benefiting from HaH or, *a fortiori*, for those who need care. Statistics on private provision are also impossible to find.

Long-term care for most of the population must, as before, be sought in informal arrangements. At the top end there is some anecdotal evidence of private sector providers stepping in to the breach by supplying care services. These started in the fields of telematics but are gradually extending into general home-help activities. This emerging market is not being monitored or coordinated by the competent authorities. Many of the new private providers, whether for profit or not, are run by former social workers who would be familiar with the Welfare Ministry. The change of supervising ministry of the HaH from welfare to employment would thus make the prospects of effective supervision, synergy between sectors and the implementation of quality standards that much more remote.

The family and its members, mostly women, would have to shoulder increasing responsibility. They may, on occasion, be helped by informal carers, most of whom would be female immigrants of previous waves of immigration from the Balkans and Eastern Europe. This market is likely to shrink as many of those immigrants of the first wave return home to escape the crisis; it may also be hit by rises in the tax obligations of self-employed workers.[10]

The main threat, though, would come from the demand side: households hit by unemployment and by liquidity squeezes can afford outsourcing care work to a smaller extent; caring obligations would revert to female family members. There has been an increase in generational cohabitation as families try to contain costs (Lyberaki and Tinios, 2014). In the stretched post-crisis income environment, pensions of older relatives are a surer source of revenue than working income. This is formulated in a widely quoted policy position, used repeatedly even by the Prime Minister, that 'pensions of grandparents cannot be reduced as they provide income for their unemployed grandchildren'.[11] Some of the tendency towards early retirement through the crisis could have been caused by the need to provide care. While those women who can retire do so, younger women, paradoxically, search actively for paid work. The 'added worker effect' of increasing labour supply dominates in the case of women; as unemployment rises, women try to compensate for the non-existence of a functioning social safety net by trying to add to family income. However, as new time use data shows, increased job search is combined with high time inputs for care on the part of women. Women thus lose out both directly in monetary terms and also indirectly by having to devote more time to informal care (Lyberaki and Tinios, 2016).

Greece is one of the countries of the EU which is ageing fastest. Nevertheless, it has yet to cope with the challenges this poses to long-term care. While an institutional framework has been in place for almost 20 years, it has proved inadequate to deal with the problems or even to provide a credible answer to how these

Greece: forced transformation 105

will be met in the future. During the crisis, focus remained on short-term public finance issues and on emergency social assistance. More long-term issues were, as before, obscured by the inability to deal with pensions conclusively.

One can only hope that time will be found for long-term care.

## Notes

1 Featherstone and Papapadimitriou (2008) provide an overview of a number of reform attempts in the pre-crisis period.
2 Stated differently, 'the buck will stop with the family', as it has most to lose by any care gaps.
3 Social enterprises and NGOs are thought to span the two types of non-state help. A legal basis for social enterprises is a relatively recent addition.
4 As hospital infrastructure is frequently financed by EU structural funds, whereas staffing and running costs come from local budgets; this could lead to overinvestment, in the sense of producing facilities which are underused. Similar effects result where health planning is dominated by the supply side.
5 A legal view of the role of local government in social policy is in Kontiadis and Apistoulas (2005).
6 Tinios (2015) provides an overview of macroeconomic and social developments up to 2015.
7 Despite the requirement that the review should be in place by October 2015, pension discussions took precedence, with the result that by April 2016 the process had yet to start.
8 However, details of how the programme would be extended to the uninsured have never been issued. How they will exercise their legal right to services thus remains unclear.
9 The legislative framework for social enterprises was provided in 2011. By 2015, there had been 430 applications, but only 40 of those were active. Licensing and other bureaucratic delays are cited as explanations (Mouriki, 2014).
10 On the grey economy, see Tatsos (2001).
11 This, as an argument for not proceeding to the first best, which would be to do something for the unemployed grandchildren directly, is rather disingenuous.

## References

Amitsis, G. (2011), *Social versus Fiscal: The future of the help at home services in the Greek social care regime*, paper presented in the 9th ESPAnet Conference 2011, 'Sustainability and Transformation of European Social Policy'', Valencia.

Amitsis, G. (2013), *Models of Residential Care in the Greek System of Social Security: Reform of Social Policies in periods of Economic Recession*, Athens: Papazisis.

Betti, F., Georgiadis, T. and Tinios, P. (2015), *Unequal Ageing in Europe: Women's Independence and Pensions*, New York: Palgrave Macmillan.

Bettio, F. and Plantenga, J. (2004), Comparing care regimes in Europe, *Feminist Economics* 10(1): 85–113.

Börsch-Supan, A. and Tinios, P. (2001), The Greek pensions system: Strategic framework for reform, In Ralph C. Bryant, Nicolas C. Garganas and George S. Tavlas (eds) *Greece's Economic Performance and Prospects*, Athens: Bank of Greece and Brookings Institution, pp. 361–451.

Featherstone, K. and Papadimitriou, D. (2008), *The Limits of Europeanisation: Reform Capacity and Public Policy in Greece*, Basingstoke: Palgrave Macmillan.

## 106 *Platon Tinios*

Ferrera, M. (1996), The southern model of welfare in social Europe, *Journal of European Social Policy* 6(1): 17–37.

Ferrera, M. (2010), The South European countries. In F.C. Castles, S. Leibfried, J. Lewis, H. Obinger and C. Pierson (eds) *The Oxford Handbook of the Welfare State*, Oxford: Oxford University Press, pp. 616–629.

Kontiadis, X. and Apistoulas, D. (2005), *Welfare State Reform and Local Government*, Athens: Papazisis.

Lyberaki, A. (2009), Is there a care gap? Who cares for whom, and how? In A. Lyberaki, P. Tinios and A. Philalithis (eds) *Life 50+: Health, Ageing and Pensions in Greece and in Europe*, Athens: Kritiki (in Greek), pp. 371–394.

Lyberaki, A. (2011), Migrant women, care work and women's employment in Greece, *Feminist Economics* 17(3): 103–131.

Lyberaki, A. and Tinios, P. (2014), The informal welfare state and the family: Invisible actors in the Greek drama, *Political Studies Review* 12(2): 193–208.

Lyberaki, A. and Tinios, P. (2016), *Can the crisis lead to backtracking on gender policies in Greece? A need to rethink gender balance policies*, Report submitted to the Hellenic Observatory, LSE on the theme "Gender and Crisis". January 2016.

Matsaganis, M. (1999), Dilemmas of welfare state reform. In M. Matsaganis (ed) *Perspectives of the Welfare State in Southern Europe*, Athens: Ellinika Grammata (in Greek), pp. 13–32.

Matsaganis, M. (2011), *Social Policy in Hard Times: Financial Crisis, Fiscal Austerity and Social Protection*, Athens: Kritiki (in Greek).

Ministry of Labour (2001), *National Action Plan for Social Inclusion 2001–2003*. http://ec.europa.eu/social/main.jsp?langId=en&catId=22.

Ministry of Labour (2003), *National Action Plan for Social Inclusion 2003–2005* (NAPincl 2003). http://ec.europa.eu/social/main.jsp?langId=en&catId=22.

Mouriki, A. (2014), *The role of local governments and civil society in addressing poverty issues in times of crisis: The case of Greece*, paper presented at an EU conference, Brussels, 'The Europe 2020 Poverty Target: Lessons Learnt and the Way Forward'.

OECD (2000), *Reforms for an Ageing Society*, Paris: OECD.

OECD (2005), *Long-Term Care for Older People*, Paris: OECD.

OECD (2011a), *Help Wanted? Providing and Paying for Long-Term Care*, Paris: OECD.

OECD (2011b), *Economic Surveys: Greece*, Paris: OECD.

OECD (2013), *Economic Surveys: Greece*, Paris: OECD.

OECD (2016), *Economic Surveys: Greece*. Paris: OECD.

Tatsos, N. (2001), *The Shadow Economy and Tax Evasion in Greece*, Athens: IOVE and Papazisis (in Greek).

Tinios, P. (2015), "Employment and Social Developments in Greece", European Parliament, Directorate General for Internal Policies, Policy Department-Economic and Scientific Policy A.

# 8 Long-term care and austerity in the UK

## A growing crisis

*Caroline Glendinning*

## 8.1 Introduction

Long-term care in the UK – especially in England – is widely argued to be in serious crisis. Not only are levels of funding and services failing to keep pace with demographic trends, but increasingly severe cuts are being made in funding. These cuts are also affecting the financial viability of the many charitable and for-profit organisations that depend on public funding to provide domiciliary and residential care services to older people. As a consequence of the funding crisis, growing numbers of older people who need help with personal care and activities of daily living are unable to access publicly funded services; those that do are likely to receive them only for short-term periods while recovering from illness. Reliance on family caregiving is increasing; older people without family carers simply risk going without basic care needs being met. Underpinning this crisis – again particularly in England – is a longer-term shift from central to local government of responsibilities for funding care. In future, access to publicly funded care services and the levels of those services are increasingly likely to be determined by the local political decisions and tax-raising capacities of individual local authorities as central government retreats from its historic fiscal equalisation role of smoothing out local taxation inequalities.

The chapter begins by outlining the funding and governance arrangements for long-term care in the UK. The fragmentation of these arrangements – in particular the separate funding and governance arrangements for the health and social care elements – is important in understanding the impacts of austerity and austerity-related policies on the levels and quality of care for older people. The chapter then summarises recent policy and practice developments that reflect aspirations to improve the quality, efficiency and effectiveness of long-term care. These developments include the introduction and extension of personalised approaches to allocating funding and delivering care; the widespread development of rehabilitation and reablement services; the twin pressures to integrate services while at the same time devolving responsibilities from central to local government; and reforms to individual rights and funding arrangements contained in the 2014 Care and Support Act. These developments provide the contexts within which increasingly stringent austerity-related measures have been introduced. The next section of the chapter details the austerity-related policies introduced by the 2010–2015

108 *Caroline Glendinning*

coalition government and the more radical proposals of the conservative government that came to power in May 2015. The last section discusses the impacts of these measures with particular focus on the extensiveness, quality and equity of services for older people and family carers and on the providers of care services. The main focus will be on developments in England, with reference to measures elsewhere in the UK where possible.

## 8.2 Long-term care: fragmented responsibilities

Long-term care is not a commonly used concept in the UK. Responsibilities for funding and providing services for older people with disabilities or serious chronic health problems are split between the National Health Service (NHS), which is separately managed in England, Scotland, Wales and Northern Ireland; local authorities in each of the four countries; and the UK-wide Department for Work and Pensions. This tripartite division has its origins in the welfare state structures established in the late 1940s.

The NHS is a universal service funded from general taxation and centrally managed within each UK country. It funds hospital, general practice, nursing, therapies, medication and community health services which are free at the point of use. It was estimated in 2006 that over £3 billion of NHS funding was contributed to long-term care in England (Wanless, 2006).

Local authorities are responsible for the funding and provision of social care – primarily personal care (help with activities of daily living) at home or in residential and nursing homes. Access to publicly funded social care depends on tests of income and assets as well as increasingly stringent assessments of need; generally, only people with very high levels of need, minimal assets and low incomes are eligible. Means-tested charges for services (copayments) are also commonly levied (in England). Older people with care and support needs who are not eligible for publicly funded social care must purchase their own, rely on family carers or manage without. Historically, local authorities have received most of their funding in the form of block grants from central government. They have some discretion over the levels and types of services they fund; therefore, access to, levels of and patterns of services to some extent vary between localities. However, current policy proposals, within England at least, increasingly emphasise the devolution of responsibility for decisions about local taxation, allocation of resources and levels of services to individual local authorities. This is likely to lead to further fragmentation and a retreat from earlier aspirations to create a national framework of entitlements, even within England, to long-term care.

The Department for Work and Pensions (DWP) administers social security cash benefits covering the extra costs of disability and care. The most important benefits for the purposes of this chapter are Attendance Allowance, which is for older people who need regular personal care or supervision, and Carers Allowance, which is for family carers with minimal income from other sources. Attendance Allowance is currently paid to 1.5 million people aged 65 years and older who need regular care or supervision, regardless of their income or asset levels. Annual

UK expenditure on Attendance Allowance is currently around £5 billion. Eligibility for Attendance Allowance is wider than the very stringent criteria now used by many local authorities to ration access to publicly funded social care, so it is received by many older people with less intensive support needs. It is commonly used to pay for low-level support such as help with shopping, gardening, cleaning and maintaining social contacts (Corden et al., 2010).

For disability and care-related social security benefits, the Department for Work and Pensions currently sets the same eligibility criteria, assessment process and benefit levels across the four constituent countries of the UK. However, following the (failed) 2014 Scottish independence referendum, Scotland has been promised devolved responsibility for deciding on eligibility for and levels of these benefits (HMG, 2015). There are also plans to reform Attendance Allowance in England, with access moving from a universal national framework and eligibility criteria to locally variable decision making (see later).

Since 2000, responsibilities for health and social care policies and associated budgets have been further fragmented following their devolution to the separate governments of England, Scotland, Wales and Northern Ireland. Scottish policies have increasingly diverged from the three other countries. Thus, Scottish legislation that came into effect in April 2016 requires the integration of health and local authority care budgets into a single local partnership for each area. Thirty-one local partnerships will together manage almost £8 million in health and social care funding. NHS and local council care services will be jointly accountable for local performance against nationally agreed outcomes and will be jointly responsible for the health and care needs of patients, with a greater emphasis on enabling people to stay in their own homes and avoiding admission to hospital or residential care (Scottish Government, 2016). A further example of Scottish divergence is that in England, Wales and Northern Ireland, eligibility for local authority-funded personal care depends on assessments of wealth/assets and income as well as level of need; eligible recipients may also be required to make copayment contributions, again depending on income level. In contrast, the Community Care and Health (Scotland) Act 2002 removed charges payable by Scottish older people for personal care services (assistance with personal hygiene, eating and drinking, mobility, management of medication and personal safety) and specialist equipment such as bath hoists and hand rails (COSLA/Scottish Government, 2010). Similarly, in 2011 the Welsh Government capped the amount that any individual is required to pay towards nonresidential social care at £60 (€76) per week (Welsh Government, 2015); no such limit exists in England.

## 8.3 Recent developments in UK long-term care

During the first decade of the century, a number of policy and practice measures aimed to improve the quality, efficiency and effectiveness of both the health and social care elements of long-term care. However, any positive outcomes from these measures are likely to be seriously constrained by the subsequent, increasingly severe austerity-related policies.

## 110  Caroline Glendinning

### 8.3.1  Personalisation and personal budgets

In response to campaigns by working-age disabled people for greater choice and control over their support arrangements, since 1997 local authorities have been able to allocate cash 'direct payments' instead of social care services in kind. How payments are used must be agreed with the local authority; they are generally used to employ a non-family carer ('personal assistant'). The direct payment option was extended to older people in 2000. However, overall take-up remained low and varied widely, both between local authorities (Fernández et al., 2007) and types of service users: older people were consistently less likely to choose the direct payment option than working-age disabled people (Leece and Bornat, 2006).

In 2008, a major programme was launched in England to expand service 'consumer' choice (Department of Health, 2008) by ensuring that everyone eligible for local authority support is offered a personal budget (PB) – a personalised funding allocation that can be used to purchase customised care and support in line with individual preferences. PBs can be taken as a cash direct payment and managed by the recipient (the preferred policy option); managed by a third-party individual or organisation; held by the local authority on behalf of the individual and used to pay for council commissioned services (the most common option for older people); or a combination of these.

A survey of English councils found that by March 2014, 81% of all people receiving local authority-funded nonresidential support were using PBs – a total of 70% of all expenditure on community-based social care. However, there remained marked variations across the English regions. Moreover, only 29% of total expenditure on PBs was in the form of cash direct payments; 47% was managed by the local authority and used to pay for local authority-commissioned services (ADASS, 2014). This indicates considerable shortfall in the policy ambition of increasing consumer choice for older social care service users.

Within the English NHS, personal health budgets (PHBs) have also been piloted for small groups of people with long-term health problems (Davidson et al., 2013; Jones et al., 2013). PHBs are now generally available for the small group of people whose health conditions are so complex and severe that they are eligible for NHS funding to cover all of their care, whether they receive this in hospital, in a residential home or in their own homes. However, take-up is still low: less than 5,000 people (of all ages) across England receive a PHB, and there are also considerable regional variations (NHS England, 2015).

Scotland has pursued similar policies, but on a slower and less radical scale. The Social Care (Self-directed Support) (Scotland) Act 2013 placed a duty on local authority social work departments to offer people eligible for social care a range of choices over how they receive their social care and support. A similar range of options for exercising this choice (through cash direct payments, third-party or local authority management) is available.

Personal budgets are far from uncontroversial. A large multi-method evaluation of the English social care pilot PB programme found little evidence of positive outcomes, including cost-effectiveness, for older people (Glendinning et al., 2008). Other commentators have criticised the appropriateness of a 'consumer' approach in social care (Barnes, 2011) and its managerialist implementation in England (Beresford, 2009). Particular concerns persist about the appropriateness of personal budgets for older people. A survey of 4,000 self-selected PB users and carers found older people were less likely than working age people to report increased control over their daily lives (TLAP, 2014). A wider research review also found little evidence of PBs leading to improvements in older people's lives; where these did occur, it was because older people had substantial help with managing their PB and employing staff (Zamfir, 2013). There is also considerable uncertainty about the benefits to family carers. On the one hand, carers may benefit from an older person's PB if this is used to fund services that relieve carers of some of their responsibilities; on the other hand, family carers may have to take on additional responsibilities for managing the budget and employing paid carers (Glendinning et al., 2015).

### 8.3.2 Rehabilitation and reablement

Since 2000, there has been considerable investment in short-term, intensive rehabilitation and reablement services – therapies and equipment – at the interfaces between acute hospital and community-based services, including social care (Department of Health, 2000). In 2010, the English government allocated an additional £70 million from the English NHS budget, plus further funding of up to £300 million per year up to 2015, to develop new rehabilitation and reablement services, particularly following periods of hospital treatment (Department of Health, 2010). This investment was followed in June 2013 by a new £3.8 billion Better Care Fund to be spent during 2015–2016 by English local authorities and NHS services working together to develop integrated services. Of this, £1 million was conditional on achieving targets to reduce emergency hospital admissions, delays in hospital discharge and admissions to long-term residential care. Achieving these targets involves the provision of effective rehabilitation services (NHS England, 2013). The Better Care Fund has been criticised as overambitious and unlikely to achieve the desired savings because of the lack of a realistic timeframe and local service capacity for planning and staff retraining; there is also very little evidence on the cost-effectiveness of integrated services (NAO, 2014).

NHS rehabilitation services are increasingly complemented by home care reablement services – short-term, intensive, goal-oriented home care services aimed at building confidence and adapting to new ways of managing routine personal care activities (including using special equipment or assistive technology). Almost all English local authorities now provide home care reablement services, free of charge, for around 6 weeks after referral; following this there is reassessment of longer-term support needs. Where service capacity is limited, people newly discharged from hospital are given priority. There is good evidence of the cost-effectiveness of home care reablement (Glendinning et al., 2010) and of the delivery arrangements likely to optimise outcomes (Rabiee and Glendinning, 2011).

These developments aim to encourage intersectoral collaboration and integration across health and social long-term care services. The 2000 investment in

112   *Caroline Glendinning*

rehabilitation services was explicitly intended to reduce delays in hospital discharge and thereby improve throughput and efficiency in the acute hospital sector. The objectives of the Better Care Fund are to promote closer working between local health and social care services and prevent older people being admitted to hospital. It is unclear how far these investments will succeed in reducing older people's dependence on services and promoting their independence and confidence, given the primary focus on service-level objectives. In particular, evidence on the longer-term benefits and effectiveness of what are essentially short-term interventions is limited (Glendinning et al., 2010).

Similar policies have been introduced in Scotland, but with a remit extended to include people with long-term health problems and vocational rehabilitation for those returning to work after a period of absence or aiming to stay in employment. Scottish policies also emphasise a holistic approach to rehabilitation, with a single point of access and services delivered by multi-disciplinary, multi-agency teams (Scottish Executive, 2007).

### 8.3.3 *Reforming social care law and funding*

Major reforms to English social care law were enacted in 2014. Two main drivers lay behind these reforms. First, in 2011, the Law Commission (an independent advisory body to the English and Welsh Governments) undertook a comprehensive review of the law on adult social care. The review noted that adult social care in England and Wales was still based on the 1948 National Assistance Act; this did not reflect subsequent major demographic and social changes. The commission recommended revising and consolidating all previous legislation into a single law governing adult social care in England and Wales. The new legislation should be underpinned by the overarching principle that adult social care must contribute to or promote individual well-being (Law Commission, 2011).

Also in 2010, the coalition government responded to long-standing concerns about funding arrangements for social care in England, in which individuals with assets (then) over £23,750 are required to pay the full costs of their care. These costs can be catastrophic if several years of expensive residential care are involved and require the older person to sell their home to pay for care – a requirement that is widely unpopular. A Commission of Enquiry led by economist Andrew Dilnot was tasked with devising a more equitable and sustainable system for funding care (it was not asked to consider the total volume of resources needed adequately to fund social care in the context of demographic change and rising demand).

The commission recommended there should be a cap (limit) on the amount any individual is required to pay towards the cost of social care over her/his lifetime of between £25,000 and £50,000. Any costs above this cap should be met by the state. Furthermore, the asset threshold for those in residential care, beyond which no means-tested local authority funding would be given, should increase from £23,750 to £100,000. However, residents of residential or nursing homes should nevertheless make standard contributions of £7,000 to £10,000 a year towards their 'hotel' (food and accommodation) costs (Commission on Funding of Care and Support, 2011).

*Long-term care and austerity in the UK*   113

Both sets of proposals were brought together in the English Care and Support Act 2014, implemented in April 2015. Equivalent legislation for Wales (Social Services and Well-being [Wales] Act 2014) comes into force in 2016.

In line with the Law Commission's recommendations, the 2014 act requires social care services to promote the well-being of older and disabled adults and family carers. Well-being includes a range of physical, mental and emotional outcomes; participation in education, training and paid work; and economic well-being. The act places new duties on local authorities to provide a range of services to prevent, delay or reduce needs for support; promote integration between social care and health services (again with the aim of promoting well-being); provide information about care options and how to access these; and promote the provision of high quality care by care provider organisations. Needs assessments should consider well-being and focus on outcomes. Family carers were given the same rights as the people they care for to assessments of their support needs.

The act also created a new framework for paying for care, originally due to come into effect in April 2016. In major modifications of the Dilnot Commission's proposals, the capital limit – the personal assets threshold above which no local authority funding would be provided – was to be set at £118,000 (not £23,750) if an individual's assets included a house, and £27,000 if not. The cap – the lifetime maximum an individual paid towards their care – was set at £72,000 (not the recommended £25,000 to £50,000). Only actual care costs would count towards the cap, not the hotel costs of residential care. Moreover, only care that a local authority would have funded to meet assessed needs, and at the level it would have paid for services to meet those needs, was to count towards the cap. Thus, any additional private spending, for example to top-up the fees of a more expensive care home above the standard rate paid by the local authority or to purchase additional domestic help, would not count towards the individual's expenditure cap. It was estimated that someone paying £25,000 a year in care home fees would take 5.5 years to reach the cap and benefit from the new arrangements, by which time they would have paid over £135,000 in fees. Even at this stage, the full costs of care home fees would not be met as the individual would still be liable for an estimated £12,000 a year in hotel costs (Clements, 2014).

The care cap proposals extended to social care the same principle of state protection from catastrophic costs provided by the NHS with respect to health care. It was estimated that 100,000 additional older people in England would begin to receive some public funding towards the costs of their care; they were likely to have relatively high needs and modest assets (between £23,250 and £150,000), so the redistributional effects of the legislation would be small (Humphries, 2013). They applied only to England.

Although welcomed in principle, implementation of the 2014 act was subject to serious criticisms from the Association of Directors of Social Services and the Local Government Association. The statutory guidance – 500 pages accompanied by 17 sets of regulations – was not approved until October 2014, leaving local authorities less than 5 months to make the necessary major reconfigurations (including workforce retraining) (Clements, 2014). Above all, the care cap proposals did not generate any overall increase in funding for social care services; at the same time they imposed new costs on local authorities in administering the reforms.

## 114  *Caroline Glendinning*

### 8.4 Austerity policies

Despite the global economic crisis of 2008, significant impacts on social care in England were not immediately apparent. A study carried out for the English Local Government Association (LGA, 2010) found little initial evidence of increased demand for long-term care services or slow-down in the introduction of personal budgets. However, there was some evidence that more social care clients were poorer and therefore contributing lower levels of means-tested copayments for social care services, which impacted overall budget levels. There were also concerns about the sustainability of smaller social care provider organisations as local authorities reduced the prices they were able to pay for services and increased competition between providers.

Explicit austerity-related policies were introduced during the 2010–2015 conservative-liberal democrat coalition government. Dominated by a conservative majority, the coalition government had an explicit policy of reducing public expenditure in order to reduce the overall spending deficit. Given the political popularity of the National Health Service, NHS funding was protected – and indeed increased in England by 19.3%, from £97.5 billion in 2010–2011 to £116.4 billion in 2015–2016. However, even this was not enough to keep pace with rising demand from a rapidly ageing population. A 2014 report spelled out the scale of the financial challenges facing the NHS (NHS, 2014) and argued for additional investment to prevent ill-health; develop new, more efficient models of care; and enact other measures to improve NHS productivity. Even these ambitious proposals to manage demand and improve productivity were estimated to leave the NHS in England short of some £8 billion a year by 2020 (Kings Fund, 2014a).

On the other hand, local government funding – and hence the funding available for social care – received no such protection. The 2010–2015 coalition government imposed significant cuts in local government spending that had a serious impact on social care. Between 2010–2011 and 2014–2015, annual surveys by the English Association of Directors of Social Services showed a total reduction of £4.6 billion in funding for adult social care – equivalent to 31% of the 2010–2011 net budget (ADASS, 2015). Overall, although numbers of people aged 65 years and older in England grew by more than 1 million between 2005–2006 and 2012–2013, spending on social care services for older people fell by £1.2 billion (15.4%). During the same period, the number of people aged 65 years and older receiving local authority-funded social care services dropped by more than a quarter, from 1,231,000 to 896,000 (Age UK, 2014).

Similar reductions were made in the funding allocated by the Westminster government to Scotland. Between 2010 and 2014, Scotland's overall budget was cut by 9% in real terms. The Scottish health budget was initially protected, but has had a 1% cut from 2015–2016. Local government budgets have experienced a 3% cut on top of smaller cuts and 'efficiency savings' over the previous 6 years, at the same time as local residential property taxes were frozen (Unison Scotland, 2014).

These measures were followed by further draconian cuts to local authority budgets announced during the first 8 months of the conservative government that came to power in May 2015. Again, these reflect a renewed determination to reduce public spending, ostensibly in order to reduce, and if possible remove altogether, the public expenditure deficit.

Again, NHS spending has to some extent been protected. Overall, total health spending in England is expected to rise by £4.5 billion in real terms between 2015–2016 and 2020–2021 – equivalent to an increase of 0.9% a year. Much of this additional funding will be allocated in 2016–2017, but it is likely to be absorbed by current budget deficits among NHS health service providers and increased pensions payments for NHS staff. With smaller increases in subsequent years, the NHS is expected to struggle to maintain current patterns and levels of services, let alone be able to invest in new models of services. Spending on public health – health education and prevention services – will fall by £800 million between 2015–2016 and 2020–2021, which will affect many services aimed at reducing needs for care (Nuffield Trust, 2015).

Again, lacking the political and public popularity of the NHS, funding for social care received no such protection. On the contrary, it has been severely hit by cuts in the allocation of funding from central government to local authorities. A cut of £0.5 billion was expected in 2015–2016; an estimated 400,000 fewer adults are expected to receive social care services in 2015–2016 than 2009–2010. Many of those who are still eligible will receive less care. Taking into account demographic increases in the numbers of older and working age disabled people, it was estimated that an additional £1.1 billion would be needed to maintain the same level of social care services in 2015–2016 as the previous year (ADASS, 2015). In response to serious concerns about the funding shortfall expressed by local authority Directors of Adult Social Care and charities representing older people, in summer 2015 the conservative government announced that implementation of the 2014 Care And Support Act cap on individual funding liabilities for long-term care, which would have involved additional local authority costs, would be postponed until 2020 – in effect until after the next election. This has raised speculation that implementation may be postponed indefinitely (Lowe, 2015). Nor is it entirely clear that the £6 billion funding previously earmarked for implementing the care funding cap reforms will remain available to local authorities to invest in social care (Age UK, 2015).

The Scottish government has sought to protect local authorities to some extent from the full impact of the Westminster government's austerity measures, by transferring an additional £250 million from the Scottish NHS budget to support local health and social care service integration. It is hoped that this integration will in due course enhance capacity in community-based services and reduce demand for expensive hospital and residential care (Scottish Government, 2015).

In autumn 2015, the conservative government announced its broader public expenditure plans for the period up to 2020. These plans hit local authority budgets – and hence social care – particularly hard. Since 2013, English local authorities have been allowed to keep half the money they raise from local business taxes; the remainder was sent to central government and redistributed in order to partially reduce regional and local inequalities, particularly between south and northern England. The autumn 2015 spending statement announced that local

## 116   *Caroline Glendinning*

authorities will be able to retain their local business taxes in full; in turn, they will receive £6.1 billion less in grants from central government by 2019–2020 (Harris, 2015). The fiscal equalisation role of central government will therefore gradually be phased out.

In addition, local authorities will be allowed to raise additional local funding for social care by increasing residential property taxes by up to 2% a year, on top of any other increases. This 2% 'precept' will be ring-fenced to be used only for social care services. The government estimated that if all local authorities raise the extra 2% in full every year, an additional £2 billion a year could be generated for social care by 2020. Additional funding for social care was also allocated through the Better Care Fund, to be used – as before – for investment in services at the social care-NHS interface aimed at reducing emergency hospital admissions and delays to hospital discharge because of a lack of community-based services. This increase was estimated to add £1.5 billion a year to the Better Care Fund by 2019–2020 (Nuffield Trust, 2015).

Three other policy measures announced by the conservative government are also likely to have significant impacts on social care. First, as part of a package of measures intended to cut public spending on social security income maintenance benefits for those in low paid employment, increases in the legal minimum wage (termed the 'national living wage') have been announced. These increases effectively shift some responsibility for income maintenance for low paid workers from the state to employers. The national living wage will be phased in up to April 2016. As care workers in residential and nursing homes and domiciliary home care services are one of the largest groups of low paid employees, the national living wage is expected significantly to increase care providers' wage bills.

Second, there are suggestions that expenditure on Attendance Allowance will be restricted or capped. As a national social security benefit with national eligibility and entitlement criteria, spending on Attendance Allowance has to date necessarily been demand-led. In 2014, an independent Commission of Enquiry into future care funding proposed that Attendance Allowance should be integrated into a single funding stream for long-term care (Kings Fund, 2014b). This suggestion now appears to have been taken up by government, with a proposal that the £5 billion Attendance Allowance budget should be transferred to local government and used to fund social care services (Brindle, 2015a).

A third measure likely to impact social care is the scrapping of a planned training scheme to create a career ladder for care workers employed in nursing homes. The scheme would have trained front-line staff to take on some of the responsibilities currently held by qualified nurses. It had been due to start in January 2016, but it has now been withdrawn (The Guardian 14 December 2015).

### 8.5   The impacts of austerity

Against a backdrop of rising demand for long-term care from increasing numbers of older people, there is increasing concern about the adequacy of funding for social care (ADASS, 2015). Analysts, professional leaders and commentators increasingly refer to the mounting crisis in the sector (Brindle, 2015b).

Total funding from central government to local authorities in England is expected to fall by 56% between 2015–2016 and 2019–2020, on top of the 37% cut experienced under the 2010–2015 coalition government (Age UK, 2015). Changes to the source of local authority revenue – particularly the increased role of local business rates and the new freedom to levy an extra 2% precept on local property taxes specifically for social care – will leave local authority budgets much more dependent on their local tax base. This raises significant concerns about the equitable distribution of funding for social care, given the wide disparities between richer and poorer areas (and particularly between northern and southern England) and therefore in the potential of local authorities to generate income from local businesses and property. Many local authorities with higher numbers of older people, and thus with higher needs for social care funding, will be able to generate much lower levels of additional resources from the new 2% precept. For example, in parts of Lincolnshire, where 30% of people are aged 65 years and older, the 2% increase would generate just under £30 per older person per year; in a wealthy outer London local authority with half that proportion of older people, the additional 2% would be expected to generate an extra £95 per older person per year (Franklin, 2015). Moreover, decisions to levy the 2% precept in full will be influenced by local political considerations. It is unlikely that all local authorities will decide to levy the full 2% increase every year for the next 4 years. The total additional revenue generated is therefore likely to be significantly lower than the £2 billion a year in cash terms by 2020 anticipated by the government (Nuffield Trust, 2015); one estimate places the additional funding likely to be generated by the precept at just £800 million (The Guardian 7 December 2015).

While the additional resources for the Better Care Fund have been welcomed, these are not due to become available until 2017–2018, when only £100 million will be made available. The full increase of £1.5 billion will only be delivered in 2019–2020, suggesting a significant immediate shortfall. Overall, spending on social care in England as a proportion of GDP will fall from 1.1% in 2015 to around 1% in 2020 – and even more if the new 2% precept generates less revenue than the £2 billion anticipated by government. This contrasts with the OECD average of 1.6% of GDP spending on long-term care and is similar to levels of spending on social care in Eastern European countries (Franklin, 2015).

### 8.5.1 The impacts on long-term care services

English home care (domiciliary care) and community-based services have been hardest hit by the cuts as local authorities have increasingly focused limited resources on those with the highest levels of need. Spending on home care services has reduced by almost a fifth (19%) between 2010–2011 and 2013–2014. This has resulted in a 15% decrease in the numbers of older people receiving local authority-funded home care, from 437,150 in 2010–2011 to 371,770 in 2013–2014. The distribution of home care services has also changed, as limited resources become increasingly focused on adults with the most intensive needs who might otherwise be at risk of admission to residential care. For example, in 2010–2011, 13.8% of home care recipients received two or less hours per

# 118    *Caroline Glendinning*

week compared with just 9.1% of recipients in 2013–2014 (Mortimer and Green, 2015). English local authority Directors of Adult Social Care anticipate that of the planned reductions in social care services for 2015–2016, 54% will be to domiciliary home care services (ADASS, 2015).

Other community-based services have also seen severe cuts. In the last three years, English local authority spending on meals on wheels has been cut by 47% (from £42.1 million to £22.3 million). As a result, there has been a 61% reduction in the numbers of people receiving meals on wheels, from 75,885 in 2010–2011 to just 29,605 in 2013–2014. Spending on day care has dropped by 30% over the same period; the number of people aged 65 years and older using local authority-commissioned or provided day care has fallen from 95,145 people in 2010–2011 to 59,300 in 2013–2014. Similarly, between 2010–2011 and 2014–2015, the numbers of older people receiving help with aids and adaptations has fallen by 83,945 as scarce resources are increasingly focused on those with highest needs (Mortimer and Green, 2015).

All these services are closely associated with prevention, support for independent living and support for informal carers, despite the new local authority duties imposed by the Care and Support Care Act 2014 to invest in services that prevent or delay needs for social care. Directors of Adult Social Care report struggling to invest in services to reduce future demand while simultaneously maintaining vital services to support those currently in greatest need. They anticipate a cash terms reduction of 6% in English local authority funding for preventive services in 2015–2016 compared with the previous year (ADASS, 2015).

The number of people supported by local authorities in residential and nursing home care also fell slightly between 2010–2011 and 2013–2014. This may reflect the growing focus of local authority support on older people in the community with the highest level needs who would otherwise be at risk of admission to institutional care. It may also reflect rising asset levels (primarily because of home ownership) among older people that disqualify them from any local authority funding.

### 8.5.2  The impacts on older people

Access to publicly funded social care in England is now highly skewed, with only a small proportion of those needing help with personal care actually receiving this through local authority-funded services or PBs. Eligibility is restricted to only those with the highest needs. Since 2008–2009, the numbers of older people receiving local authority-funded care has fallen by 30%; by 2015 there were 0.5 million fewer people (of all ages) receiving care than in 2008–2009 (Franklin, 2015). Between 2010 and 2015, more than 400,000 older people were unable to access the care they needed because of cuts in services (Nuffield Trust, 2015).

Research conducted in 2014 estimated that 870,000 older people aged between 65 and 89 in England had one or more personal care needs that were unmet. Almost a third of older people who reported difficulty in carrying out essential activities of daily living, such as getting out of bed, washing, using the toilet or eating, received no help from either paid care workers or family carers (Age UK,

*Long-term care and austerity in the UK*  119

2014). Another analysis using data from the English Longitudinal Study of Ageing estimated that in 2012–2013 there were 1.86 million people aged 50 years and older in England with unmet care needs – an increase of 120,000 since 2006–2007 (Franklin, 2015). Within the older population, women are more likely than men to have one or more unmet needs. The risk of having unmet needs increases with age; almost 78% of those aged 85 to 89 years report at least one unmet need. Older people who are single or divorced are also more likely than those with partners or spouses to have unmet care needs (Mortimer and Green, 2015).

### 8.5.3 Private care markets

This significant shortfall in the coverage of publicly funded social care services has helped to create a growing privately funded care market in England, with increasing numbers of older people who are assessed as having insufficiently severe needs and/or income or assets that are too high to qualify for local authority-funded services instead paying for social care from their own resources (Baxter and Glendinning, 2014). An estimated 43% of older and physically disabled adults living in residential homes (i.e. those with the most intensive care needs) meet the entire cost of their care themselves, The proportion of 'self-funders' in residential care rises to 57% if people topping up local authority fees with additional private spending to meet the costs of care home fees that are higher than the local authority will pay for are included (LaingBuisson, 2013, cited in Humphries, 2013). In addition, some 70,000 people living at home pay privately for all their personal care, and a further 200,000 pay from their own private resources for help with domestic tasks (instrumental activities of daily living) such as shopping and cooking (Humphries, 2013). The proposed cap on individual responsibilities for funding care would have reduced these liabilities to some extent, particularly among those older people who currently fund the entire costs of their residential care. This has now been postponed until at least 2020. Additionally, the proposed transfer of the social security Attendance Allowance benefit budget to local authorities to spend on social care services threatens those older people who need some help with personal care or domestic tasks at home but whose needs are not assessed as sufficiently serious to qualify for local authority-funded services. The benefit is awarded using different eligibility criteria from those employed by local authorities and is commonly used by recipients to fund low-level services, including help from voluntary organisations and friends, that help to prevent deteriorations in health and independence and avoid moves to expensive residential care (Corden et al., 2010). Given the significant underfunding of local authority care and the fact that the transferred resources will not be ring-fenced, they are likely to be used to help meet the significant shortfall in funding for services for people with the most severe support needs.

### 8.5.4 The impacts on family caregivers

There is emerging evidence of increased burdens falling on unpaid family caregivers. Across the UK, the total number of carers increased by 11% between 2001 and 2011 (Carers UK, 2014). According to the 2011 census, some 6.5 million

120    *Caroline Glendinning*

people across the UK provide unpaid care to relatives and close friends. A survey of 4,500 family carers found 48% struggling to make ends meet financially; 82% reported caring had had a negative impact on their health; and three-quarters expressed concern about the impact of caring on their health in the future (Carers UK, 2015).

Large numbers of unpaid carers are themselves elderly; in 2014, 20.5% of older people provided unpaid care – a total of 1.3 million across the UK. Older people often provide more intensive care than the population of unpaid carers as a whole: over a third of older carers care for 20 or more hours a week, and more than a quarter care for 50 or more hours a week (Mortimer and Green, 2015).

Analysis of 2011 census data shows an inverse relationship between the incidence of informal caregiving and the levels of additional revenue likely to be generated by the new 2% local authority social care precept. In other words, because of variability in local authorities' tax base, the precept is expected to generate significantly less money in those local authorities where there is a higher reliance on unpaid care (Franklin, 2015).

### 8.5.5  *The impacts on care markets*

A further major consequence of the reductions in English local authority funding for social care is an increasingly fragile social care market. Since 1993 there has been a massive shift from social care services provided by local authorities to provision by private (charity or for-profit) organisations. Funding for these services comes from direct local authority contracts, individual PBs or private purchase. In 1992, the private sector supplied just 2% of English home care contact hours; by 2013, this was 89% (Humphries, 2013). Some 92% of all English nursing and residential care home places for older people are now supplied by private and voluntary sector providers (Humphries, 2013). Outsourcing and contracting of NHS services to private providers in England is also increasing.

The Care and Support Act 2014 requires English local authorities to promote effective local care markets, ensuring a variety of providers and high quality services for older people to choose from. However, the funding shortfall is having an increasing impact on care providers, particularly smaller ones, as for several years local authorities have frozen the fees they pay for the supply of home and residential care or only increased fees below inflation. Cuts in individual PB levels, as local authorities tighten their budgets, also reduce demand in local care markets. Over half of English Directors of Adult Social Care reported in 2015 that care provider organisations in their area were facing financial difficulties (ADASS, 2015).

Care providers themselves report increasing problems in recruiting and retaining staff. In 2013–2014, the Care Quality Commission (which regulates and inspects service providers across the health and social care sectors) reported that one in five English nursing homes did not have enough staff on duty to ensure residents received safe care (CQC, 2015). Vacancy rates for nurses working in social care (mainly in homes for older people and people with severe learning disabilities) are 9%; over the past 2 years, the largest groups of nursing homes reported a 55% increase in the use of temporary agency staff to fill permanent staffing shortfalls. Staffing problems are exacerbated by the fact that nurses working in social care are, on average, older than those working in the NHS, so proportionally more are close to or are at retirement age (Brindle, 2015b). The decision to cut a training programme that would have developed the nursing-related skills of care workers in nursing homes will increase these staffing pressures.

The reasons behind the growing crisis in care are contested; some commentators argue that large residential care providers are prone to crisis because they use debt-based financial engineering models (as developed by private equity) to maximize profit (Burns et al., 2016). As an illustration of the growing crisis, in late 2015 the largest UK provider of residential care services announced plans to close seven homes in Northern Ireland – a move that relatives warned could kill residents because of the stress of moving (The Guardian 4 December 2015). The largest English home care services provider, employing 15,000 care workers, has recently recorded a loss of £220 million, and several other care providers are reported to be seeking buyers or early exits from loss-making local authority contracts (Brindle, 2015b). Shortfalls in the availability of domiciliary or residential care will have immediate serious knock-on effects on demands for NHS services and the achievement of Better Care Fund objectives.

The introduction of the national living wage by April 2016 will further increase pressures on care providers, who bear the responsibility and risk of increasing pay levels for their staff. The cost of implementing the national living wage across the English social care sector is estimated to be £800 million (Nuffield Trust, 2015). This is unlikely to be matched by increased payments from local authorities to care providers, adding further to the fragility of local care markets.

The pressures on care providers are of course felt by care workers and their clients. The Care Quality Commission reported in April 2015 that 8.7% of social care providers were inadequate and a further 31.9% required improvement (CQC, 2015). The quality of home care has been a concern for some years. A highly critical report from the Equality and Human Rights Commission found many examples of poor quality care, including 15-minute visits from home care staff which did not allow even basic personal care needs to be met; clients unable to influence the timing of visits; neglect of clients' basic hygiene; poor staff awareness and training; and a failure to respect clients' dignity and privacy (EHRC, 2011).

## 8.6 Conclusions

Without the protection of the political and public popularity enjoyed by the NHS, social care in the UK – particularly in England – is in crisis. This crisis has developed rapidly since 2010, as two successive governments have reduced funding for local government services, of which the most significant element is adult social care. The prospects for the years up to 2020 are increasingly grim.

Within this deteriorating context, recent policy and practice aspirations – particularly the introduction of personalised funding and the 2014 Care and Support Act – seem unlikely to be realised. Already far lower proportions of older people

## 122   *Caroline Glendinning*

than other groups of disabled adults opt for direct payments, and as the size of individual PBs are squeezed, options to spend these limited resources in different, more creative ways, are reduced (Glasby et al., 2015). The new legal responsibilities of local authorities to delay and prevent needs for care are also unlikely to be met, as local authorities struggle to support even those with the highest levels of care needs. Over the coming years, the ability of care provider organisations to recruit, train and retain staff and provide good quality care seems increasingly fragile, as they struggle to meet increased wage bills. Major threats to their viability and the wider capacity of local care markets seem likely.

Some additional funding has been made available through the Better Care Fund for the development of services at the boundaries of acute hospital and social care. Similar funding has been transferred from the Scottish NHS budget for similar purposes. These resources are linked to clear objectives of improving integration between services. However, the environment in which health and social care partners are now working is far from favourable: 'the intense financial pressures facing public services . . . mean that potential partners are having to navigate a much more complex, congested environment and . . . develop local relationships in incredibly stressful and difficult conditions' (Glasby et al., 2015: 95). Moreover, the focus of new service investments on hospital admission and discharge overlooks the broader functions of social care: to maintain independent living, support social participation and promote quality of life.

Of greatest concern, shifts in sources of funding for social care, from central to local government, herald a retreat from any concept of social care as a universal service with (approximately) similar eligibility thresholds and levels of provision across England. This is in addition to the variability already found across the four countries of the UK. In future, access to social care and the types and levels of services will depend increasingly on local decision making and priorities. While this is consistent with the current conservative government's policies favouring greater local devolution, it is incompatible with any notion that access to publicly funded support to counteract the frailties of old age is a basic citizenship right for frail older people.

## References

ADASS (2014), National personalisation survey 2014. *National Overview Report.* http://www.adass.org.uk/PersonalisationSurvey2014 downloaded 8 June 2015.

ADASS (2015), Budget survey 2015. http://www.adass.org.uk/budget-survey-2015 downloaded 8 June 2015.

Age UK (2014), Older people with care needs not getting crucial help. http://www.ageuk.org.uk/latest-press/archive/older-people-care-needs-not-getting-help/ downloaded 8 June 2015.

Age UK (2015), *Consultation Response Spending Review 2015*, London: Age UK. www.ageuk.org.uk/professionals/policy (Accessed: 25 November 2015).

Barnes, M. (2011), Abandoning care? A critical perspective on personalisation from an ethic of care, *Ethics and Social Welfare* 5(2): 153–167.

Baxter, K. and Glendinning, C. (2014), People who fund their own social care: A scoping review, *SSCR 2619, NIHR School for Social Care Research*, SPRU: University of York.

*Long-term care and austerity in the UK* 123

Beresford, P. (2009), Whose personalisation? *Compass*, London 47: 1–5.

Brindle, D. (2015a), Fears of benefit cap for older people if councils take charge, *The Guardian*, 17 December 2015.

Brindle, D. (2015b), The outlook for social care is grim – unless more workers are recruited, *The Guardian*, 18 November 2015. http://www.theguardian.com/society/2015/nov/18/social-care-workers-increased-demand-unpaid-care downloaded 4 January 2015.

Burns, D., Cowie, L., Earle, J., Folkman, P., Froud, J., Hyde, P., Johal, S., Rees Jones, I., Killett, A. and Williams, K. (2016), *Where Does the Money Go? Financialised Chains and the Crisis in Residential Care*. Centre for Research on Socio-Cultural Change, University of Manchester.

Carers UK (2014), *Facts about Carers: Policy Briefing*, London: Carers UK.

Carers UK (2015), Carers call for more support. http://www.carersuk.org/news-and-campaigns/press-releases/carers-call-for-more-support-as-new-figures-reveal-worrying-impact-of-caring downloaded 8 June 2015.

Clements, L. (2014), The care act 2014 updated overview. http://www.lukeclements.co.uk/whats-new/ downloaded 8 June 2015.

Commission on Funding of Care and Support (2011), *Fairer Care Funding – the Report of the Commission on Funding of Care and Support (Dilnot Report)*, London: Stationery Office. http://webarchive.nationalarchives.gov.uk/20130221130239/http://www.dilnot-commission.dh.gov.uk/our-report/ downloaded 9 June 2015.

Corden, A., Sainsbury, R., Irvine, A. and Clarke, S. (2010), *The impact of disability living allowance and attendance allowance: Findings from exploratory qualitative research*. Department for Work and Pensions Research Report, No. 649. Norwich: HMSO.

COSLA/Scottish Government (2010), Free personal and nursing care. www.gov.scot/Resource/Doc/305166/0095748.pdf downloaded 31 May 2015.

CQC (2015) *The State of Health Care and Adult Social Care in England 2013/14*, Newcastle: Care Quality Commission. http://www.cqc.org.uk/content/state-care-201314#asc downloaded 8 June 2015.

Davidson, J., Baxter, K., Glendinning, C. and Irvine, A. (2013), Choosing health: Qualitative evidence on the experiences of personal health budget holders, *Journal of Health Services Research and Policy*, 18(2S): 50–58.

Department of Health (2000), *The NHS Plan: A Plan for Investment: A Plan for Reform, Cmnd 4818*, London: HMSO.

Department of Health (2008), *Transforming Social Care, Local Authority Circular Letter 2008 (1): Gateway ref: 9337*, London: Department of Health.

Department of Health (2010), £70million support to help people in their homes after illness or injury, Press release 5 October. http://www.dh.gov.uk/en/MediaCentre/PressreleasesDH_120118 downloaded 27 August 2011.

EHRC (2011), *Close to Home: An Inquiry into Older People and Human Rights in Home Care*, Manchester: Equality and Human Rights Commission. http://www.equalityhumanrights.com/publication/close-home-inquiry-older-people-and-human-rights-home-care-executive-summary downloaded 8 June 2015.

Fernández, J.L., Kendall, J., Davey, V. and Knapp, M. (2007), Direct payments in England: Factors linked to variations in local provision, *Journal of Social Policy* 36: 97–122.

Franklin, B. (2015), *The End of Formal Adult Social Care Funding: A Provocation by the ILC-UK*, London: Centre for Later Life Funding.

Glasby, J., Miller, R. and Needham, C. (2015), Adult social care. In L. Foster, A. Brunton, C. Deeming, and T. Haux (eds) *In Defence of Welfare Social Policy Association*. http://www.social-policy.org.uk/what-we-do/publications/in-defence-of-welfare-2 downloaded 5 January 2015.

## 124   *Caroline Glendinning*

Glendinning, C., Challis, D., Fernández, J.L., Jacobs, S., Jones, K., Knapp, M., Manthorpe, J., Moran, N., Netten, A., Stevens, M. and Wilberforce, M. (2008), *IBSEN: National Evaluation of the Individual Budgets Pilot Programme*, York: Social Policy Research Unit, University of York.

Glendinning, C., Jones, K., Baxter, K., Arksey, H., Rabiee, P., Forder, J. and Wilde, A. (2010), *Home Care Re-Ablement Services: Investigating the Longer-Term Impacts (Prospective Longitudinal Study)*. Social Policy Research Unit, York: University of York.

Glendinning, C., Mitchell, W. and Brooks, J. (2015), Ambiguity in practice? Carers' roles in personalised social care in England, *Health and Social Care in the Community* 23(1): 23–32.

*The Guardian* (4 December 2015), Care home closures: Relatives fear move could kill residents.

*The Guardian* (7 December 2015), Plan to offset care cuts with local tax 'falls £1.2 billion short'.

*The Guardian* (14 December 2015), Scheme to boost staff in nursing homes is scrapped.

Harris, J. (2015), Will the rot stop when even the parks are flogged off? *The Guardian*, 27 November 2015.

HMG (2015), *Scotland in the United Kingdom: An Enduring Settlement, Cm 8990*, London: HM Government.

Humphries, R. (2013), *Paying for Social Care: Beyond Dilnot*, London: Kings Fund.

Jones, K., Forder, J., Caiels, J., Welch, E., Glendinning, C. and Windle, K. (2013), Personalisation in the health care system: Do personal health budgets impact on outcomes and cost? *Journal of Health Services Research and Policy* 18(2S): 59–67.

Kings Fund (2014a), No escaping the financial challenge facing the NHS: Our response to NHS England's Five Year Forward View. http://www.kingsfund.org.uk/press/press-releases downloaded 16 December 2015.

Kings Fund (2014b), A new settlement for Health and Social Care (Barker Commission), London, Kings Fund. http://www.kingsfund.org.uk/publications/new-settlement-health-and-social-care downloaded 8 June 2015.

LaingBuisson (2013), *Market Survey of Older People*, London: LaingBuisson.

Law Commission (2011), *Adult Social Care, HC941*, London: Stationery Office.

Leece, J. and Bornat, J. (2006), *Developments in Direct Payments*, Bristol: Policy Press.

LGA (2010), *The Impact of the Economic Slowdown on Adult Social Care*, London: Local Government Association.

Lowe, S. (2015), Care cap delayed. http://ageukblog.org.uk/2015/07/20/care-cap-delayed/?itv=1078503&itc=0&ito=8155 downloaded 26 July 2015.

Mortimer, J. and Green, M. (2015), *Briefing: The Health and Care of Older People in England 2015*, London: Age UK.

NAO (2014), *Planning for the Better Care Fund, HC 781 Session 2014–15*, London: National Audit Office.

NHS England (2013), Everyone Counts: Planning Patients 2014/15–2018/19.

NHS England (2014), *NHS Five Year Forward View*, London: NHS England.

NHS England (2015) Personal Health Budgets: National Progress Update November 2015. http://www.personalhealthbudgets.england.nhs.uk/_library/PHB_progress_update downloaded 15 December 2015.

Nuffield Trust (2015) The spending review: what does it mean for health and social care? www.nuffieldtrust.org.uk/publications downloaded 18 December 2015.

Rabiee, P. and Glendinning, C. (2011), Organisation and delivery of home care reablement – what makes a difference? *Health and Social Care in the Community* 19(5): 495–503.

Scottish Executive (2007), Co-ordinated, integrated and fit for purpose. A delivery framework for adult rehabilitation in Scotland. http://www.gov.scot/Publications/2007/02/20154247/12 downloaded 26 March 2016.

Scottish Government (2015), Budget: Local government funding. www.scotland.gov.uk/News/Budget-Local-Government-funding-2084.aspx downloaded 26 March 2016.

Scottish Government (2016), Health and social care integration due to go live. http://news.scotland.gov.uk/News/Health-social-care-integration-due-to-go-live-23be.aspx downloaded 26 March 2016.

TLAP (2014), Third national personal budget survey, think local act personal. http://www.thinklocalactpersonal.org.uk/Latest/Resource/?cid=10343 downloaded 8 June 2015.

Unison Scotland (2014), The cuts don't work: The impact of 'austerity' cuts on Scotland's public services. www.unison.org.uk/news/article/2014/06/impact-of-austerity-in-scotland downloaded 26 March 2016.

Wanless, D. (2006), *Securing Good Care for Older People: Taking a Long-Term View*, London: Kings Fund.

Welsh Government (2015), Paying for care. www.gov.wales/topics/health/socialcare/care/?lang=en Downloaded 26 March 2016.

Zamfir, M. (2013), Personalisation through personal budgets: Its effectiveness for older adults in social care services: Findings from an English based literature review, *Research, Policy and Planning* 30(2): 77–90.

# 9 Paradoxical decisions in German long-term care

## Expansion of benefits as a cost-containment strategy

*Margitta Mätzke and Tobias Wiß*

### 9.1 Introduction: the question of expansion

Discussions about long-term care date back to the 1970s in Germany, when proposals about how to finance and organize care for older people were first broadly debated (Zängl, 2015: 240). These concerns were first addressed in legislation in the 1988 health reform (Zängl, 2015), but in subsequent public policy debates, long-term care policy increasingly took shape as a policy field distinct from health or pension policy. Debate led to policy initiative, so that in 1994–1995, a long-term care insurance scheme (LTCI) was created. Questions of financing LTC took center stage in the policymaking process from the beginning, as possibilities of taking financial burdens for long-term care from the municipal social assistance system while at the same time avoiding additional payroll tax burdens were principal concerns of LTC policy (Roth and Rothgang, 2001: 292). In that sense, the motif of cost containment has shaped long-term care policy from its inception, and it has remained a central aspect of discussions and reform conceptions ever since (Theobald, 2012: 62; 2015: 38). An explicit requirement to pay attention to stable contribution rates was written in the law (Paquet and Jacobs, 2015: 3). Austerity has also been a reality, as benefits were not adjusted to the development of prices for care services, so that the real value of long-term care insurance benefits has steadily declined since the mid-1990s (Paquet and Jacobs, 2015: 4; Roth and Rothgang, 2001: 302). Since LTCI benefits are capped and not meant to cover the full cost of care, increasing out-of-pocket payments have been the result of this development. Internationally comparative accounts therefore emphasize the theme of austerity, at times even retrenchment, and the fact that expenditure for long-term care services in Germany is below average on a European scale (Pavolini and Theobald, 2015: 472).

The austerity narrative captures only part of the story, however. While the development of benefits may have lagged far behind the growth of needs, the long-term care sector has steadily expanded. This holds for overall expenditures – €26 billion in 2014 compared to €17 billion in 2000 (Bundesministerium für Gesundheit, 2016a); it holds for the number of people receiving benefits – 2.6 million in 2014 compared to 1.8 billion in 2000 (Bundesministerium für Gesundheit, 2016b); and most importantly, it holds for the scope of tasks and services receiving public financing, which has been broadened and enriched

*Paradoxical decisions in German LTC*  127

especially in recent years. For instance, this pertains to long-term care benefits for people suffering from dementia, which have become part of the benefit package only recently, or several measures aimed at improving working conditions for informal caregivers (Meißner, 2014: 62). Expansion in that sense was robust and never contested in principle, and it took place especially in the years since the economic crisis. Although the German economy recovered from the crisis surprisingly well, consolidation of public finances has been a major issue in public policymaking, particularly when it comes to the large expensive spending programs of the German welfare state, and yet, the financial crisis did not have major effects on long-term care in Germany. In this the country's experience diverges from that of other European countries such as Spain, Great Britain, or Finland, where long-term care benefits have been cut explicitly in the wake of the crisis (Waldhausen, 2014: 11). Measures of the 2014–2015 long-term care reform established regular reviews of benefit amounts relative to the cost of care services (Hagen and Rothgang, 2014: 9), and this monitoring system is in the process of evolving into a regular and obligatory indexing scheme (Paquet and Jacobs, 2015: 4). The most recent reform of long-term care policy, which will take effect in 2017, increases benefits in both home care and residential care (Rothgang, 2015: 806). Lawmakers deliberately made sure that existing beneficiaries all experience rising benefits (Rothgang and Kalwitzki, 2015: 47), and the latest reform will result in drastic growth of costs that are most likely not covered by the contribution rate increases already enacted (Walendzik et al., 2015: 21).

This strong expansion is puzzling, Germany's good economic performance notwithstanding. It is puzzling because there is very little in long-term care policy that can be construed in a social investment perspective. Social investment policies, that is, policies that seek to "minimize the intergenerational transfer of poverty as well as to ensure that the population is well prepared for the likely employment conditions (less job security; more precarious forms of employment) of contemporary economies" (Jenson, 2009: 447; see also Esping-Andersen, 2002) are the one area in which we still see expansionary social policy activism today. Care for the elderly may be an increasingly urgent necessity and a growing economic sector and labor market, and there may also be strong moral obligations to cater to the growing needs, but there is little by way of investment in future economic competitiveness in that sector of the social protection system. Expansion is also puzzling in Germany's welfare system, because, as Bonoli (2007) aptly argues, we should not see responses to new social risks, such as long-term care needs or the needs of caring relatives, that easily in a mature "industrial welfare state". Given the cost of the social insurance system's obligations to provide social protection for "old" industrial risks, such as unemployment or old age, there should be little scope for initiatives to cater to the needs of other sectors of society, such as caregivers or frail elderly in need of long-term care. Yet, we do see such initiatives, especially since 2008. We observe not only quantitative expansion of the cost and number of recipients in the long-term care system, which could be seen as straightforward outgrowth of demographic and socioeconomic trends, but we also encounter deliberate decisions to broaden the scope of benefits, improve the

128   *Margitta Mätzke and Tobias Wiß*

conditions of access, and take into account a fuller set of conditions that could make older people eligible to social care. Why is this so? Why do we see this rather unbroken and uncontested expansion in the qualitative substance and scope of long-term care benefits, especially in the aftermath of the economic crisis? Why do we see a discourse of budget consolidation, spending cuts, and cost containment paired with the willingness to extend the scope of entitlements to long-term care benefits beyond what it had been for 20 years?

The answer we advance in this chapter is focused on design features of the German long-term care system itself. That system, we submit, has two traits that render it potentially dangerous for any austerity-minded government. First, it has grown into a structure that is extremely unwieldy and extremely difficult to control, let alone steer. At the same time, due to its specific design of benefit entitlements, organization, and governance structures, it has the potential to create financial obligations for central and local governments that are likewise extremely difficult to control. People in need of long-term care are entitled to social assistance benefits once their own financial resources are exhausted. Therefore, there is the potential of uncontrolled, socioeconomically driven cost increases, and these will fall within the jurisdiction of local governments. The story of long-term care policy is a story of attempts at curbing this uncontrolled growth of entitlements and demands. It is the attempt at trading regulated and rational expansion for unbridled growth.

The next section of the chapter takes a look at the structures, benefits, and institutions of the long-term care system that cause German long-term care benefits to fall short of needs and in that sense generate a condition of permanent austerity and at the same time a constant drive toward expansion. Section 9.3 analyzes the resulting policy dynamics within the unwieldy system of German long-term care to show how the prospect of escalating demands on the system poses a serious threat. Section 9.4 traces the measures and underlying conceptions of recent reforms and is joined, in the concluding section 9.5, by broader considerations on how the fear of unbridled growth informs highly expansive reform measures.

## 9.2   Design of an unwieldy long-term care system

Once a long-term care policy crystallized out of the host of municipal and central government activities at financing and providing care for older people, German lawmakers opted for a social insurance solution as financing scheme (Ranci and Pavolini, 2015: 273). While this system does indeed share many features of the other four social insurance branches in the German welfare state (social health insurance, accident insurance, pension insurance, and unemployment insurance), there are crucial points at which the "fifth column" diverges from the classical principles of social insurance: the connection with the labor market and employment system is rather weak, as dependency at old age is not a work-related risk (Landenberger, 1994: 319, 327). There is a combination of cash benefits with in-kind benefits, and benefit recipients can choose between the two (Evers, 1995). There is also an overall limit to the benefits paid out of long-term care insurance. The last aspect, the cap on benefits, is the most important idiosyncrasy. Not only is

*Paradoxical decisions in German LTC* 129

it consequential for the governance of the long-term care sector (Rothgang, 1994: 183), but observers have also criticized the insurance solution for its somewhat questionable distributive results because as a financing scheme it privileges middle income people (Landenberger, 1994: 331) and protects their savings and their children's inheritance, whereas with the capped benefits that cover only part of the cost of care, low-income beneficiaries will not be lifted out of social assistance (Dudey, 1991: 357). There were also concerns at the time that capped benefits might become the model for other social insurance schemes as well (Landenberger, 1994: 324). In spite of all these peculiarities and concerns, however, the path dependent solution prevailed in the process of introducing long-term care insurance (Götting and Hinrichs, 1993; Rothgang, 1994), holding on to the familiar organizational template as a source of legitimacy (Lessenich, 2003: 233) while enacting innovative elements under the umbrella of overall institutional continuity (Lessenich, 2003: 217).

In the structure of benefits and services, German long-term care insurance makes a distinction between home care and residential care, and it decrees a principle for home care before residential care. The fifth social insurance branch covers expenses for the care of older people only partially. The main aim is to reduce – but not to fully cover – the care-related personal and financial burdens that people in need of care and their relatives experience, leaving ample room for informal care arrangements. LTCI has a dual structure, with a statutory system covering 71 million insured persons and a mandatory private LTCI (covering 10 million people) for those not covered by the statutory LTCI. The public branch is part of Germany's social insurance system. All employees insured in one of the public health insurance funds are covered by statutory LTCI, while the private mandatory system is for those who have private health insurance (the self-employed and employees with annual salaries over €56,250 in 2016). Private long-term care insurers must guarantee benefits and services equivalent to those of the statutory long-term care insurance system (see Rothgang, 2011). Taken together, the public and the private LTCI systems cover the entire population so that long-term care has long been the only social risk for which the German welfare state provides universal coverage (health insurance followed suit in 2009).

### 9.2.1 Benefits

Persons in need of care are entitled to LTCI benefits and services irrespective of their age, income, and wealth. Beyond LTCI, they are entitled to receive benefits from the social assistance system if they or their relatives are not able to pay for expenses not covered by the LTCI. In other words, entitlement to benefits is based on strictly need-based criteria. Beneficiaries who fall back on social assistance are subject to means testing, but for all care recipients, need is assessed based on medical criteria. An expert of the medical review board of the statutory health insurance, usually a physician or nurse, judges, according to a set of criteria, which activities of daily living a person can perform. Based on the result, the person who applied for care services is assigned one of three care levels. Persons in care level 1 get the lowest and persons in care level 3 get the highest amount of

## 130   *Margitta Mätzke and Tobias Wiß*

cash or in-kind benefits. In the current system, benefits depend on the care level and whether recipients receive care at home or in a nursing home. For care level 1, LTCI covers €468 in home care and €1,065 in residential care; for care level 2, it is €1,144 and €1,330; and for care level 3, it is €1,612 for both home care and residential care (Hoffer and Schölkopf, 2014; Statistisches Bundesamt, 2015a). Recipients of home-care benefits can get additional benefits such as day or night care, short-term care, and support for changes in the living environment. A recent policy innovation responding to the growing problem of dementia allows persons with permanent serious limitations in activities of daily living skills to receive additional benefits. The main aim of the LTCI is to provide differentiated and flexible benefits, such that care recipients can stay at home as long as possible. There is regional variation in the strictness with which medical criteria are applied in the tests of eligibility and, as a result, in the number persons entitled to benefits (Schulz, 2010: 7). There is also variation across the *Bundesländer* in the prices negotiated between care providers and LTCI funds (Eifert and Rothgang, 1999; Rothgang and Kalwitzki, 2015: 52). However, there is a uniform catalog of benefits that can be paid by the LTCI and also a uniform contribution rate in all places.

### 9.2.2  Financing

In the statutory system, employees and their employers pay equal contributions. Between 1995 and 2008, the level of LCTI contributions to the statutory long-term care insurance remained stable at 1.7% of pre-tax incomes. Since then, contribution hikes (increase to 1.95% in 2008, to 2.05% in 2013, and to 2.35% in 2015) set in to finance higher expenses. Contributions are paid up to an income ceiling of €50,850 (2016); pensioners pay both the employer and the employee parts of LTCI contributions. A decision of the federal constitutional court mandated that people over age 23 who do not have children have to pay a surcharge of 0.25% as of January 1, 2005. Revenues and expenses have both been increasing since the introduction of the LTCI. Between 22% and 25% of LTCI expenses are for cash transfers, while 41% to 49% are for residential care (Bundesministerium für Gesundheit, 2016a). The cap on benefits makes substantial private copayments necessary. Care recipients or their relatives have to fully cover the cost of room and board in residential care and partly even the care expenses (Rothgang and Kalwitzki, 2015: 10; Schulz, 2010: 7,), which amounts to some degree of inequality in access to care services (Theobald, 2004).

### 9.2.3  Recipient rates

Recent data about the development of LTCI recipient rates show an increase from 2 million recipients in 1999 to more than 2.6 million in 2013 (Statistisches Bundesamt, 2015a). Almost three quarters of all beneficiaries receive home-based care and almost half of all care recipients are cared for by relatives. Only 30% are in residential care (Figure 9.1).

The development of long-term care recipient rates by care level (Figure 9.2) reveals shifts of emphasis among the care levels. Between 1999 and 2013, growth

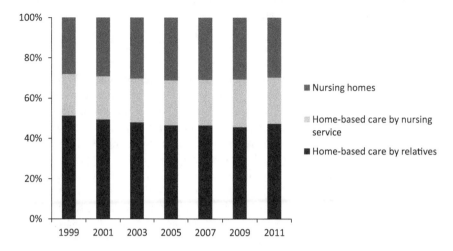

*Figure 9.1* Long-term care recipient rates by care institution
Source: Authors' illustration based on Statistisches Bundesamt (2015a).

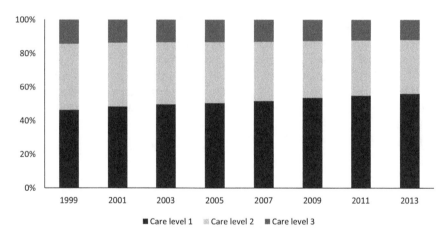

*Figure 9.2* Long-term care recipient rates by care level (percentage)
Source: Authors' illustration based on Statistisches Bundesamt (2015a).

was strongest for persons with the lowest benefits (care level 1). The proportions of care recipients of care levels 2 and 3 have been declining from 39% to 32% and from 14% to 12%, respectively. Although the total number of long-term care recipients increases, most of the new persons in care receive benefits at level 1, and this dampens the increase in overall expenses somewhat. In line with recipient rates, the number of long-term care providers increased in the past decade. In 2013, 12,745 companies or organizations offered home-care services (in 1999 it was 10,820) and 13,030 institutions offered residential care (in 1999 it was 8,859) (Bundesministerium für Gesundheit, 2016c).

### 9.2.4 Who cares?

Beyond families, who shoulders the lion's share of long-term care (Wetzstein et al., 2015), three groups of outpatient and residential care providers can be distinguished: private for-profit care services or nursing homes, private not-for-profit care services or nursing homes (e.g. *Arbeiterwohlfahrt, Caritas,* and *Paritätischer Wohlfahrtsverband*), and public care services and nursing homes. The amount of professional home-care service has expanded, especially in the private sector (Schulz, 2010: 15). In the last 15 years, a massive shift from private not-for-profit outpatient services to private for-profit services has taken place (Figure 9.3). Private for-profit services as a proportion of all home-care service providers increased from 51% in 1999 to 64% in 2013. At the same time, the share of private not-for-profit service providers went down to 35% in 2013 from 47% in 1999. When considering not institutions but care recipients, private not-for-profit services lost even more ground. In 1999, they provided care for 63% of all outpatient long-term care recipients. In 2013, they provided care for only half of all care recipients; the other half received care from private for-profit firms. The public outpatient long-term care services hardly play any role.

The development is similar for residential long-term care services, although here private not-for-profit services are more common. Private not-for-profit nursing homes still dominate the market, but their share decreased from 57% in 1999 to 54% in 2013, whereas private for-profit nursing homes increased from 35% in 1999 to 41% in 2013 (authors' calculation based on Statistisches Bundesamt, 2015c). The decrease of private not-for-profit and the increase in private for-profit

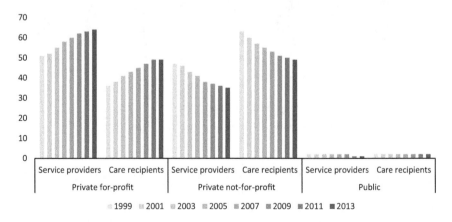

*Figure 9.3* Outpatient long-term care service providers (number and density) (percentage)
Source: Authors' calculations based on Statistisches Bundesamt (2015b).

residential care is even stronger in terms of available beds. Public nursing homes play a bigger role for residential care as compared with outpatient care, but their shares for nursing homes and available beds halved between 1999 and 2013 to only 5% and 6%, respectively.

What do the institutions and structures of long-term care outlined in this section imply for the character and the governance structure of the long-term care sector in Germany? Why is the system prone to growth, although everyone talks about cost containment? The next section of the chapter provides answers to these questions.

## 9.3 Characteristics and governance structures in German long-term care

Typical of a conservative welfare state, but typical even of elder care almost everywhere, the family plays a very important role as provider of long-term care for the elderly. There is a strong normative preference for family-based elder care in Germany (Pfau-Effinger et al., 2008: 90–93), and as this is endorsed, welcomed, and to some extent even supported in the country's long-term care system, which is classified as a "traditional informal care-led model" (Pavolini and Ranci, 2008: 250). Long-term care insurance, with the possibility it offers of receiving home care and choosing the cash transfer over in-kind benefits, still relies on the family. This is in line with the concept of optional familialism, in which public or market-provided care services only partially unburden families' caring responsibilities (Leitner, 2003: 359). More than 70% of people in need of care are cared for in their homes by ambulatory care providers, relatives, or a combination of both (Wetzstein et al., 2015: 2), and almost half of all care recipients are cared for by their relatives (see Figure 9.1). Caregivers are primarily women, especially in cases where the volume of care work is high (Wetzstein et al., 2015: 8), and it places high burdens on well-being and health of caregivers (Schulz, 2010: 12).

Interpretation of the influence of long-term care policy on this "familiarist" care regime is fraught with ambiguities because of the double-edged nature of public support for family care activities. On the one hand, these policies rely on the care work in families, thus reconfirming the role of the family, especially in the welfare mix. On the other hand, there is institutional recognition and institutional support for this work (Bode, 2016: 5), installing measures that seek to improve caregivers' chances at combining their care obligations with formal employment while at the same time promoting professionalized (not-for-profit and for-profit) home-care services for older people. This growing sector of elder-care providers has led some observers to conclude that the German long-term care system is not very conservative but actually quite liberal (see, for instance, Riedel et al., 2015).

Demographic trends give rise to the expectation of drastic increases in the need for professional care in the future, while trends in female labor force participation will lower the number of women available for care work (Häcker and Raffelhüschen, 2007). Worries about a strong trend toward an expansion of residential care, resulting in strong increases in the cost of elder care had plagued

134    *Margitta Mätzke and Tobias Wiß*

policymakers in the field of long-term care from the beginning (Götting and Hinrichs, 1993: 65), explain governments' reluctance to explicitly address the problem to begin with. These worries turned out to be without cause, because there was no movement into the nursing home at massive scale, and there is in fact a strong preference for home care. Erosion of the potential of caregivers has not materialized and will not become manifest in the short run, because as of now the baby boomers are still available as caregivers (Hackmann and Moog, 2010: 118). In the medium and long run, however, there will be a strong increase in the need for professional elder care, necessitating improved working conditions for care workers (Hackmann and Moog, 2010; Hämel and Schaeffer, 2013). This demographic/socioeconomic scenario produces a very specific perception of the policy challenges in long-term care policy: a prospect of ever-increasing need for elder care paired with declining societal caregiving resources, which will call for policies that seek to tap into the shrinking reservoir of family care services as long as possible while trying to discourage the (alleged) over-use of residential care (Zängl, 2015: 248). The preference for home care is an explicit part the policy paradigm underlying German long-term care policy, and it is explicitly written into the law (Kantel, 2000: 1079).

### 9.3.1 The role of the market in long-term care

While the family has long played the dominant part in caring for older people, long-term care policies as of the 1990s have contributed to changing this pattern, introducing a much larger role of economic logics into the system. This was the case not so much with regard to social insurance financing but much more so on the side of care delivery: a large number of private, for-profit providers of long-term care services entered the system after long-term care insurance was introduced (Evans et al., 2014: 126; see also Figure 9.3). This development was and is deliberate and welcomed. Care recipients are required to choose between cash benefits and in-kind benefits and among different providers of outpatient and residential care, forming one way in which market logics have been becoming more salient (Theobald, 2015: 30). This is not without consequences for care delivery, employment patterns, and working conditions (Theobald, 2012: 67–69). "Economic pressures, competition and an increasing share of for profit provides have resulted in a rise of precarious employment" (Theobald, 2015: 35). In the actual delivery of care, economic pressures are manifest in increased requirements of documentation and speedy delivery of narrow sets of tasks, leaving little room for communication with care recipients, a tendency that has sometimes been labeled "tailorization" of care (Pfau-Effinger et al., 2008: 85; Ranci and Pavolini, 2015: 280). The result of these economic logics has been paradoxical effects on work and employment in the elder-care sector. Despite the fact that the care sector has been growing, precarious work in that sector has been growing as well, partly because of labor policies of employers (both for profit and non-profit) in the sector, but partly also because the collective actors in the sector's industrial relations system are fragmented and disorganized (Evans et al., 2014: 128), which has disintegrating effects on labor relations in the health and social care sectors.

Economic logics are also at the root of (perceived) quality problems, especially in the case of ambulatory care services, and these quality problems are one reason why many care recipients prefer family care (Pfau-Effinger et al., 2008: 95).

### 9.3.2 Governance of long-term care

With regard to governance, the most significant characteristic of long-term care insurance in Germany is the cap on benefits (Kantel, 2000: 1083), and this is the aspect in which long-term care insurance diverges most sharply from the classical social insurance model. Long-term care insurance covers only about 58% of costs for home-based and residential care service provision (Pavolini and Theobald, 2015: 472), which is in line with Ranci and Pavolini (2015) calling German long-term care "a weak social right". This character of covering only parts of the cost of care has never been challenged or changed, even in the most recent reforms that resulted in more benefits for more people (Rothgang and Kalwitzki, 2015: 52).

#### Consumer choice as regulatory tool

The cap on benefits is an important part in the governance model that lawmakers had in mind when they enacted long-term care insurance. That model values autonomous decision making on the part of care recipients; with regard to providers, it entails diversity and the plurality (Riedel et al., 2015: 6). This is explicitly endorsed in the law as including not-for-profit as well as private for-profit providers (Evers, 1995: 26). The emancipatory potential of choice only partially informed this preference for diversity. More importantly, the idea of choice converged with new public management ideas of market coordination and the efficiency enhancing effects of consumer autonomy (Ranci and Pavolini, 2015: 274). In the everyday practice of long-term care, the idea has been slow to arrive at providers and caregivers who do not fully endorse the perception of older people in need of long-term care as customers (Evers and Rauch, 1999: 178). Nevertheless, the idea of care recipients acting as consumers, who, by exercising their right to choose among different options, install market competition is prevalent. This is largely a theoretical model, placing too high a burden on the shoulders of care recipients, who are often overwhelmed by the need to decide about the type and the provider of care (Paquet and Jacobs, 2015: 4). That this unrealism severely limits the emancipatory potential of choice (Pfau-Effinger et al., 2008: 86) has been of little concern for efficiency-minded policy makers. The market model constructs care recipients as consumers. In that context, the cap on benefits is absolutely crucial because it is the one feature in the long-term care system that could, in theory, secure price-elastic demand on the part of beneficiaries (Eifert and Rothgang, 1999: 449; Rothgang, 2000: 431). The competition model is not consistently implemented. On the one hand, this is because "consumer choice" has hardly any regulatory leverage in the sector; on the other hand, there are too many attempts at public capacity planning and political intervention for market coordination to unfold any efficiency-enhancing effects (Rothgang, 2000: 444).

## 136    *Margitta Mätzke and Tobias Wiß*

### Traditional corporatist governance modes

Most observers and scholars are not primarily interested in the question of when and why market competition is *not* properly implemented, however. Instead, the way in which quasi markets disrupt traditional structures of coordination is the prevalent issue. The traditional welfare mix in social service fields was highly organized, characterized by stable relationships and cooperative problem solving. Quasi market governance materialized in a new "contract culture" (Bode, 2006: 347) that disrupted these relationships and resulted in not only more heterogeneous provider structures (Evers and Rauch, 1999: 173) but also more fragile networks of actors and cooperative relations. The outgrowth is a "diversified but fragmented care infrastructure" in which different financing schemes (contributory social insurance, tax-financed social assistance, competition-oriented health insurance) exist alongside each other (Bode, 2016: 12) on different government levels (Hoberg and Klie, 2015: 28) in ways that are overall poorly integrated. There has also been a decline in the role of peak associations and greater responsibilities of individual providers (Roth, 1999: 420; Strünck, 2000: 991). Corporatist governance is still present, but it is not as dominant as it used to be (Roth, 1999: 428). The social service sector has become disorganized in the sense that "long-established patterns of system-wide coordination . . . turn into volatile and heterogeneous configurations" (Bode, 2006: 347). The partnership between the state and the voluntary sector, or the participation of civil society in the social welfare sector, is being transformed (Bode, 2006: 348) into a structure with much less public control (Strünck, 2000: 994).

### Government regulation and capacity planning

Shrinking public control is not only a direct result of the decision to rely on market coordination (Evers, 1995: 26; Evers and Rauch, 1999); it also derives from the way in which responsibility for securing sufficient supply of long-term care services is structured. The original idea of capacity planning was one of dual financing, with *Bundesländer* and municipalities being in charge of securing an adequate care infrastructure and the social insurance scheme being in charge of operating costs. Since it is not the *Länder* but long-term care insurance funds that are responsible for securing adequate supply, there are no incentives for *Länder* or municipalities to invest much, so investment costs are often borne by residents of elder-care facilities (Eifert and Rothgang, 1999: 448). Capacity planning on the part of long-term care insurance funds remained an empty phrase (Paquet and Jacobs, 2015: 6), but there is no scope for public capacity planning either, a fact on which the Netherlands and Germany are exceptional in Europe (Riedel et al., 2015: 6; Schulz, 2010: 7f).

### Long-term care insurance funds as a regulatory hub

Competition plays an important role in the regulatory model of long-term care, but this model is very different from the one installed at roughly the same time (the beginning of the 1990s) in the health care system (Rothgang, 2000: 427). In

*Paradoxical decisions in German LTC*   137

long-term care, it is competition among providers, rather than financers, that is supposed to unfold beneficial effects (Strünck, 2000: 989; Paquet and Jacobs, 2015: 4), and long-term care insurance funds have no part in this because there is no parameter in which they would have any room for maneuver. At the same time, long-term care insurance funds are organizationally located within the health insurance funds and, in many respects, such as contracting with providers for all types of in-kind benefits or defining their membership communities, they follow health insurance logics (Paquet and Jacobs, 2015: 3). In some cases, their staff is the health insurance funds' staff, but because of the radically different structural contexts and competitive environments in which the two social insurance branches operate, organizational integration has not led to improved cooperation or better management of thresholds between health care and long-term care (Paquet and Jacobs, 2015: 4 f; Rothgang, 2016). Most importantly, though, because they have to cover only a fixed amount of the cost of long-term care, there are no strong incentives for long-term care insurance funds to strive for cost containment (Paquet and Jacobs, 2015: 3 f), such that there is a constant danger of an upward trend in user charges.

Market competition is supposed to ensure efficiency gains and contain the growth of expenditures for long-term care. In the competitive order of long-term care, however, there is no actor or group of actors who would have a strong interest in or would be in a position to make sure elder care is available at good quality and moderate cost. Care recipients are not in a position to exercise the type of fully autonomous and well-informed consumer choice that would enable them to act as a regulatory core of the system. Traditional governance modes are in a state of disarray. *Bundesländer* and municipalities are constrained in their regional and local planning capacities, and the long-term care insurance funds are not in a position of becoming, nor do they have incentives to become, key players in the regulation of care service provision and cost control. Therefore, the system is not self-regulating, and especially the cost dynamic has the potential of becoming a major problem. Long-term care insurance was installed to take financial burdens off the municipal social assistance system, which had previously picked up a large share of the cost of residential long-term care (Hoffer and Schölkopf, 2014: 22). This goal has partially been reached in the sense that the fifth social insurance branch did reduce the number of older people in need of social assistance because of their care needs (Roth and Rothgang, 2001: 297). LTCI's capped benefits did not suffice to end the practice of financing residential care from social assistance benefits altogether (Hoberg and Klie, 2015: 27). The practice is problematic, because social assistance is paid out of local communities' budgets, where municipalities, unlike the social insurance system, have no secured and earmarked funding for social assistance needs (Künzel, 2015: 36). Therefore, cost explosion remains a constant threat for public sector actors after all. It is this threat that has informed policymaking in the field of long-term care, especially in recent years.

## 9.4 Recent long-term care reforms

Long-term care reform activity in the last 10 years, under varying governments, has expanded services and benefits, made LTCI benefits available for larger numbers of people, and, as a result, has enacted higher contribution rates to satisfy the

## 138 *Margitta Mätzke and Tobias Wiß*

rising financial demands of the long-term care system. It has also strengthened home-care services and rehabilitation measures and sought to improve caregivers' working conditions, enabling them to better reconcile their care obligations with formal employment (Rothgang and Kalwitzki, 2015; Steffen, 2015). Paradoxical as this seems, this has been a "cost containment strategy" – the attempt to make home care more attractive, to keep people out of the nursing homes, and to prevent costly residential care, thereby curbing the flood of claims on the resources of the tax-financed local social assistance system. Part of the recent policy development has also been significant qualitative improvements in the criteria of access to benefits and the range of services and social benefits available to both caregivers and care recipients.

### 9.4.1 The broader concept of care

A reform of long-term care in 2008 increased the benefit amounts for home-care services stepwise by 2012, and for residential care only for people in need of higher levels of care. The reform also introduced the category of "limitations in activities of daily living skills", making long-term care insurance benefits available for people suffering from dementia who had previously not been fully entitled to receive benefits. Before the 2008 reform, care needs had been assessed almost exclusively on the basis of medical assessments, taking into account physical needs only. The 2008 reform also strengthened home-care services by creating local care centers and establishing a right for care recipients and caregivers to receive long-term care counseling. A reform of the year 2015 (*Pflegestärkungsgesetz I*) further extended benefit amounts and increased the number of nurses in the residential care segment. This reform was most important in that it introduced indexation of the caps on cash and in-kind benefits in line with the inflation rate, ending the erosion of benefit levels that had plagued the system previously. The reform also set up a care fund to stabilize the development of the long-term care insurance contributions. Every year, 0.1% of the contribution revenue is to be paid into the care fund.

The German long-term care system will change considerably in 2017 with the revision of the definition of care need and the assessment procedure used to identify care needs, which is essential for the level of benefits and services. The 2016–2017 reform (*Pflegestärkungsgesetz II*, enacted in 2015) increases the number of criteria for the judgment of whether a person needs care from 30 to 77, and it increases and modifies the number of care levels to five, allowing for more precision in the assessment of need. The reform has a strong expansive thrust, and it will result in increasing expenses for long-term care (Walendzik et al., 2015). But it also fixed a "birth defect of long-term care insurance in Germany", which had long been criticized for its extremely narrow definition of being in need of care and that focused almost exclusively on medical conditions (Rothgang and Kalwitzki, 2015: 53). The new system measures both physical and cognitive impairments, resulting in higher care recipient rates. A further novelty are more equal copayments across the different care levels. So far, copayments have been increasing with the care level, making care expensive for those with more impairments (Kantel, 2000) and often resulting in a tendency to seek residential care because benefits were higher for residential care. Upgrading home care reduces the financial burdens for the families of care patients in high care levels, and it also reduces the financial burdens for the social assistance scheme, because this is the social protection system that has to step in once private resources are exhausted. The ministry of health estimated that the 2016–2017, reform will result in more persons entitled to elderly care – in particular dementia patients – thanks to the modifications in the criteria of access. The LCTI will receive an additional €5 billion per year from 2017 on (Bundesministerium für Gesundheit, 2015). To finance the expansion of services and benefits for more recipients, the reforms increased the contribution rate from 1.7% (1.95% for childless persons) in 2007 to 2.55% (2.8%) in 2017.

### 9.4.2 *Modernizing long-term care: reconciliation, monitoring quality, and promoting rehabilitation*

The demographic development and the increasing female labor force participation will soon result in declining societal care resources and the need of more professional care. Improving reconciliation of family care and formal employment seems to be promising as a way of tapping into societal resources of families as caregivers (Stüben and von Schwanenflügel, 2015). Starting in 2008, all employees have been entitled to take up to 10 days of leave for organizing care for relatives in situations of acute need. In addition, employees in firms with more than 15 employees can take up to six months of unpaid leave of absence, fully or partly, for the purpose of caring for relatives at home.

In terms of the quality of long-term care, the 2008 reform introduced new instruments for quality monitoring of residential care, including a requirement to publish the annual quality inspection of the medical review board of the statutory health insurance. The hope is that this will result in competition-based and quality criteria based on transparent, reliable, and comparative information about conditions in the different residential care facilities. Moreover, quality audits must take place more frequently since 2011 (Schulz, 2010: 19). To control the quality of care for those receiving cash benefits at home, the beneficiaries have to arrange (twice per year if graded at care levels 1 and 2 and quarterly if graded at care level 3) reviews of their personal and home-care situations by professional caregivers. As an additional part of the care assessment, rehabilitation measures need to be considered since 2008, and residential care providers get a bonus payment if they succeed in placing a care beneficiary in a lower care level.

## 9.5 Conclusions

The years since the financial crisis have witnessed long-term care expansion. This was not only due to increasing needs and gradually declining family resources. Much of the expansion was due to deliberate decisions to improve the quality

## 140   Margitta Mätzke and Tobias Wiß

of care, especially in the home-care sector. Recent reforms have attempted to strengthen elements of rehabilitation, albeit with only limited results (Hoberg and Klie, 2015: 19; Rothgang, 2016); to extend rights to caregivers that allow them to reconcile work and care obligations; and to move away from a purely medical approach to assessing need toward one that takes competence coping with everyday life into account in a that encourages care at home even in cases where cognitive impairments are the main reason of care dependency. All these measures can be seen as attempts to remedy the reactive, rather than proactive, orientation of long-term care (Kantel, 2000: 1079) that has characterized long-term care institutions. In that sense, one could (with some measure of goodwill) read a social investment spirit into the recent reform activism in the field of long-term care.

All these measures have also, however, been informed by the intention to contain an uncontrolled rise of expenses. Increasing life expectancy results in greater numbers of people in need of care, but there are declining resources for providing care in the modern labor market and family structures. The Federal Statistical Office estimates that 3.4 million person will receive elderly care in 2030, almost 700,000 more than today (Statistisches Bundesamt, 2010: 27). Long-term care reforms that try to accomplish a better match between the need for home-based care and available support are also a response to this prospect of strong and uncontrolled expansion. This prospect is a real possibility because the long-term care sector has a governance structure that gives public policy makers and regulators very little by way of planning capacity, regulatory leverage, or other ways to control performance and cost in the long-term care sector.

Thus, besides the motif of trying to rationalize and to control expansion, characteristics of the decision-making structures and the unwieldiness of the long-term care system itself account for the timing and the substantive contents of some of the policies. Policy processes in the German political system and LTC policy have always been extremely slow (Katzenstein, 1987), so policies reflecting discourses and reform proposals that have been items in political debates for a long time (Mätzke and Ostner, 2010) should not astonish us greatly. That policy proposals and policy solutions reflect the perceptions of powerful actors within that slow and unwieldy decision structure should not astonish us greatly either. In these perceptions, expansion reflects *fears of alternatives* on the part of policy makers and administrators of the system. Measures that help caregivers to reconcile their care obligations with labor market participation reflect an underlying objective of seeking to tap into the reservoir of inexpensive informal care by family members instead of professional home care. Measures that address the problem of cognitive limitations and enable people to stay in their own homes reflect an underlying wariness of residential care in cases of (mild) dementia. And last but not least, measures that expand the benefits of long-term care insurance seek to prevent dependence on social assistance benefits to which people in need of care would otherwise be entitled. In that sense, therefore, explicit long-term care policy dates back to the late 1980s and discussions about long-term care in Germany date back to the 1970s, but the structural public policy challenge actually originated as early as 1961, when the Federal Republic of Germany recognized social assistance as an individual entitlement and universal right. Since then, there

*Paradoxical decisions in German LTC* 141

have been limits to the extent to which demographic and social problems of the magnitude of long-term care can be entirely ignored and left to the private sector and society to resolve.

## References

Bode, Ingo (2006), Disorganized welfare mixes: Voluntary agencies and new governance regimes in Western Europe, *Journal of European Social Policy* 16(4): 346–359.

Bode, Ingo (2016), The changing governance of domiciliary elderly care in Germany. Unpublished paper presented at the workshop of the *COST ACTION IS 1102: SO.S Cohesion: Social Services, Welfare States and Places*, Kassel.

Bonoli, Giuliano (2007), Time matters: Postindustrialization, new social risks, and welfare state adaptation in advanced industrial democracies, *Comparative Political Studies* 40(5): 495–520.

Bundesministerium für Gesundheit (2015), Pressemitteilung vom 13.11.2015. Gröhe: Verbesserungen für Pflegebedürftige und Angehörige – Bundestag beschliesst das Zweite Pflegestärkungsgesetz. http://www.bmg.bund.de/fileadmin/dateien/Pressemitteilungen/2015/2015_04/151113-43_PM_PSG_II.pdf (Accessed: 10 March 2016).

Bundesministerium für Gesundheit (2016a), Die Finanzentwicklung der sozialen Pflegeversicherung. http://www.bmg.bund.de/fileadmin/dateien/Downloads/Statistiken/Pflege versicherung/Finanzentwicklung_Pflegeversicherung_xls/03-Finanzentwicklung-der-sozialen-Pflegeversicherung.pdf (Accessed: 4 March 2016).

Bundesministerium für Gesundheit (2016b), Leistungsempfänger der sozialen Pflegeversicherung nach Altersgruppen. http://www.bmg.bund.de/fileadmin/dateien/Downloads/Statistiken/Pflegeversicherung/Leistungsempfaenger_Altersgruppen/05-Leistungsempfaenger-der-sozialen-PV-nach-Altersgruppen_2014.pdf (Accessed: 4 March 2016).

Bundesministerium für Gesundheit (2016c), Zahlen und Fakten zur Pflegeversicherung. http://www.bmg.bund.de/fileadmin/dateien/Downloads/Statistiken/Pflegeversicherung/Zahlen_und_Fakten/Zahlen_und_Fakten_01–2016.pdf (Accessed: 4 March 2016).

Dudey, Stefan (1991), Verteilungswirkungen einer gesetzlichen Pflegeversicherung, *Wirtschaftsdienst* 7: 356–359.

Eifert, Barbara and Rothgang, Heinz (1999), Marktliche und planerische Elemente bei der Umsetzung des PflegeVG auf Länderebene, *Zeitschrift für Sozialreform* 45: 447–464.

Esping-Andersen, Gøsta (2002), A child-centered social investment strategy. In Gøsta Esping-Andersen (ed) *Why We Need a New Welfare State*. Oxford, New York: Oxford University Press, pp. 26–67.

Evans, Michaela, Thiele, Günter, Ziegler, Kai and Risthaus, Franziska (2014), Zwischen Ökonomisierungsangst und Wachstumseuphorie: Zur Governance der Arbeit im Pflegesektor, *Vierteljahreshefte zur Wirtschaftsforschung* 83(4): 123–136.

Evers, Adalbert (1995), Die Pflegeversicherung: Ein mixtum compositum im Prozess der politischen Einigung, *Sozialer Fortschritt* 44(2): 23–28.

Evers, Adalbert and Rauch, Ulrich (1999), Ambulante Altenpflege–Umbau oder Abbau kommunaler Verantwortlichkeiten, *Zeitschrift für Sozialreform Jg* 45: 170–185.

Götting, Ulrike and Hinrichs, Karl (1993), Probleme der politischen Kompromißbildung bei der gesetzlichen Absicherung des Pflegefallrisikos – Eine vorläufige Bilanz, *Politische Vierteljahresschrift* 34(1): 47–71.

Häcker, Jasmin and Raffelhüschen, Bernd (2007), Zukünftige Pflege ohne Familie: Konsequenzen des "Heimsog-Effekts", *Zeitschrift für Sozialreform* 53(4): 391–422.

Hackmann, Tobias and Moog, Stefan (2010), Pflege im Spannungsfeld von Angebot und Nachfrage, *Zeitschrift für Sozialreform* 56(1): 113–137.

142  *Margitta Mätzke and Tobias Wiß*

Hagen, Kornelia and Rothgang, Heinz (2014), Erfolge und Misserfolge der Pflegeversicherung – Ihre Weiterentwicklung bleibt notwendig, *Vierteljahreshefte zur Wirtschaftsforschung* 83(4): 5–20.

Hämel, Kerstin and Schaeffer, Doris (2013), Who cares? Fachkräftemangel in der Pflege, *Zeitschrift für Sozialreform* 59(4): 413–431.

Hoberg, Rolf and Klie, Thomas (2015), Strukturreform Pflege und Teilhabe. Erster Teil: Zwischen Cure und Care, Kommunen und Sozialversicherung, *Sozialer Fortschritt* 64(1–2): 27–33.

Hoffer, Heike and Schölkopf, Martin (2014), 20 Jahre Gesetzliche Pflegeversicherung – Mythen und Falkten, *Vierteljahreshefte zur Wirtschaftsforschung* 83(4): 21–41.

Jenson, Jane (2009), Lost in translation: The social investment perspective and gender equality, *Social Politics* 19(2): 446–483.

Kantel, Dieter (2000), Das Gesetz der Pflegeversicherung: Je pflegebedürftiger, desto weniger Hilfe, *Zeitschrift für Sozialreform* 46(12): 1075–1088.

Katzenstein, Peter J. (1987), *Policy and Politics in West Germany: The Growth of a Semisovereign State*, Philadelphia: Temple University Press.

Künzel, Gerd (2015), Strukturreform Pflege und Teilhabe: Zweiter Teil: Die Rolle der Kommunen und die Schnittstelle zur Eingliederungshilfe, *Sozialer Fortschritt* 64(1–2): 33–40.

Landenberger, Margarete (1994), Pflegeversicherung als Vorbote eines anderen Sozialstaates, *Zeitschrift für Sozialreform* 40(5): 314–342.

Leitner, Sigrid (2003), Varieties of familiarism: The caring function of the family in comparative perspective, *European Societies* 5(4): 353–375.

Lessenich, Stephan (2003), *Dynamischer Immobilismus: Kontinuität und Wandel im deutschen Sozialmodell*, Frankfurt / New York: Campus Verlag.

Mätzke, Margitta and Ostner, Ilona (2010), The role of old ideas in the New German family policy agenda, *German Policy Studies* 6(3), pp. 119–163.

Meißner, Thomas (2014), Erste Pflegestärkungsgesetz verabschiedet, *Heilberufe / Das Pflegemagazin* 66(2): 62–63.

Paquet, Robert and Jacobs, Klaus (2015), Die Pflegeversicherung als Sozialversicherung – institutionelle Rahmenbedingungen und Grenzen, *Sozialer Fortschritt* 64(1–2): 1–7.

Pavolini, Emmanuele and Ranci, Costanzo (2008), Restructuring the welfare state: Reforms in long-term care in Western European countries, *Journal of European Social Policy*, 18(3): 246–259.

Pavolini, Emmanuele and Theobald, Hildegard (2015), Long-term care policies. In Ellen Kuhlmann, Blank, H. Robert, Ivy Lynn Bourgeault and Claus Wendt (eds) *The Palgrave International Handbook of Healthcare Policy and Governance*, Basingstoke: Palgrave Macmillan, pp. 462–478.

Pfau-Effinger, Birgit, Och, Rainer and Eichler, Melanie (2008), Ökonomisierung, Pflegepolitik und Strukturen der Pflege älterer Menschen. In Adalbert Evers and Rolf G. Heinze (eds) *Sozialpolitik. Ökonomisierung und Entgrenzung*, Wiesbaden: VS Verlag, pp. 83–98.

Ranci, Costanzo and Pavolini, Emmanuele (2015), Not all that glitters is gold: Long-term care reforms in the last two decades in Europe, *Journal of European Social Policy* 25(3): 270–285.

Riedel, Monika, Kraus, Markus and Mayer, Susanne (2015), Organization and supply of long-term care services for the elderly: A bird's-eye view of old and new EU member states, *Social Policy & Administration* Online first: 1–22.

Roth, Günter (1999), Auflösung oder Konsolidierung korporatistischer Strukturen durch die Pflegeversicherung, *Zeitschrift für Sozialreform* 45(5): 418–446.

Roth, Günter and Rothgang, Heinz (2001), Sozialhilfe und Pflegebedürftigkeit: Analyse der Zielerreichung und Zielverfehlung der Gesetzlichen Pflegeversicherung nach fünf jahren, *Zeitschrift für Gerontologie und Geriatrie* 34(4): 292–305.

Rothgang, Heinz (1994), Die Einführung der Pflegeversicherung – Ist das Sozialversicherungsprinzip am Ende? *Leviathan – Sonderheft* 22(14): 164–185.

Rothgang, Heinz (2000), Wettbewerb in der Pflegeversicherung, *Zeitschrift für Sozialreform* 46(5): 423–448.

Rothgang, Heinz (2011), Solidarität in der Pflegeversicherung: Das Verhältnis von Sozialer Pflegeversicherung und Privater Pflegeversicherung, *Sozialer Fortschritt* 60(4–5): 81–87.

Rothgang, Heinz (2015), Was lange währt wird endlich teuer, *Wirtschaftsdienst* 12: 806.

Rothgang, Heinz (2016), Ordnungspolitische Weiterentwicklung durch mehr Wettbewerb in der Pflegeversicherung? *Gesundheits- und Sozialpolitik* 70(1): 19–24.

Rothgang, Heinz and Kalwitzki, Thomas (2015), Pflegestärkungsgesetz II: Eine erstaunlich großzügige Reform, *Gesundheits- und Sozialpolitik* 69(5): 46–54.

Schulz, Erika (2010), *The long-term care system for the elderly in Germay*. ENEPRI Research Report 78. Brussels: European Network of Economic Policy Research Institutes.

Statistisches Bundesamt (2010). *Demografischer Wandel in Deutschland. Heft 2: Auswirkungen auf Krankenhausbehandlungen und Pflegebedürftige im Bund und in den Ländern*, Wiesbaden: Statistisches Bundesamt.

Statistisches Bundesamt (2015a), *Pflegestatistik 2013: Pflege im Rahmen der Pflegeversicherung – Deutschlandergebnisse*, Wiesbaden: Statistisches Bundesamt.

Statistisches Bundesamt (2015b), Pflegestatistik – Ambulante Pflegedienste und von ambulanten Pflegediensten betreute Pflegebedürftige (Anzahl und Dichte). http://www.gbe-bund.de/oowa921-install/servlet/oowa/aw92/WS0100/_XWD_FORMPROC?TARGET=&PAGE=_XWD_308&OPINDEX=1&HANDLER=XS_ROTATE_ADVANCED&DATACUBE=_XWD_336&D.000=DOWN&D.001=PAGE&D.100=ACROSS&D.983=ACROSS (Accessed: 7 March 2016).

Statistisches Bundesamt (2015c), Pflegestatistik – Pflegeheime und verfügbare Plätze in Pflegeheimen. http://www.gbe-bund.de/oowa921-install/servlet/oowa/aw92/WS0100/_XWD_FORMPROC?TARGET=&PAGE=_XWD_208&OPINDEX=1&HANDLER=XS_ROTATE_ADVANCED&DATACUBE=_XWD_236&D.000=DOWN&D.001=PAGE&D.100=ACROSS&D.983=ACROSS (Accessed: 7 March 2016).

Steffen, Johannes (2015), Sozialpolitische Chronik. http://www.portal-sozialpolitik.de/uploads/sopo/pdf/Sozialpolitische-Chronik.pdf (Accessed: 7 March 2016).

Strünck, Christoph (2000), Verhandelte Sozialpolitik – Die Pflegeversicherung als Arena neuer Machtbeziehungen, *Zeitschrift für Sozialreform* 46(4): 988–1002.

Stüben, Christine and von Schwanenflügel, Matthias (2015), Vereinbarkeit von Familie, Pflege und Beruf: die neuen gesetzlichen Regelungen als Unterstützung für Pflegebedürftige und Angehörige, *Gesundheits- und Sozialpolitik* 69(1): 76–79.

Theobald, Hildegard (2004), *Title: Collection Title Folio No. SP I 2004–302*, Berlin: Library/Archive.

Theobald, Hildegard (2012), Combining welfare mix and new public management: The case of long-term care insurance in Germany, *International Journal of Social Welfare* 21: S61–S74.

Theobald, Hildegard (2015), Marketization and managerialization of long-term care policies in a comparative perspective. In Tanja Klenk and Emmanuele Pavolini (eds) *Restructuring Welfare Governance. Marketization, Managerialism and Welfare State Professionalism*, Cheltenham: Edward Elgar, pp. 27–45.

## 144   *Margitta Mätzke and Tobias Wiß*

Waldhausen, A. (2014), *Care services in crisis? Long-term care in times of European economic and financial crisis*. Observatory for Sociopolitical Developments in Europe Working Paper No. 8, edited by Institute for Social Work and Social Education, Frankfurt/M: Institute for Social Work and Social Education.

Walendzik, Anke, Lux, Gerald, van der Linde, Kirsten and Wasem, Jürgen (2015), *Finanzielle Auswirkungen der formalen Überleitung auf Basis der Pflegestärkungsgesetze für die gesetzliche Pflegeversicherung (Soziale Pflegeversicherung und Private Pflegeversicherung.* IBES Diskussionsbeitrag No. 215.

Wetzstein, Matthias, Rommel, Alexander and Lange, Cornelia (2015), Pflegende Angehörige – Deutschlands größter Pflegedienst, *GBE Kompakt. Zahlen und Trends aus der Gesundheitsberichterstattung des Bundes* 6(3): 1–12.

Zängl, Peter (2015), Eine kurze Retrospektive auf die lange Entwicklungsgeschichte der Pflegeversicherung, *Zukunft der Pflege: 20 Jahre Norddeutsches Zentrum zur Weiterentwicklung der Pflege*, 233–252.

# 10 Long-term care expenditures in Finland

*Ismo Linnosmaa and Lien Nguyen*

## 10.1 Introduction

The demand and utilization of long-term care is projected to increase due to population ageing. Given the expected increase in longevity, population ageing is projected to affect the top of the population pyramids in particular. According to long-term projections in Europe, the size of the population aged 80 years and older is expected to triple between 2008 and 2060 (European Commission, 2009). Such a demographic change is likely to increase demand for and utilization of long-term care, since the need for care and support is high among the very old.

Long-term care is defined as sustained help and support that is needed to cope and sometimes to survive when physical and/or cognitive disabilities impair the ability to perform the activities of daily living such as eating, bathing, dressing and walking (Grabowski, 2008). Definitions of long-term care often also include long-term health problems and older age as factors that create a need for help and support (e.g. Netten et al., 2012).

LTC can be formal or informal and it can be provided in homes, care homes or day centres (Frank, 2012; Netten et al., 2012). Definitions of long-term care often emphasize social care needs and services (Grabowski, 2008; Netten et al., 2012), but long-term care for older people contains the elements of both social and health care. In practice, it may be difficult to disentangle the social and health components of care from each other. In Finland, municipalities have often integrated home care in a way that the same person provides both nursing support and support for a client's ADL problems. Given the difficulties of drawing clear boundaries between health and social care, definitions of LTC often explicitly include health care services (e.g. Brown and Finkelstein, 2011; Frank, 2012).

In this chapter, we describe the expenditures and financing of LTC during the period from 2000 to 2013 as well as recent policy reforms and developments in the marketization of LTC in Finland. In particular, we are interested in changes in Finnish LTC that have occurred following the global economic crisis of 2008. Section 10. 2 provides a short description of Finnish LTC services and their organisation and financing. To give a wider framework to the analysis, section 10.3 describes the economic growth and public spending in Finland in recent decades. An analysis of LTC expenditures and their financing follows in sections 10.4 and 10.5. In section 10.6, we describe the most recent policy initiatives in the field of LTC and ageing policy in Finland. Section 10.7 summarizes our findings.

## 10.2 Long-term care in Finland

We first give an overview of LTC services, the legal background and the organisation and financing of LTC in Finland. Our main focus is on care services for older people; we will not, for example, consider care and services provided for young persons with disabilities.

### *10.2.1 Long-term care and services for older people in Finland*

Both formal and informal care are provided for the older population in Finland. Formal services can be classified into community care and institutional care (Noro et al., 2014). Community care contains care support for family carers (*omaishoitajat*) and cared-for people, home care, support services (e.g. meals on wheels and cleaning), and care provided at day centres, service centres and sheltered housing facilities with and without 24-hour assistance. Institutional care consists of LTC in older people's homes and in primary health care. Sheltered housing with 24-hour assistance is often very similar to institutional care with regards to patients' needs, and for this reason, the term *round-the-clock care* (Colombo et al., 2011; Noro et al., 2014) has been adopted. Round-the-clock care is understood to consist of institutional care and care provided in sheltered housing facilities with 24-hour assistance.

A family carer is a person who takes care of a relative or otherwise close person. Family carers pledge to undertake care duties by signing a care contract with the municipality of residence (i.e. local authority) (Linnosmaa et al., 2014). Care support is a benefit package consisting of a carer allowance and services provided for both the carer and the cared-for person. Persons in need of care may apply for the care support package from their municipality of residence. Before support is granted, the cared-for person's need for support and care, the carer's applicability to take up care duties and the living environment are assessed (Linnosmaa et al., 2014). The minimum payment for family carers is €300 per month.[1] Family carers are eligible for three days of care leave (respite) a month during periods when they are committed to round-the-clock care. Municipalities are obligated to arrange respite care for the time of the care leave.

The amount of informal care supplied is difficult to estimate exactly, but lower and upper bounds for the number of informal carers can be estimated. Family carers are part of the informal carer pool since family care requires no formal qualifications. In 2014, there were 43,235 family carers in Finland (Sotkanet, 2016). This figure includes carers who take care of people aged younger than 65 years. As 67 per cent of cared-for people are 65 years or older (Sotkanet, 2016), one can estimate that approximately 28,970 carers provide care for older people. It is known that not all informal carers sign a contract with their municipality of residence (e.g. Vilkko et al., 2014), and hence the figure presumably defines the lower bound of the number of informal carers taking care of older persons.

To approximate the upper bound of the number of informal carers providing care for older people, one can estimate the number of people helping a relative or friend who is not able to manage daily activities because of disability, sickness or old age. The survey on welfare and services in Finland (HYPA) asked about this type of care from a representative sample of Finnish citizens in 2006, 2009 and 2013. According to the latest findings in 2013, 29.7[2] per cent of respondents (N = 4,226) said that they had provided such help and support to relatives and friends (Vilkko et al., 2014). At the population level, this implies that approximately 1.2 million Finns would provide help to relatives and friends whose functional ability had declined because of sickness, disability or old age. Approximately one quarter of helpers considered themselves the principal helper of the person receiving help (Vilkko et al., 2014).

### 10.2.2 Organisation and financing of services for older people

Several laws and decrees in Finland steer the organisation and financing of health and social care services, including LTC provided to older people. The act on government grants for social welfare and health care[3] defines the responsibilities of the state government, regional state administrative agencies, and the municipalities in planning and organising social and health care services. The Law on Social Care[4] and the Health Care Act (1326/2010) aim at promoting and maintaining welfare, health and social security by providing each Finnish citizen with equal access to health and social care services. Financing of health and social care services is regulated by an act[5] and a decree[6] on user fees and the Act on Government Grants on Municipal Basic Services.[7]

The recently introduced Act on Supporting the Functional Capacity of the Older Population and on Social and Health Services for Older Persons (980/2012) regulates the assessment of the service needs and the provision of health and social services for older people.

Municipalities are responsible for organising health and social care services,[8] including LTC. Municipalities can do this in several ways. They can produce the services themselves via public facilities or in cooperation with other municipalities, or they can purchase the services from the state, other municipalities or private providers. Municipalities may also grant a voucher to a service user who can use the voucher to purchase the service from a preferred private provider. The municipality granting the voucher is committed to paying for the service up to the value of the voucher.

The two most important financiers of the services provided for older people in Finland are the state government and municipalities (Linnosmaa, 2014). The state government allocates state subsidies (or state grants) to municipalities. Since state subsidies are not given for specific purposes (i.e. they are not earmarked), municipalities are free to decide how to use them (Seppälä and Pekurinen, 2014). Municipalities finance the organisation of health and social care of older people through the returns from municipal taxation, state subsidies and user fees. The maximum fees that municipalities can charge are regulated by a decree.[9] The maximum user fees are generally means-tested, and home care fees also depend on the size of the household to which the service user belongs.

The Finnish LTC system is based on the idea that anyone in need of care has access to services. If a person thinks that she is in need of LTC, she may contact the municipality of residence (i.e. local authority).[10] Municipal health and social care professionals assess the person's needs for social and health care services. After the assessment, the municipality is responsible for drawing up a service plan defining what kind of health and social care services are required to support the person's well-being, health, functional capacity and independent living. The views of the older person should also be recorded in the service plan. The municipality then makes the final decision about the provision of services. As there is no national definition of the need for care (Johansson, 2010), there is regional variation in the provision of and access to LTC in Finland.

## 10.3 Economic and demographic development in Finland

The Finnish economy is currently weak. The EU has continued its steady economic recovery, but Finland has not properly recovered from the industrial collapse that began in 2008. The global recession, the collapse of the telecommunications industry in Finland, the contraction of the paper industry and the Russian recession have resulted in decreased output (Figure 10.1). The cessation of productivity growth in Finland is unprecedented. Employment has been on a downward path (see, e.g., OECD, 2016.) The present crisis in manufacturing is quite different from the recession that Finland experienced in the early 1990s and more difficult in many respects.

Gross domestic product (GDP) volume in Finland in 2015 expanded 0.5 per cent over the previous year for the first time since 2012 (Official Statistics of Finland, 2016a). GDP growth in Finland was some 0.5 per cent both in 1976 and

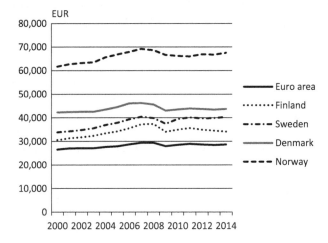

*Figure 10.1* Real GDP per capita (2010 = 100) in 2000–2014
Source: Data from EuroStat (2016a).

*Long-term care expenditures in Finland* 149

2015, reaching a peak of 5.7 per cent in 1980 and the lowest record of –8.3 per cent in 2009. After the years of positive growth in 2010–2011, Finland went back into recession in 2012 and contracted by 0.7 per cent in 2014.

In Finland, GDP per capita in 2015 was €37,819 (Statistics Finland, 2016a). Among the four Nordic countries, GDP per capita in 2014 (2010 = 100) was highest in Norway (€67,500) and lowest in Finland (€34,100), which was still above the average GDP per capita in the EU area (€28,600) (Figure 10.1). It has been expected that the acceleration in economic growth will continue through 2016 and 2017 (European Commission, 2016).

The unemployment rate was 6.4 per cent in 2008 and 7.7 per cent in 2012. The unemployment rate in 2015 was 9.4 per cent compared with a rate of 8.7 per cent in 2014, and it is expected to remain at the same level for years to come (European Commission, 2016).

### 10.3.1 Public sector surplus in comparison to European countries since 2008

The Finnish recession and rapidly increasing age-related expenditures affected public expenditures and the debt ratio. Between 2008 and 2015, the share of age-related expenditures to GDP increased by 10 percentage points (Figure 10.2). Half of the decline in 2014 was due to higher social benefit payments largely related to ageing and higher unemployment (OECD, 2016).

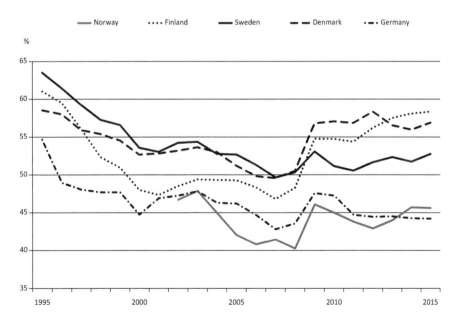

*Figure 10.2* Government spending as a share of GDP in 1995–2015
Source: Data from EuroStat (2016b).

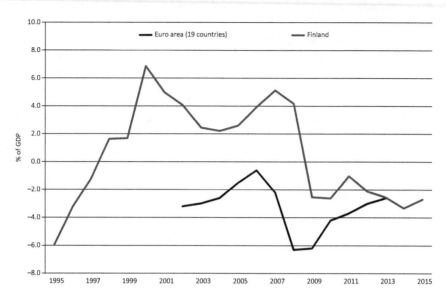

*Figure 10.3* General government deficit and surplus in 1995–2015
Source: Data from EuroStat (2016c), Statistics Finland (2016c).

In 2015, government spending relative to GDP in Finland was the highest in the OECD. It was 58.3 per cent in Finland and was lowest in Switzerland at 33.7 per cent; it was around 45.6 to 56.9 per cent in the other Nordic countries (OECD, 2016). During the period from 1995 to 2015, the ratio of government spending to GDP in Finland was at its highest level in 1995 at 61.1 per cent and reached its lowest level at 46.8 per cent in 2007. In 2008, this ratio was 48.3 per cent, and in 2009 it increased to 54.8 per cent, after which it has increased to 58.1 per cent (Figure 10.2).

Since 2009, budget surpluses in the period 1998–2008 have turned into deficits, which took place for seven consecutive years (Official Statistics of Finland, 2016a). The general government deficit was €5.7 billion in 2015, compared with €6.5 billion in 2014, when the deficit surpassed 3.3 per cent of GDP for the first time since the mid-1990s (Figure 10.3). In 2015, the deficit was slightly lower, though it still exceeded 2.7 per cent of GDP. Thus, this deficit relative to GDP went below 3 per cent, which is used as a reference value in the EU.

### 10.3.2 Demographic development in Finland

The population of Finland is greying rapidly. Ageing in Finland has been taking place noticeably earlier and slightly more intensely than in most European countries (Heikkilä, 2012; Karisto, 2007; Piekkola, 2004). The most significant change in the Finnish age structure has been due to the baby boomers born during the second half of the 1940s who have been retiring since the beginning of the 2010s.[11]

The number of older people (65 years old or older) exceeded 1 million in 2012. In 2014, 20 per cent of people in Finland were aged 65 years and older. The

*Long-term care expenditures in Finland* 151

corresponding figure in 1990 was 13.5 per cent, which gradually increased to 15 per cent in 2000 and 16.7 per cent in 2008. The proportion of people aged 75 years or older was 5.7 in 1990, from which it increased evenly on average by 0.12 percentage points each year until 2014, when it was 8.7 per cent. The ratio of people aged 75 years or older to every 100 children aged under 15 years was 29.4 in 1990, 49.9 in 2011 and 53.1 in 2014.[12] It is estimated that older people (65 years and older) and the older old (75 years and older) will comprise 26.3 and 15.8 per cent of the population by 2040, respectively, and will be 29.4 and 17.8 per cent by 2065, respectively (Official Statistics of Finland, 2016b).

The life expectancy of a newborn child in Finland increased from 70.1 years to 81.1 years in the period from 1971 to 2014 (Statistics Finland, 2016b). The latest figure was one year higher than the OECD average of 80 years. For those born in 2014, life expectancy for women was 84.1 years compared with 78.4 for men, and the corresponding figures for the EU (28 countries) were 83.6 years for women and 78.1 years for men (EuroStat, 2016d).

The total dependency ratio (TDR) in Finland is now one of the highest among the OECD countries, and it will not improve for decades.[13] The TDR was 57.1 in 2014. The lowest ratio since 1917, at 46.7, was recorded in 1984. It is projected that the TDR will exceed a value of 60 by 2017, 70 by 2032 and 76 by 2060 (Official Statistics Finland, 2016b). Also by 2065, the proportion of those aged 65 or older in the total population is expected to increase to 29.4, while the youngest group aged under 15 years and the working age population will be 14.1 per cent and 56.4 per cent, respectively (Official Statistics of Finland, 2016b).

Among the four Nordic countries, in 1995 the old-age dependency ratio (OADR)[14] was 21.1 in Finland, 24.8 in Norway and 27.4 in Sweden (Figure 10.4).

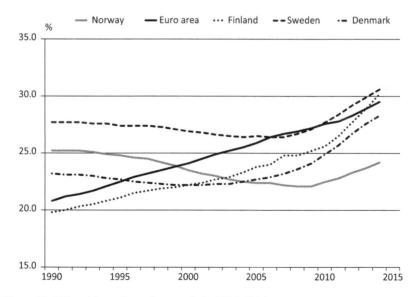

*Figure 10.4* The old-age dependency ratio in 1994–2014
Source: Data from EuroStat (2016e).

152  *Ismo Linnosmaa and Lien Nguyen*

In 2014, Finland had an OADR of 30.2, higher than that of the EU (18 countries) on average (29.5), but lower than the ratio of Sweden (30.6) (EuroStat, 2016e).

Lengthened life expectancy has increased the number of older people. This not only means a rise in pension expenditure but also a greater need for both social and health care services. Further, technological advances and patients' expectations have also put pressure on expenditures. To ensure both fiscal sustainability and well-being in the longer term, there is a need to reduce fragmentation in the health care system and to have better coordination between primary and specialised health care (OECD, 2016) and social care. These are the goals of the current reform in Finnish social and health care, which the current government plans to implement in 2019.

## 10.4  Expenditures on long-term care

In order to describe the expenditures of LTC for older people in Finland, we utilize data from the annual statistical report on Health Expenditure and Financing (HEF) (Terveyden ja hyvinvoinnin laitos, 2015). The data compilation in the HEF statistics uses the concepts and classifications of the OECD System of Health Accounts (SHA) Version 1.0 (OECD, 2000). The principles of calculating outputs and expenditures follow those used in national accounting: the value of the market output is computed using basic prices, while the value of the nonmarket output is based on production costs.

Since the basic statistics include only institutional care provided for older people,[15] more comprehensive data on expenditures on care for older people have been produced for the purposes of national reporting in Finland. In addition to institutional care, the HEF statistics include expenditures on LTC in primary health care, home care and other services for older people. Both operating and investment expenditures are included in the HEF statistics, but in the following sections we concentrate on operating expenditures only.

### 10.4.1  Total expenditures

The varying line in Figure 10.5 describes the development of total expenditures on care for older persons in 2013 prices over the time period from 2000 to 2013 in Finland. Total expenditures in 2013 prices were computed using the total expenditures in current prices (Terveyden ja hyvinvoinnin laitos, 2015) and the health care price index, with 2013 as the base year. We also computed the total expenditures in real terms using the social and health care price index, but since the resulting time series differed only slightly, we decided to use the health care price index. The straight line in Figure 10.5 describes the predicted total expenditures in 2013 prices, where the predicted values were computed by fitting a linear model to the data for the years 2000 to 2009.

The total expenditures in 2013 prices were €2.4 billion in 2000 and €3.6 billion in 2013, indicating a growth of 52 per cent in real expenditures over that time period. The annual growth of total expenditures was steady from the year 2000

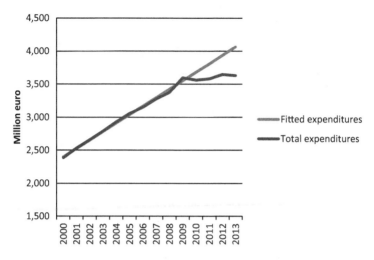

*Figure 10.5* Total expenditures in 2013 prices on care for older persons in Finland, 2000–2013 (in million euros)

up to the year 2009 (Figure 10.5). For those years, the annual growth rates varied between 3 and 6 per cent (Figure 10.6). There was a sudden surge in the growth of real spending in 2009, but since then the annual growth of the total expenditures has been less than 2 per cent (Figure 10.6). In 2010 and 2013, the real expenditures were reduced in comparison to the previous years.

Figures 10.5 and 10.6 indicate that the annual growth rates for total expenditures have been significantly lower after 2009 than before. The model predicting total expenditures using historical data (Figure 10.5) clearly overestimates the development of total expenditures for the time period from 2010 to 2013. Before 2009, the average annual growth rate for total expenditures was 4.3 per cent, which exceeds the annual growth rates of real spending for the years 2010 to 2013 by more than 1 percentage point[16] (Figure 10.6).

To see if the decline in the growth rates of total expenditures is associated with a decline in the need for LTC, we next examine the development of per capita expenditures in Finland for individuals aged 65 years or older.[17] Hence, we assume that the number of individuals aged 65 years or older and the need for LTC are positively associated.

Figure 10.7 illustrates the developments of per capita expenditures in 2013 prices for members of the population aged 65 years and older (left scale) and the size of the 65 and older population (right scale) in Finland from 2000 to 2013. The number of people aged 65 years or older grew constantly, from approximately 777,000 individuals in 2000 to more than 1 million individuals in 2013. Expenditures per capita grew up to the year 2009, though after that we observed a sharp decline in per capita spending. The expenditures per capita decreased from €3,950

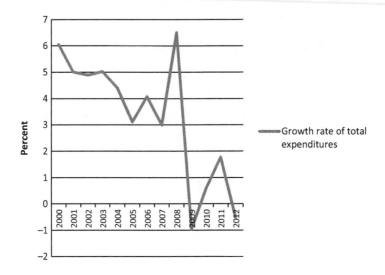

*Figure 10.6* Growth rates of the total expenditures, 2001–2013 (percentage)

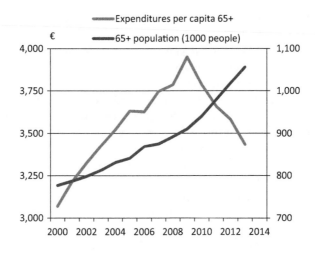

*Figure 10.7* Per capita expenditures for individuals older than 65 years (euros) and the size of the 65 and older population (1,000 people)

per person aged 65 and older in 2009 to €3435 in 2013. The decline in per capita expenditures was due to the reduced growth in total expenditures (Figure 10.5) and the increase in the size of 65 and older population, assumed to be positively correlated with the increase in the need of care.

## 10.4.2 Expenditures on institutional care, home care and other services

In this section, we classify the total expenditures on care for older people into expenditures on institutional care, LTC in primary health care, home care and other services for older people. Institutional care includes both public and private LTC provided for older people in their homes and other institutional facilities. LTC in primary health care is the sustained care (over 90 days) provided for individuals aged 65 years or older in public health centres in Finland. Home care contains both private and public long-term nursing and personal care services provided to older care recipients at home or in community-based settings, like sheltered housing. The last category, other services, includes expenditures on care for older people provided in private and public sheltered housing with and without 24-hour assistance, family care, day and service centres and care allowances for family carers.

Figure 10.8 displays the development of total expenditures in 2013 prices for each of these categories over the time period from 2000 to 2013. Institutional care, LTC provided in health centres and other services experienced the most significant changes from 2000 to 2013. The real expenditures on LTC in institutional care and primary health care have decreased from €815 million to €717 million, and from €465 million to €337 million, respectively. The changes have not taken place steadily from one year to another, but the biggest reductions have occurred likewise after the year 2009. Indeed, real spending in institutional care grew from €815 million in 2000 to €929 million in 2009, while the corresponding change in primary health care was from €465 million in 2000 to €540 million in 2009.

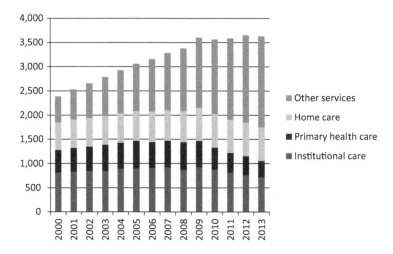

*Figure 10.8* Real expenditures on institutional care, primary health care, home care and other services, 2000–2013 (in million euros)

The category of other services has experienced the largest change in quantitative terms over the period from 2000 to 2013. The real expenditures in other services grew from €536 million in 2000 to €1.9 billion in 2009. Expenditures in 2013 were 3.5 times the expenditures in 2000, which implies a 251 per cent growth. It is worth noting that the expenditure growth in other services has not slowed after 2009.

The development in Figure 10.8 reflects the structural change that has been taking place in round-the-clock care in Finland for the last 15 to 20 years. LTC provided in institutional care and health centres has been reduced and more LTC has been produced in sheltered housing units with 24-hour assistance. The care provided for the 65 and older population in institutional care and primary health care declined from 12.4 million inpatient days in 2000 to 6.8 million inpatient days in 2013, while over the same period, inpatient days for the 65 and older population in sheltered housing with 24-hour assistance increased from 2.4 million inpatient days to 12.2 million days (Sotkanet, 2016). The development of inpatient days in institutional care, primary health care and sheltered housing with 24-hour assistance (Figure 10.9) is similar to the development of the real expenditures on institutional care, primary health care and other services (Figure 10.8). Hence, the observed changes in the expenditure data reflect the underlying structural change in round-the-clock care.

Municipalities have various economic incentives to purchase inpatient care from sheltered housing units with 24-hour assistance rather than from old people's homes or primary health care. First, an inpatient day in sheltered housing facilities with 24-hour assistance is less expensive than an inpatient day in an old people's home or primary health care (Kapiainen et al., 2014). Second, while municipalities are responsible for patients' pharmaceutical expenditures in old

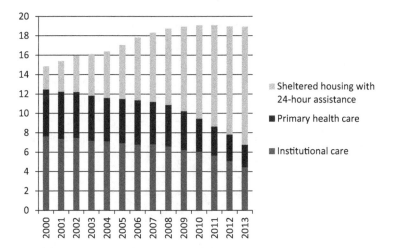

*Figure 10.9* Inpatient days in institutional care, primary health care and sheltered housing with 24-hour assistance, 2000–2013 (in million days)

Long-term care expenditures in Finland  157

people's homes or primary health care, they do not have to pay for the drug costs in sheltered housing units since these costs are covered by the National Health Insurance (NHI) scheme of Kela (the Finnish Social Insurance Institution) and patients' fees (Blomgren and Einiö, 2015). The underlying reason for this is that sheltered housing is part of community care, where patients together with the NHI are responsible for paying for their pharmaceutical expenditures. This creates an economic incentive for municipalities to shift pharmaceutical expenditures to patients and the NHI by purchasing more care from sheltered housing units with 24-hour assistance. See Grabowsky (2007) for a more general discussion about cost shifting in LTC.

### 10.4.3 The share of private care

As described, each individual municipality can organize care services for older persons by itself or in cooperation with other municipalities and by buying services from the state and private providers in the market. HEF statistics allow us to split the total LTC expenditures into expenditures from public production (henceforth public expenditures) and purchases from private providers (henceforth private expenditures) in institutional care (old people's homes and other institutional facilities), home care and other services for older persons. Although some municipalities have recently outsourced primary health care to private providers, all primary health care was public in Finland under the period of examination.

Table 10.1 describes the share of private expenditures in institutional, home care and other services for older persons in 2000 to 2013 (Terveyden ja hyvinvoinnin laitos, 2015). In institutional care, the share of private expenditures has been around 20 per cent of total expenditures in 2000. The share shows an increasing trend until 2005 (24.0 per cent), after which it shows a decreasing trend to 2013 (16.5 per cent). In home care, the share of the private expenditures has stayed around 6.4 to 8.1 per cent over the years 2000 to 2013. The share of private expenditures is the highest in other services, which reflects the fact that a large share of the care provided in sheltered housing facilities in Finland is private. In 2009, the shares of private production (in private for-profit providers and not-for-profit organisations) in all sheltered housing facilities and sheltered housing facilities with 24-hour assistance were 52 and 55 per cent, respectively (Terveyden ja hyvinvoinnin laitos, 2011).

From municipalities' annual operational economies, the cost category 'purchases of customer services from others' describes the purchases of customer services from enterprises and organisations in the third sector (Kuntaliitto, 2012). As argued by Valkama et al. (2013), the growth of this category over a certain period of time suggests that outsourcing for the private sector has risen in the organisation of customer services, but probably the trend also implies that competitive tendering has increased to the same extent. However, municipalities' economic statistics have not been able to capture precise information on these trends or forms of tendering. Moreover, the tendency may indicate that services organised by municipal cooperation have begun to replace services that municipalities

*Table 10.1* The share of private expenditures in institutional care, home care and other services for older persons (percentage)

| Year | 2000 | 2001 | 2002 | 2003 | 2004 | 2005 | 2006 | 2007 | 2008 | 2009 | 2010 | 2011 | 2012 | 2013 |
|---|---|---|---|---|---|---|---|---|---|---|---|---|---|---|
| Institutional care | 19.9 | 20.3 | 20.9 | 21.1 | 22.3 | 24.0 | 21.3 | 20.9 | 21.9 | 19.6 | 19.2 | 17.9 | 17.6 | 16.5 |
| Home care | 6.4 | 7.3 | 8.0 | 8.0 | 8.1 | 7.8 | 7.3 | 6.9 | 7.3 | 6.5 | 6.9 | 6.8 | 6.5 | 6.7 |
| Other services | 54.8 | 56.0 | 56.1 | 58.5 | 57.3 | 57.4 | 61.0 | 60.0 | 59.9 | 60.3 | 59.4 | 58.6 | 57.1 | 59.2 |

purchased from the private sector. As for this observation, purchases of customer services (for institutional care services for older people, home care services and other services for older persons and people with disabilities, 2011 = 100) from other municipalities and federations of municipalities overwhelmingly grew in the period from 2006 to 2014 (Statistics Finland, 2016d, the authors' own calculations; Valkama et al., 2013).

Considering municipal institutional services for older people, purchases of customer services from others (i.e. enterprises and organisations in the third sector) gradually decreased in absolute terms after 2006 (Figure 10.10). Similarly, purchases of home care services from others have also dropped to some degree after 2006 (from 2006 to 2014). Indeed, the most pronounced growth in customer purchases from others has happened in the category of 'other services for older persons and people with disabilities'. This service category contains, among other things, service centres, group homes, and sheltered housing with and without 24-hour service.

Between 2006 and 2014, in terms of real expenditures, purchases of institutional elderly care services from others in municipalities fell about 42 per cent, and those of home care services from others fell by nearly 10 per cent, while those of other services for older persons and people with disabilities grew by 69 per cent (Figure 10.10). The corresponding figures for similar purchases in the period from 2001 to 2011 in municipalities were −14.4, −8.5 and 139.9 per cent according to Valkama and colleagues (2013). Clear changes in the purchases of these service types took place mainly in the period from 2008 to 2010: those purchases of institutional care services for older people fell after 2008 and those of home care services fell after 2010. The purchases of other services in 2010 were lower than in 2009, while purchases in 2013 increased 10.3 per cent in comparison to

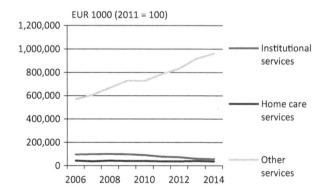

*Figure 10.10* Municipalities' purchases of institutional care services for older people, home care services and other services for older persons and people with disabilities (2011 = 100) from organisations and enterprises, 2006–2014

Data source: Statistics Finland (2016d)

160　*Ismo Linnosmaa and Lien Nguyen*

2012, constituting the highest annual growth in the period from 2006 to 2014 (Figure 10.10).

As municipalities' purchases of home care services have decreased, it has been left to private provision/production to meet the service needs, and service consumption is reliant on households' own direct purchases. In fact, a fundamental transformation in home care services has taken place in Finland that brought about, among other things, privatisation, the integration of health and social care and a growing dependence on informal carers (Kröger and Leinonen, 2012). Customers' direct purchases of for-profit services have been supported more and more by tax reductions and vouchers, while at the same time municipal care service provisions have more and more been outsourced to for-profit providers (Lith, 2013).

It seems that these days, quasi-markets prevailing among the municipalities challenge the purchase of services provided by enterprises and organisations. The share of customer services for older persons and people with disabilities based on municipal cooperation has clearly increased since 2006. This trend is in part explained by the reform to restructure municipalities and services (known as the PARAS project) initiated in 2007 (Meklin and Pekola-Sjöblom, 2013). The reform aimed to strengthen local government and service structures to ensure better productivity of local government activities. According to the state policy alignment,[18] this objective can be achieved by forming larger catchment areas for services provided by single municipalities in which the population base is inadequate or small and by increasing cooperation between municipalities. Hence, the municipalities have had an opportunity to build up mutual cooperation between themselves, which has likewise resulted in markets for themselves.

Municipal services for older people are outsourced with competitive tendering public procurements or without competitive tendering by, for example, making direct purchases and cooperating with other municipalities. Care services purchased from others are nowadays more often invited tenders, while purchases from other municipalities and federations of municipalities are not invited to bid (e.g. Aho and Junnila, 2012; Laamanen et al., 2008; Tynkkynen et al., 2013).

## 10.5  Financing of long-term care

We turn to analysing the financing of LTC in Finland. To accomplish this, we use annual statistics on social protection expenditures and financing (SPEF) (Terveyden ja hyvinvoinnin laitos, 2016). The SPEF data follow the accounting principles of the European System of Integrated Social Protection Statistics (Eurostat, 2012). The SPEF statistics collect data on costs and financing of social protection activities by the state government, municipalities, nonprofit organisations and other organisations.

Due to the different accounting principles applied in the HEF and SPEF statistics, the two data sources provide different and incomparable estimates for total expenditures of care for older persons in Finland. In this section, we decided to use the SPEF data, as they give a more comprehensive and detailed picture of the

*Long-term care expenditures in Finland* 161

financing of care for older persons in Finland. An additional feature of the SPEF data is that they contain explicit information about user fees in LTC.

The social protection activities in SPEF include both in cash and in-kind (services) benefits to households and individuals with a defined set of needs or risks. For in-kind benefits in old age, the SPEF data include institutional care; home care; care allowance; care provided in sheltered housing facilities, day centres and service centres; family care and other services. The LTC provided for older people in primary health care is not reported under this heading since the data are included under the heading of sickness and health (Terveyden ja hyvinvoinnin laitos, 2016). This is one reporting difference between the SPEF and HEF data.

Municipalities pay the largest share of LTC expenditures in Finland (Figure 10.11). In 2013, municipalities paid €1.5 billion and were responsible for the 53.2 per cent of gross expenditures. The portion of total gross expenditures to be financed by the municipalities has fallen from 62 per cent in 2000. The decline was not steady, but the funding share of the municipalities first declined to 50 per cent in 2010 and has increased after that year to be more than 53 per cent. Hence, the financing burden of municipalities in the financing of LTC became heavier after the 2008 financial crisis.

The state government has paid from 20 to 30 per cent of gross expenditures in the period under examination. In 2000, the state government was responsible for the 21 per cent of gross expenditures. This share went up to 30 per cent by 2010 but came down to 29 per cent in 2013. The state government paid €845 million of gross expenditures in 2013.

Service users paid €519 million in user fees in 2013. The user fees covered from 17 up to 19 per cent of gross expenditures on care for older persons over the

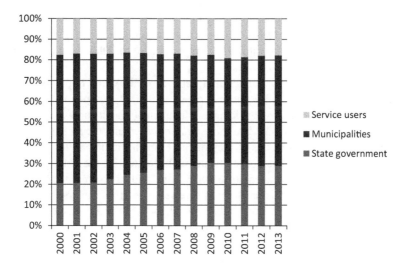

*Figure 10.11* Shares of state government, municipalities and user fees in the financing of LTC in Finland (percentage)

162    *Ismo Linnosmaa and Lien Nguyen*

period from 2000 to 2013. The funding share of user fees reached its maximum of 19 per cent of gross expenditures in 2010, though the share came down by one percentage point to 18 per cent in 2013.

## 10.6  Recent policy initiatives in Finnish long-term care

A long-term trend in the Finnish ageing policy has been to support ageing at home or in home-like settings (e.g. residential care homes) and reduce long-term care in old people's homes and primary health care (Noro et al., 2014). The trend has been supported in practice by quality recommendations and legislative reforms.

Quality recommendations have been issued in Finland three times in the last decade and a half in 2001, 2008 and 2013. Recommendations have been developed to support the development and evaluation activities in municipalities. They aim at ensuring both healthy and capable ageing and effective and high-quality services for the older population (Sosiaali-ja terveysministeriö ja Kuntaliitto, 2013). Quality recommendations are given on inclusion, living environment, securing healthy and capable ageing, quality and coverage of services, informal care and management. For example, it is recommended that 91 to 92 per cent of 75 and older population should live in their own homes and 2 to 3 per cent should be in institutional care (old people's homes or primary health care) by 2017 in Finland. Although recommendations about how to organize and develop care for older persons have no legal force, they have been considered useful by municipal decision makers (Sosiaali- ja terveysministeriö ja Kuntaliitto, 2013).

The Act on Supporting the Functional Capacity of the Older Population and on Social and Health Services for Older Persons (980/2012) was introduced in July 2013. One of the objectives of the new legislation was to strengthen and support the move from institutional care to home care or home-like settings. The law also aimed at promoting and supporting the right of older persons to high-quality services that support the well-being, health and functional capacity of older people and at improving the possibilities of older people to influence more decision making that affects their own lives.

The Act on Supporting the Functional Capacity of the Older Population and on Social and Health Services for Older Persons (980/2012) complements the existing legislation on organisation, pricing and financing of health and social care services (e.g. the Law on Social Care [*Sosiaalihuoltolaki*] and the Health Care Act). The law regulates the responsibilities of the Finnish municipalities to promote well-being, health, functional capacity and inclusion among the older population; to find out about services needs of older people; and to respond to the need by providing high-quality social and health care services. It also steers the provision of service quality in facilities providing social and health care services for older persons. For example, the 20th article of the law states that a facility should have enough personnel with qualifications that suit the clients' needs. The law includes similar articles on the management and premises of care facilities.

In the current legislation, family carers are eligible for care leave (respite) during periods when they are committed to round-the-clock care. This implies that not all family carers have access to care leaves and breaks from care duties. The current government aims to support family care by extending the right to care leave for all family carers contracted to their municipality of residence. In addition, the government plans on decreeing on the responsibilities of municipalities to provide services and medical examinations to support the family carer's health and well-being. At the time this chapter was written, these legislative changes were in the form of a government bill, though it had not yet passed through the parliamentary proceedings.

By strengthening the possibilities of home care and family care, the current government aims to reduce the costs of institutional LTC. This hinges on the degree to which home care and family care will serve to substitute for institutional care (Bolin et al., 2008; Van Houtven and Norton, 2004) and the relative prices of home care and institutional care. It is worth noting that home care can become an expensive alternative if the number of home care visits is high due to high dependence and complex medical problems of the cared-for person (Guo et al., 2015).

## 10.7 Summary and conclusions

Economic growth has been weak in Finland since the economic crisis in 2008. GDP growth in Finland has been lower than 0.5 per cent in recent years. This has also had implications for public spending and expenditures on LTC services for the older population. Our descriptive analysis on the LTC service system in Finland has shown the following:

- The growth rate of total expenditures on care for older people has been lower since the crisis than in the years before the crisis.
- There are no signs that the diminished growth would be caused by a reduced need for LTC.
- There has been a structural change in round-the-clock care, where the emphasis has shifted away from institutional care to community care and care offered in sheltered housing facilities in particular, as well as a tendency towards the integration of informal family care into the formal care system.
- After the crisis in 2008, Finnish municipalities have paid a slightly growing share of total elderly care expenditures.
- It seems that broader cooperation among the municipalities has been set up as mutual municipal purchases of customer services of other services for older people and people with disabilities has increased since the mid-2000s, while the private provision of institutional care services for older people fell after 2008.

The most recent policy initiatives for LTC also reflect the economic situation in Finland. By supporting the possibilities for ageing at home instead of in institutions, recent reforms aim at reducing total expenditures on LTC. Our analysis has indicated that the growth rate of LTC expenditures has already declined since the economic crisis in 2008. Whether the most recent policy initiatives on strengthening home and family care will reduce the growth of LTC expenditures further depends on the substitutability of home care for institutional care, but also on their relative prices. The effectiveness of these measures remains to be seen.

## 164 Ismo Linnosmaa and Lien Nguyen

## Notes

1 *Laki omaishoidon tuesta* 937/2005.
2 This figure was 30.2 per cent in 2006 and 29.1 per cent in 2009.
3 *Laki sosiaali-ja terveydenhuollon suunnittelusta ja valtionavustuksesta* 733/1992.
4 *Sosiaalihuoltolaki* 1301/2014.
5 *Laki sosiaali-ja terveydenhuollon asiakasmaksuista* 734/1992.
6 *Asetus sosiaali-ja terveydenhuollon asiakasmaksuista* 912/1992.
7 *Laki kunnan peruspalvelujen valtionosuudesta* 1704/2009.
8 *Laki sosiaali-ja terveydenhuollon suunnittelusta ja valtionavustuksesta* 733/1992.
9 *Asetus sosiaali-ja terveydenhuollon asiakasmaksuista* 912/1992.
10 Act on Supporting the Functional Capacity of the Older Population and on Social and Health Care Services of Older Persons 980/2012.
11 The old-age retirement age specified by the National Pensions Act in Finland is 65 years. With the implementation of the earnings-related pension reform in 2005, a working person can flexibly retire between the ages of 63 and 68.
12 The share of those aged at least 65 years was equal to the share of children under 16 years old in 2008 (16.7 per cent), after which it increased evenly until 2014 (19.9 per cent).
13 The total dependency ratio is defined as the ratio of young dependents (aged 0–14 years) and old dependents (older people aged 65 or over) to the working-age population (aged 15–64 years). This indicator provides a broad indicator of the pressures on social spending arising from demographic changes. The ratio is expressed as the number of dependents per 100 people aged 15 to 64 years.
14 The old-age dependency ratio is the ratio of the number of people aged 65 and older (age when they are generally economically inactive) to the number of people aged between 15 and 64 years. The value is expressed as the number of older people per 100 people aged 15 to 64 years.
15 In this section and in section 10.5, we use the term *institutional care* to refer to care provided in old people's homes and other institutional facilities, since this is the terminology used in the HEF statistics. In general terminology, institutional care refers to care provided in old people's homes and primary health care (section 10.2).
16 We also extended the analysis to the years 1995 to 1999. With this extension, roughly the same conclusions held. The most notable exception was the year 1997, when total expenditures decreased 1.2 per cent. In 1998, the annual growth rate of total expenditures was 1.6 per cent. For the years 1996 and 1999, the growth rates were 3 and 2.3 per cent, respectively, which clearly exceeding the annual growth rates after the year 2009.
17 Per capita expenditures for individuals aged 65 or older is computed by the ratio REXP/POP65+, where REXP is the total expenditures in 2013 prices and POP65+ is the number of individuals aged 65 or older.
18 Act on Restructuring Local Government and Services 169/2007.

## References

Aho, T. and Junnila, M. (2012), Kilpailutus sosiaali- ja terveyspalveluissa. Tampere Juvenes Print, https://www.tekes.fi/globalassets/global/ohjelmat-ja-palvelut/ohjelmat/innovaatiot-sosiaali – ja-terveyspalveluissa/kilpailutus_sote.pdf (Accessed: 5 May 2016).
Blomgren, J. and Einio, E. (2015), Laitoshoidon vähenemisen yhteys ikääntyneiden muihin pitkäaikaishoidon palveluihin ja sairausvakuutuksen korvaamien lääkkeiden kustannuksiin vuosina 2000–2013, *Yhteiskuntapolitiikka* 80: 334–347.
Bolin, K., Lindgren, B. and Lundborg, P. (2008), Informal and formal care among single-living elderly in Europe, *Health Economics* 17: 393–409.
Brown, J. and Finkelstein, A. (2011), *Insuring long-term care in the US, National Bureau of Economic Research*, Working Paper 17451. doi:10.3386/w17451.

*Long-term care expenditures in Finland* 165

Colombo, F., Llena-Nozal, A., Mercier, J. and Tjadens, F. (2011), *Help Wanted? Providing and Paying for Long-Term Care*, OECD Health Policy Studies, Paris: OECD.

European Commission (2009), 2009 Ageing report: Economic and budgetary projections for the EU-27 member states (2008–2060). *European Economy* 2, EC Directorate-General for Economic and Financial Affairs, Luxemburg (Accessed: 20 May 2016).

European Commission (2016), Country Report Finland 2015. Commission staff working document. (In Finnish, Suomen maaraportti 2016. Komission yksiköiden valmisteluasiakirja.) Brussel 26.2.2016. http://ec.europa.eu/europe2020/pdf/csr2016/cr2016_finland_fi.pdf (Accessed: 3 April 2016).

EuroStat (2012), *ESSPROS Manual and User Guidelines*. Luxemburg: The European System of Integrated Social Protection Statistics (ESSPROS), Publication Office of the European Union.

EuroStat (2016a), Statistical Office of the European Communities, database. Real GDP per capita, growth rate and totals. http://ec.europa.eu/eurostat/data/database (Accessed: 26 March 2016).

EuroStat (2016b), Statistical Office of the European Communities, database. General government spending. http://ec.europa.eu/eurostat/data/database (Accessed: 24 March 2016).

EuroStat (2016c), Statistical Office of the European Communities, database. General government deficit and surplus. http://ec.europa.eu/eurostat/data/database (Accessed: 24 March 2016).

EuroStat (2016d), Statistical Office of the European Communities, database. Life expectancy at birth. http://ec.europa.eu/eurostat/data/database (Accessed: 25 March 2016).

EuroStat (2016e), Statistical Office of the European Communities, database. Old age dependency ratio per 100 persons. http://ec.europa.eu/eurostat/data/database (Accessed: 26 March 2016).

Frank, R.G. (2012), Long-term care financing in the United States: Sources and institutions, *Applied Economic Perspectives and Policy* 34: 333−345.

Grabowski, D.C. (2007), Medicare and Medicaid: Conflicting incentives for long-term care, *The Milbank Quarterly* 85: 571−610.

Grabowski, D.C. (2008), The market for long-term care services, *Inquiry* 45: 58−74.

Guo, J., Konetzka, R.T. and Manning, W.G. (2015), The causal effects of home care use on institutional long-term care utilization and expenditures, *Health Economics* 24: 4–17.

Heikkilä, E. (2012), Labour market participation of immigrants in Finland and its regions. The European Social Science History Conference, Glasgow, Scotland, UK, 11–14 April 2012. Siirtolaisinstituutti, Institute of Migration, Turku. www.migrationinstitute.fi (Accessed: 29 March 2016).

Johansson, E. (2010), *The long-term care system for the elderly in Finland.* Enepri Research Report 76, Contribution to WP1 of the ANCIEN Project.

Kapiainen, S., Väisänen, A. and Haula, T. (2014), Terveyden- ja sosiaalihuollon yksikkökustannukset Suomessa vuonna 2011, Terveyden ja hyvinvoinnin laitos, Raportti 3/2014, Tampere Juvenes Print.

Karisto, A. (2007), Finnish baby boomers and the emergence of the third age, *International Journal of Ageing and Later Life* 2: 91–108.

Kröger, T. and Leinonen, A. (2012), Transformation by stealth: The retargeting of home care services in Finland, *Health and Social Care in the Community* 20: 319–327.

Kuntaliitto (2012), Kuntien ja kuntayhtymien talous- ja toimintatilaston luokitukset 2012. Helsinki. www.kunnat.net (Accessed: 5 May 2016).

Laamanen, R., Simonsen-Rehn, N., Suominen, S., Øvretveitd, J. and Brommels, M. (2008), Outsourcing primary health care services – How politicians explain the grounds for their decisions, *Health Policy* 88: 294–307. doi:10.1016/j.healthpol.2008.04.001.

166    *Ismo Linnosmaa and Lien Nguyen*

Lith, P. (2013), Yksityiset sosiaali- ja terveyspalvelut. Raportti yksityisestä palvelutarjonnasta ja yritysten kasvusta sekä julkisista hankinnoista ja toiminnan kehittämisestä sosiaali- ja terveyspalveluissa. TEM raportteja 34/2013. Ministry of Employment and the Economy (in Finland).

Linnosmaa, I., Jokinen, S., Vilkko, A. and Siljander, E. (2014), *Omaishoidon tuki. Selvitys omaishoidon tuen palkkioista ja palveluista kunnissa vuonna 2012, Terveyden ja hyvinvoinnin laitos*, Raportti 9/2014, Tampere: Juvenes Print.

Linnosmaa, I. (2014), *Vanhustenhuolto teoksessa Seppälä ja Pekurinen (toim.) Sosiaali- ja terveydenhuollon keskeiset rahavirrat, Terveyden ja hyvinvoinnin laitos*, Raportti 22/2014, Tampere: Juvenes Print.

Meklin, P. and Pekola-Sjöblom, M. (eds) (2013), *The Reform to Restructure Municipalities and Services in Finland: A Research Perspective*. Evaluation Research Programme ARTTU Studies No. 23. Helsinki: Association of Finnish Local and Regional Authorities.

Netten, A., Burge, P., Malley, J., Potoglou, D., Towers, A-M., Brazier, J., Flynn, T., Forder, J. and Wall, B. (2012), Outcomes of social care for adults: Developing a preference-weighted measure, *Health Technology Assessment* 16: 1–166. doi:10.3310/hta16160.

Noro, A., Mäkelä, M., Jussmäki, T. and Finne-Soveri, H. (2014), *Ikäihmisten palvelut murroksessa teoksessa: Noro A, Alastalo H (eds.) Vanhuspalvelulain 980/2012 toimeenpanon seuranta. Tilanne ennen lain voimaantuloa vuonna 2013, Terveyden ja hyvinvoinnin laitos*, Raportti 13/2014, Tampere: Juvenes Print.

OECD (2000), *A System of Health Accounts*, Paris: OECD.

OECD (2016), *OECD Economic Surveys: Finland 2016*, Paris: OECD. https://www.oecd.org/eco/surveys/Overview-OECD-Finland-2016.pdf (Accessed: 29 March 2016).

Official Statistics of Finland (2016a), *National Account 2015. Economy 2015 (in Finnish, Kansantalouden tilinpito 2015. Kansantalous 2016)*. Helsinki: Statistics Finland. http://www.stat.fi/til/vtp/2015/vtp_2015_2016–03–16_fi.pdf (Accessed: 29 March 2016).

Official Statistics of Finland (2016b), *Population Forecast. Population 2015 (in Finnish, Väestöennuste. Väestö 2015)*. Helsinki: Statistics Finland. http://www.stat.fi/til/vaenn/2015/vaenn_2015_2015–10–30_fi.pdf (Accessed: 30 March 2016).

Piekkola, H. (2004), *Demographic aspects of ageing and time use in a set of European countries*. ETLA Discussion Paper No. 899. The Research Institute of the Finnish Economy, Helsinki. www.etla.fi (Accessed: 29 March 2016).

Seppälä, T. and Pekurinen, M. (2014), *Sosiaali- ja terveydenhuollon keskeiset rahavirrat, Terveyden ja hyvinvoinnin laitos*, Raportti 22/2014, Tampere: Juvenes Print.

Sosiaali-ja terveysministeriö ja Kuntaliitto (2013), *Laatusuositus hyvän ikääntymisen turvaamiseksi ja palvelujen parantamiseksi, Sosiaali- ja terveysministeriön julkaisuja 11*, Helsinki: Sosiaali- ja terveysministeriö.

Sotkanet (2016), Statistics and Indicator Bank. Helsinki: National Institute for Health and Welfare. www.sotkanet.fi (Accessed: 15 March 2016).

Statistics Finland (2016a), Bruttokansantuote (BKT) markkinahintaan 1975–2015*. Helsinki: Tilastokeskus. http://www.stat.fi/til/vtp/2015/vtp_2015_2016–03–16_tau_001_fi.html (Accessed: 26 May 2016).

Statistics Finland (2016b), StatFin Database. Väestö, vastasyntyneiden elinajanodote 1971–2014. http://pxnet2.stat.fi/PXWeb/pxweb/fi/StatFin/ (Accessed: 26 March 2016).

Statistics Finland (2016c), StatFin Database. General government deficit and surplus. www.tilastokeskus.fi (Accessed: 27 March 2016).

Statistics Finland (2016d), StatFin Database. Julkinen talous, kuntien ja kuntayhtymien talous ja toiminta, kuntien käyttötalous. http://pxnet2.stat.fi/PXWeb/pxweb/fi/StatFin/ (Accessed: 2 May 2016).

## Long-term care expenditures in Finland 167

Terveyden ja hyvinvoinnin laitos (2011), *Yksityinen palvelutuotanto sosiaali- ja terveyspalveluissa 2009, Tilastoraportti 33/2011*, Tampere: Juvenes Print.

Terveyden ja hyvinvoinnin laitos (2015). *Terveydenhuollon menot ja rahoitus 2013, Tilastoraportti 6/2015*, Tampere: Juvenes Print.

Terveyden ja hyvinvoinnin laitos (2016), *Sosiaalimenot ja rahoitus 2014, Tilastoraportti 2/2016*, Tampere: Juvenes Print.

Tynkkynen, L.-K., Keskimäki, I. and Lehto, J. (2013), Purchaser–provider splits in health care – The case of Finland, *Health Policy* 111: 221–225. doi:10.1016/j. healthpol.2013.05.012.

Vilkko, A., Muuri, A., Saarikalle, K., Noro, A., Finne-Soveri, H. and Jokinen, S. (2014), Läheisavun moninaisuus. In M. Vaarama, S. Karvonen, L. Kestilä, P. Moisio and A. Muuri (ed) *Suomalaisten hyvinvointi 2014, Terveyden ja hyvinvoinnin laitos*, Tampere: Juvenes Print, pp. 222–237.

Valkama, P., Kallio, O. and Tukiainen J (2013), Ulkoistaminen ja kilpailuttaminen vanhuspalveluiden näennäismarkkinoilla, *Janus* 21: 345–365.

Van Houtven, C. and Norton, E. (2004), Informal care and health care use of older adults, *Journal of Health Economics* 23: 1159–1180.

## Acts and decrees

Act on Restructuring Local Government and Services 169/2007

Act on Supporting the Functional Capacity of the Older Population and on Social and Health Services for Older Persons 980/2012

*Asetus sosiaali-ja terveydenhuollon asiakasmaksuista* 912/1992

The Health Care Act 1326/2010

*Laki kunnan peruspalvelujen valtionosuudesta* 1704/2009

*Laki omaishoidon tuesta* 937/2005

*Laki sosiaali-ja terveydenhuollon suunnittelusta ja valtionavustuksesta* 733/1992

*Laki sosiaali-ja terveydenhuollon asiakasmaksuista* 734/1992

The Law on Social Care (*Sosiaalihuoltolaki*) 1301/2014

# 11 Long-term care in Denmark, with an eye to the other Nordic welfare states

*Bent Greve*

## 11.1 Introduction

Welfare states are under constant change and have been ever since they were developed and known by the words *welfare state*. Types of changes, using Farnworth and Irving (2011), range from small incremental adjustments to "earthquake transitions", although the main tendency, at least in the Nordic welfare states, seems to be the former. Over time, this can change the historical path in a very different direction. There are also debates on whether convergence in the European welfare states can be seen. This article focuses on the ongoing development within the LTC system in the Nordic countries, especially Denmark, and the specific area of elderly care. Long-term care for people with disabilities is not included in the analysis, except when data do not make a distinction between different groups in need of care.

The reason for this choice is that in the area of LTC, many different strands of arguments are used for alterations. Ongoing demographic changes, economic constraints, involvement of civil society and use of market mechanism are all elements in the changes within LTC (Pavolini and Ranci, 2008). There was a real growth in expenditures on LTC from 2005 to 2011 in most countries within the OECD area, with the exception of Hungary and Finland (OECD, 2013c). There is also an expected increase in the years to come due to the demographic change of there being more elderly and more people who are very old (de la Maisonneuve and Martins, 2014), although healthy ageing might reduce the pressure. How to measure and understand change, especially if the focus is on the quality of care, can be very difficult. It is also an area where informal and formal care works along the same lines and where the boundaries between civil society, state and market are under constant change. There are also challenges to understanding the balance between the actors.

Therefore, the universal Nordic welfare states are an interesting choice for study given their historical commitment to a universal approach to welfare and a high degree of state involvement in the welfare service area. This is due to the emphasis on defamilialism as a central aspect in the Nordic welfare state model, and LTC is an area where this in principle can be seen. The extra focus on Denmark is due to the author's more detailed knowledge about Denmark, including work on commissions and national reports.

The next section deals more precisely with core aspects such as demography and economic constraints. In section 11.3, the central theme is how to analyse and measure quality in the delivery of LTC care, as this can be seen as an important parameter to control if the market is more involved in the delivery of care. However, it is also related to both public and civil society involvement in care. Thus, the ability to measure and understand quality is a central analytical issue for the chapter in understanding welfare development in long-term care.

Welfare regime clustering is the structuring device using a small-n comparative analysis (Vis, 2013) and using the four Nordic countries to look into similar designs (Ragin, 1987) and at differences among the four countries in order to determine whether the Nordic countries are more similar or whether they have moved apart at least somewhat.

Thus, overall the chapter focuses on and analyses whether the Nordic welfare states – often depicted as universal – look the same and whether universalism and professional care are still central in the delivery and financing of LTC.

## 11.2 Central issues

The issue of how welfare states should cope with the possible increasing number of frail elderly is not new. In 1999, the OECD argued in favour of an active ageing policy that included how to integrate support and provision of support, informal care and long-term care with other social policies (Jacobzone, 1999).

In general, "LTC is interpreted as a set of medical, social and personal care services provided on a regular basis for people who need help with ADLs" (Swartz, 2013, p. 400). Swartz also points to that 60 to 70 % of people who need LTC in the OECD area receive it informally from relatives. The consequences for those delivering the informal long-term care are also important as they can vary between increasing well-being to increasing stress and dissatisfaction with life, and they might also reduce the opportunity for employment (Heger, 2014). In this chapter, LTC will be understood as a more permanent need for care for people with disabilities and elderly. Due to data limitations I will focus especially on the elderly. Given the increased focus on rehabilitation, the boundaries between care and long-term care can be blurred. It seems that rehabilitation can reduce the need for support, but not completely remove the need.

There are many and varied ways to provide LTC (Claid Dale et al., 2012), including a variety in who provides care and how it is paid for (general taxation, social insurance, user charges, pure private), and many combinations thereof. The variations in informal and formal care are wide, and, the combination of support in private homes and in residential care and the rules regarding right to care also result in a plethora of variations across the European countries. They can be means-tested, based upon evaluation of what the elderly can do themselves and mixed with the partners'/spouses' roles. Informal caregivers may have a lower level of well-being (Verbaekel, 2014) and, this must then be weighed against the economic cost of a type of needed support. There might also be a trade-off between work and family life (Greve, 2012), as children have to provide informal care to their parent(s). Whether children (including grandchildren) care for older (grand)parents can be important, as informal care might reduce the need for public sector involvement. If this involvement, especially if it is due to reciprocity and, therefore, different kinds of economic incentives cannot be expected to have any large impact on the number of people doing voluntary care, then the size of informal care can be difficult to estimate. The continuation in the delivery of care might stop at any time. The degree of help seems to be higher in the Southern and Eastern European welfare states than in the Nordic and Continental welfare states (Brugiavini, et al., 2013).

There are therefore also many different issues to consider, such as how responsibilities are divided between society, the person and his/her family; whether low-income people (welfare assistance approach) or people with specific needs will be supported; whether a social insurance approach or a more universal approach will be used; what the role of national/local level is; how to finance the elderly activities; and how to combine income, housing and LTC assistance (Swartz, 2013). The borderlines between long-term care and health care are not always distinct given that the very frail elderly often will be in need both of care and health treatment, and often their needs might shift between the two areas.

Furthermore, for efficiency, is it better to have a common way of financing either through taxes and duties or through an obligatory social insurance (Barr, 2010). A person does not know ahead of time whether he/she will be in need of care; therefore, if everyone saved money for this in advance, many households would need to put away much of their income for this purpose. This would result in a dramatic difference of equality in access to care given that some people would not be able to afford necessary and potentially expensive care. So, left to itself, the market fails to provide care to all people who are not able to take care of themselves, including those who do not have relatives to take over.

Still, the way to finance long-term care is very different, complex and ever-evolving. It ranges from universal to comprehensive to means-tested funding and included a variety of user charges, targeting and user-choice, and it is mixed in many ways (OECD, 2011). The degree of devolution is also very diverse (see the more precise description of the Nordic countries and see Chapter 8 in this book regarding the UK).

The many and different pressures on the welfare states have for long been debated in many countries (for a recent overview, see Schubert, Villota and Kuhlmann, 2015), including in many small European welfare states.[1] Therefore, I will not provide a long description of this or of why the demographic changes imply specific challenges in the area of LTC; I will, however, stress that this is logical given that those in need of LTC are primarily elderly people, and the sheer increase in the number of elderly over time will have an impact on the overall level of spending. With future expected development implies a continuous cost pressure in the area (see de la Maisonneuve and Martins, 2014). The focus here is on change in care for the elderly and on understanding quality in long-term care.

## 11.3 What is quality in long-term care?

Quality in the delivery of welfare services is an important issue, and this has been an issue related to marketization in the Nordic countries. Here the focus is on the overall level, whereas more specific elements in the Nordic countries will be addressed in section 11.5.

Quality can be described by Donebedians framework linking quality with structure, process and outcome, where structural measures include material or human resources related to the provision of services and process and outcome indicators include possible measurement in achieving clinical relevant goals (OECD, 2013a). The OECD (2013a) also points to that quality dimensions can include:

- Effectiveness and care safety
- Patient-centeredness and responsiveness
- Care coordination.

A core issue is that the approach to and use of quality as a steering instrument in the area has been less strong than in health care partly due to the difficulty in defining quality. At the same time, given the economic constraints, it is not only quality that is of importance, but also the ability to have the best performance in a combination of resources and quality expected. Performance can be related to the following:

- Quality of life of LTC users
- Quality of care
- Equity of LTC systems
- Total burden of LTC (public financial as well as informal caregiving) (Mot et al., 2012).

OECD further points to the following elements to include in the understanding and measurement of quality of care: effectiveness, safety, responsiveness, coordination, timeliness, continuity and integration of the provided care. Thus, in this perspective, economic considerations (e.g. effectiveness) relate to the care quality.

There are thus different possible outcomes of LTC: functional ability, other health status measure, and health-related quality of life. Compared to the area of health care, the problem is that perfect recovery is not an option. Despite this, rehabilitation has become a cornerstone in Nordic welfare states in order to cope with cost pressure and quality of life for the elderly.

OECD (2013b) defines quality as

> Good quality of LTC maintains or, when feasible, improves the functional and health outcomes of frail, the chronically ill and the physically disabled old people. Three aspects are generally accepted as critical to quality of care: effectiveness and safety, patient-centeredness and responsiveness, and care co-ordination. LTC includes a range of personal care services to help disabled

172    *Bent Greve*

people with basic activities of daily living (ADL), as well as basic medical services, nursing care, prevention, rehabilitation or palliative care. It can also include domestic help and help with administrative tasks.

(p. 2.)

A Swedish study (Stolt, Blomqvist and Winblad, 2011) pointed to 12 indicators (3 on process and 9 on structural factors): participation, employment, basic competences, advanced competences, full-time employment, employee turnover, hourly employment, shared accommodation, individual facilities, food alternatives, nightly fast and management.

These two ways (OECD and the Swedish study) of looking into quality point out that there is a need to know the numbers receiving care and to have information on staff and spending. In principle, users' evaluations could give some information; however, this is difficult in the area of long-term care given the situations of many of those in need of care, especially people with dementia.

These two ways will be used as a guideline, although little factual information and few measurements of the quality of care are available. This will be combined with information on how to combine work and family life, as this is also an issue in quality of life. A core problem is that it is difficult to be against quality (Dahl, 2012), but it is not easy to agree on what quality is. Although it is argued that the measurement of long-term care quality is developing, this is happening very slowly (OECD, 2013a), and there is still a long way to go due to the complexity of and integration and use of different mixes in the provision in long-term care.

## 11.4  Recent developments in the Nordic welfare state: an empirical focus

This section will first present some empirical data on the development mainly since the year 2000. Data availability is not always simple because there are differences in the way countries measure and inform on this. There is also difference between the details in the data from OECD and the EU (Council of European Union, 2014). This implies that comparison should be done with caution, albeit this is less of a problem when only having the Nordic countries involved in the comparison, although here measuring size and quality of the LTC is difficult (Meagher and Szebehely, 2013). It is even more difficult to get good data related to quality of care, and often there is a larger problem related to comparing data over a longer time span. Following is some central quantitative information on the development in the Nordic welfare states. It is not possible to get data on the size and use of welfare technology.

The empirical description starts with Table 11.1, which presents the proportion of elderly receiving care either at home or in an institution.

The data in Table 11.1 show, not surprisingly, that there is a clear connection between age and the need of formalised long-term care; the needs of those over the age of 80 are higher than those below. Data (not in the table) indicate that in all countries women receive care at a higher rate than men. The main reason for

*Table 11.1* Proportion of those above the aged 65 years and older and aged 80 and older receiving care at home or in institutions

| | *2000* | *2005* | *2008* | *2010* | *2012* | *2013* | *2014* |
|---|---|---|---|---|---|---|---|
| **Above age of 65 at home** | | | | | | | |
| Denmark | 12.4 | 12.8 | 14.1 | 13 | 11.6 | — | — |
| Finland | 8.2 | 7.7 | 7.3 | 7.4 | 7.2 | 7.1 | — |
| Norway | — | 11.9 | 12.5 | 12.5 | 12.1 | 11.9 | 11.7 |
| Sweden | 9.6 | 10.2 | 11.4 | 12.2 | 11.7 | 11.4 | — |
| **Above age of 80 at home** | | | | | | | |
| Denmark | 31.3 | 31.6 | 37.4 | 35.9 | 34 | — | — |
| Finland | 21 | 19.7 | 18.4 | 18.7 | 18.5 | 18.5 | — |
| Norway | 21.4 | 20.6 | 27.2 | 27.7 | 28.1 | 28.1 | 28.2 |
| Sweden | — | 22.2 | 23.0 | 28.5 | 28.6 | 29.6 | — |
| **Above age of 65 in institutions** | | | | | | | |
| Denmark | — | — | 4.9 | 4.6 | 4.2 | 4 | 3.9 |
| Finland | 3.6 | 4.2 | 4.7 | 4.9 | 4.8 | 4.7 | — |
| Norway | 5.9 | 5.7 | 5.5 | 5.6 | 5.2 | 4.9 | 4.7 |
| Sweden | 7.7 | 6.5 | 6.0 | 5.4 | 4.9 | 4.9 | — |
| **Above age of 80 in institutions** | | | | | | | |
| Denmark | — | — | 13.9 | 13.7 | 13.1 | 12.6 | 12.7 |
| Finland | 11.2 | 12.2 | 12.8 | 13.2 | 12.8 | 12.8 | — |
| Norway | — | 14.6 | 14.2 | 14.5 | 14.2 | 13.8 | 13.6 |
| Sweden | 20.9 | 16.7 | 15.7 | 14.8 | 14.1 | — | — |

Note: A problem in comparison here is that for the number of people receiving care, and especially the care at home, the number of hours with support might be changed so that the same relative proportion receiving care can disguise both an expansion and a retrenchment.

Source: OECD, Long-term care dataset, 2015 (http://stats.oecd.org/index.aspx?DataSetCode=HEALTH_STAT).

174   *Bent Greve*

this is that women live longer, and therefore they are more often single when they become frail; conversely, many women take care of the men in these age groups. With the exception of the proportion receiving care at home being in Finland than in the other Nordic countries, there is a strong similarity among the persons getting care, and there has also been a tendency for them to look more like each other. Whether the elderly get more informal care is difficult to depict, but Tables 11.5, 11.6, and 11.7 later in the chapter seem to show a slightly higher pressure on families in Finland.

It is difficult to interpret the development since the year 2000, as this can be explained by at least three different elements:

1   Retrenchment, especially after the financial crisis
2   Substitutions between home care and institutional care
3   Impact of rehabilitation, enablement and use of welfare technology.

For Sweden, for example, the development since 2000 in the proportion of those receiving care in institutions has been dramatically reduced, although only so that the level now is on par with other Nordic countries. An increase in the proportion of elderly above the age of 80 receiving care at home in Sweden indicates a shift and also more use of rehabilitation; at the same time there has been a relative decline in the number receiving care at institutions. There also seems to be a slight tendency toward a reduction in line with the expectation that people are not only living longer but they are also more healthy than earlier, combined with use of rehabilitation, assistive use of IT and reablement. Preventive initiatives might have had an impact, although the size is difficult to measure. Still, healthy ageing could be attributed, at least partly, to focusing on a healthier lifestyle and to changes in homes that make them better for elderly people. These elements of a possible reduction in pressure on long-term care will further be touched upon later. In Norway, there seems to have been an increase in the number of elderly receiving care at home without any reduction in the proportion at the institutions.

The preventative elements seem to have had an impact, especially in Sweden, on the number of beds available for the elderly (Table 11.2). The data overall do not lend support to a reduction in delivery of care and spending in the wake of the financial crisis, as the development towards reduction in institutional care took place before the start of the financial crisis. A problem in the analysis is that the number receiving care at home do not indicate the number of hours care is delivered. Data from Denmark from 2008 to 2014 do not show any changes, with an average number of hours per week being 3.7 (both personal and practical help in the private homes) (Statistikbanken AED021, http://www.statistikbanken.dk/AED021). The picture is the same in Norway, where since 2008 there has been an increase in the average weekly number of hours of support provided in the private homes for those aged 67 years and older. However, in Sweden, there has been decline (although data is from 2001–2012) "both in the coverage and intensity of eldercare services" (Ulmanen and Szebehely, 2015, p. 83). The picture is thus not the same in all Nordic countries, but to argue that there has just been retrenchment would not paint a correct picture.

*Long-term care in Denmark* 175

*Table 11.2* Number of beds per 1,000 people aged 65 years and older in the Nordic countries since 2000

|         | 2000 | 2005 | 2008 | 2010 | 2012 | 2013 |
|---------|------|------|------|------|------|------|
| Denmark | 58.3 | 54.5 | 54.0 | 51.9 | 48.7 | —    |
| Finland | 44.5 | 51.6 | 61.6 | 64.1 | 61.7 | 60.5 |
| Norway  | —    | 60.5 | 59.6 | 57.2 | 54.3 | —    |
| Sweden  | 98.5 | 88.4 | 84.1 | 78.9 | 72.2 | 69.6 |

Source: OECD, Long-term care dataset, 2015 (http://stats.oecd.org/index.aspx?DataSetCode= HEALTH_STAT).

Again, this also points to the expectation that care, especially for elderly in need of long-term care, will to a larger degree either receive informal care or support in their private homes, as in recent years there has been a decline in the availability of beds, especially in Sweden, again with changes starting before the financial crisis. There is no systematic information on the number of informal workers over time or for all four countries.

Table 11.3 shows the percentages of nurses and formal carers for those above the age of 65.

The difference in the data is an indication that the information in the area is not necessarily systematic. Given the relatively high agreement in the level of persons receiving care among the countries, one should not expect such large differences in the availability of carers. It might be a consequence of the fact that the border between health and social care in the area is not (at least statistically) clear. This is further underlined by the fact that the overall difference in the level of spending is not that big across the four countries (see Table 11.4).

Table 11.4 shows the increase in spending on long-term care since 2000. This is mainly due to the demographic change, but presumably it is also due to the increase in care for other people in need of long-term care, as data do not distinguish between care for elderly and other people in need of long-term care, such as people with disabilities. However, the rise of 0.6% in Sweden from 2000 to 2005 could again be an indicator that data quality in the area still is under development. Comparing the Nordic countries, the difference here is also very limited, with Sweden being the highest spender in the area. The rather stable development is once again an indicator that the fiscal crisis did not seem to have an impact on spending in this area.

A way to compare the spending is to look into both real growth in GDP and development of people who might be in need of long-term care. Table 11.5 shows the relation between development in real GDP and change in the population for those aged 75 and older.

Given the real increase in GDP, the table indicates that in all the Nordic countries there has been an increase in real spending on elderly since 2000. The reason why this also has been the case in Finland, despite the falling ration to GDP (see Table 11.4) is that there has since 2000 been an increase from 1.8% of GDP to 2.6%, and even after the financial crisis, there was an increase in spending. Data do not point to a retrenchment in spending in the area.

176    *Bent Greve*

*Table 11.3* Percentage of nurses and formal carers in for the total population aged 65 years and older

|         | 2000 | 2005 | 2008 | 2010 | 2012 | 2013 |
|---------|------|------|------|------|------|------|
| Denmark | 8.8  | 9.6  | 9.1  | 8.9  | 8.5  | —    |
| Norway  | —    | 23.1 | 24.5 | 24.2 | 23.5 | 23.1 |
| Sweden  | 13.8 | 14.3 | 13.8 | 13.1 | 12.5 | 12.3 |

Note: This is based upon head counts, so it is not a full-time equivalent. No data available for Finland.

Source: OECD, Long-term care dataset, 2015 (http://stats.oecd.org/index.aspx?DataSetCode=HEALTH_STAT).

*Table 11.4* Spending on long-term care as percentages of GDP since 2000 in the Nordic countries

| Year    | 2000 | 2005 | 2008 | 2010 | 2012 | 2013 | 2014 |
|---------|------|------|------|------|------|------|------|
| Denmark | —    | 2.3  | 2.4  | 2.6  | 2.5  | 2.5  | —    |
| Finland | 1.8  | 2.1  | 2.2  | 2.5  | 2.6  | 2.6  | —    |
| Norway  | 1.9  | 2.2  | 2.3  | 2.6  | 2.6  | 2.6  | 2.7  |
| Sweden  | 0.6  | 3.5  | 3.5  | 3.6  | 3.6  | 3.4  | —    |

Source: Data from OECD.Stat.

*Table 11.5* The real GDP/+75 demographic ratio since 2000

| GEO/TIME | 2000  | 2005  | 2008  | 2010  | 2012  | 2013  | 2014  |
|----------|-------|-------|-------|-------|-------|-------|-------|
| Denmark  | 100.0 | 106.6 | 110.1 | 105.7 | 104.9 | 103.3 | 102.7 |
| Finland  | 100.0 | 105.2 | 105.6 | 95.1  | 92.8  | 89.9  | 88.1  |
| Sweden   | 100.0 | 112.7 | 120.4 | 120.9 | 124.0 | 125.4 | 127.3 |
| Norway   | 100.0 | 110.5 | 115.7 | 114.3 | 119.6 | 120.9 | 123.5 |

Note: Both indexes calculated with 2000 = 100 in order to calculate the composite index of development,

Source: Calculated based upon Eurostat data on GDP in fixed price and demographic development for those above the age of 75 since 2000.

A central issue has been how the possibly changed roles between state and civil society might influence quality of life not only for those using long-term care but also for members of the family, such as in the work-life balance. Table 11.6 shows whether care responsibilities (without distinguishing between children and/or elderly) influence ability to concentrate at work.

The data are an indication that for most people this does not seem to be a central issue, although the position is better in the Nordic countries than it is on average in the EU. The data do not imply whether this is due to the availability of care facilities, companies' policies or collective agreements or having no dependent children and/or elderly to take care of. Still, the data can be an indication that the

*Long-term care in Denmark*  177

*Table 11.6* How often is it difficult to concentrate at work because of care responsibilities?

|  | Several times a week | Several times a month | Several times a year | Less often or rarely | Never |
|---|---|---|---|---|---|
| Denmark | 1.0 | 4.4 | 7.4 | 25.5 | 61.7 |
| Finland | 1.1 | 6.9 | 9.0 | 39.0 | 43.9 |
| Sweden | 2.8 | 4.6 | 8.3 | 31.6 | 52.6 |
| EU | 4.1 | 10.1 | 11.6 | 29.1 | 45.3 |

Note: Data for Norway is not available.

Source: Date from European Quality of Life, 2012 (http://www.eurofound.europa.eu/surveys/european-quality-of-life-surveys/european-quality-of-life-survey-2012).

more developed service welfare states imply a lower risk of lack of concentration at the work place, thereby implying higher productivity and thus can be seen as a social investment (Greve, 2015).

Part of the story, or the opposite side of the coin, relates to whether work has an impact on how to solve the conflict between work and family life. This is indicated in Table 11.7.

The picture is slightly different from that in Table 11.6, as many more people now find that it is difficult to fulfil family responsibilities because of time spent at their jobs. In a given month, the number of people who find it difficult varies between one sixth of the population in Denmark and Finland and one fourth of the population in Sweden and 3 out of 10 people in the EU. Thus, the Nordic countries in general seem better able to juggle the work-family balance, but these data reflect not only long-term care but also care for children.

Table 11.8 looks more specifically into caring for the elderly or people with disabilities.

The lowest percentage of people involved can be found in Denmark and Sweden and the highest in Finland, but again, this is lower on average than in the EU countries. If taking 'once or twice' into account, Finland has a higher share than in the EU. There thus seem to be many who are not involved in caring, but there are around 8 to 10% who are often involved during a week. This implies that caring for a dependent person can have an impact on the quality of life for many people not only in the Nordic welfare states but also in Europe. Looking at the age profile of those involved, the most frequent age group is those between 50 and 64 years of age, presumably an indication that, as indicated earlier, many women do not have a spouse/partner when they are in need as elderly.

At the same time, the Nordic countries do not score highest on the opinion of the quality of long-term care. Based upon questions on a scale from 1 to 10 (1 being very poor quality, 10 being very high quality), Denmark's score is 6.7, Finland's is 6.3 and Sweden's is 5.7. The score of Sweden is even below the EU average of 5.8. At the top are Luxembourg with 7.6, Malta with 7.3 and Belgium with 7.1. This is an indication of that even if service is available, the perceived quality by the citizens is lower in the Nordic countries. Whether this is due to higher expectations or actual lower quality of care cannot be concluded from the available data.

178　*Bent Greve*

*Table 11.7* How often difficult to fulfil family responsibility because of time spent at job?

|  | Several times a week | Several times a month | Several times a year | Less often or rarely | Never |
|---|---|---|---|---|---|
| Denmark | 3.7 | 13.2 | 8.5 | 32.7 | 41.8 |
| Finland | 3.2 | 14.2 | 14.8 | 39.0 | 28.7 |
| Sweden | 6.6 | 17.7 | 14.4 | 34.4 | 26.9 |
| EU | 10.5 | 19.2 | 14.5 | 26.2 | 29.6 |

Note: No data for Norway available

Source: European Quality of Life, 2012 (http://www.eurofound.europa.eu/surveys/european-quality-of-life-surveys/european-quality-of-life-survey-2012).

*Table 11.8* How often are you involved in caring for elderly or disabled relatives?

|  | Every day | Several days a week | Once or twice a week | Less often | Never | Age group(s) with most frequent involvement |
|---|---|---|---|---|---|---|
| Denmark | 1.3 | 1.6 | 3.6 | 11.9 | 81.6 | 50–64 |
| Finland | 3.3 | 3.5 | 8.4 | 30.3 | 54.5 | 50–64 |
| Sweden | 1.6 | 2.0 | 4.6 | 19.8 | 72.0 | 50–64, 65+ |
| EU | 5.9 | 3.6 | 4.5 | 10.5 | 75.5 | 50–64 |

Note: No data for Norway.

Source: European Quality of Life, 2012 (http://www.eurofound.europa.eu/surveys/european-quality-of-life-surveys/european-quality-of-life-survey-2012).

## 11.5　Development in elder-care policies: central changes

Care for the elderly has not just been developed from one day to another. There is a relatively long tradition, although care for the elderly was a latecomer in social policy. This is partly because life expectancy was lower earlier and the families, to a large extent, took care of the frail elderly. In this section, more space will be devoted to Denmark, which is seen as a good case for the development in the Nordic welfare states; however, in relation to marketization, a comparison with the other Nordic countries will be given. First is a short depiction of the systems, recent development and policy measures. This is mainly based upon country descriptions in Council of the European Union (2014).

Denmark has, as indicated in section 11.3, a comprehensive system with some tendency for retrenchment, given a restructuring of the system. This restructuring, though, was built upon prevention, rehabilitation and reablement. Retrenchment is witnessed by the decline in the number of users and, since 2008, a decline of around 15% in the number of hours allocated per week. From 2011 to 2012, there was also a slight decline in the number of full-time workers in long-term care. Whether the decline is real retrenchment or a success due to rehabilitation can be difficult to determine.

Finland also has a very decentralised system that combines institutional care and home care, but is at the same time an example of the problems with the boundaries between long-term care and health care, including what is labelled inpatient departments of health care centres de facto is hospital beds that are long-term care. In 2011, 2.2 % of those above the age of 65 received care in institutional homes, and a further 3.6 % received support in sheltered housing, where the aim, like in Denmark, is to have care for independent elderly so they can continue to live in their private homes. Regarding quality, since 2001 there have been national guidelines for quality in long-term care, with a focus on service needs, service structure and promotion of welfare, including a guideline for the ratio of personnel per recipient of care. Quality here also focuses on geriatric assessment. In 2012, new legislation was enacted with a focus not only on service provided at home but also on institutional care if this can secure a safe and dignified life. Furthermore, there was an increased focus, as in the other Nordic countries, on people with dementia, given that 13,000 people in Finland are diagnosed every year.

In Sweden, it is the municipalities who are responsible, and this has been the case since 1992. There is a user charge related to long-term care, whether home based or in a care home, the cared for must still have 5,000 Swedish Krone in disposable income after paying for the services and taxes. In order to help with prevention, like in Denmark health checks have been established that should increase health and well-being as well as provide guidelines related to how to prevent, for example, falls. A central body assesses the quality of care, and since 2014 there are new binding regulations regarding dementia care. There has been a decline in the number of people living in care homes, and there is stable support in private homes, albeit with a larger focus on those most in need and fewer people receiving less than 10 hours per week in support. The development of a more market-based system has implied that large companies have taken over a large share of the care (and the data are not only for long-term care). In 2012, private companies delivered 87 billion Swedish Kroner and 17 billion came from nonprofit actors, totalling 104 billion, and number which has doubled since 2005 (Werne and Unsgaard, 2014).

In Denmark, social policy has often been decided as compromises between classes, and large political compromises. This has often been done after work in commissions prepared for the changes. In the early 1980s there was an elderly commission with reports in 1980, 1981 and 1982 that became very influential in the way care for the elderly was developed. Central was that the elderly should be able to stay in their homes as long as possible, and it was also a first indication that choice for the individual could become an issue. Self-determination and continuity were other central aspects. The economic situations of elderly people living in old-age homes were changed; instead of receiving pocket money, they got the full universal pension and were then required to pay for rent, heating, cleaning, food and other expenses out of the pension to the local municipality. After these formal changes took place, many elderly were left with very little money (Greve, 2002). Self-determination and influence were seen not only as for the individual but also for the group of elderly; therefore, all municipalities have elderly councils with the aim of giving advice to the municipality and a system where the elderly can complain about decided levels of care and services.

## 180    *Bent Greve*

The focus on self-determination and continuity included a change in the year 2000 so that elderly could make changes in the form and type of care delivered; for example, instead of cleaning they might sometimes want to take a short walk or talk about relatives. This was labelled *flexible home care*. In 2003, this was further followed up by free choice of provider. This later implied a much more marketised welfare system, especially in relation to cleaning in homes for the elderly, because the elderly chose private providers. However, recent years have seen a growing number of private providers going bankrupt.

Denmark has, in the line with the administration of social care in the other Nordic countries, a strong focus and high reliance on a decentralised system, which implies that the local municipalities were the ones responsible for the delivery of care for elderly in need. The possible conflict between central rules and local administration was the reason that "quality standards" were introduced (Petersen, Petersen and Christiansen, 2014). These main aim of these quality standards was to describe the amount of time and the different types of support the elderly could get. However, there is no clear indication of how to compare quality other than indicating to the elderly what they can expect of services, and there is no clear indication of how to judge it, so the area is still based on the discretion of the social workers within the framework set by the local municipality's political decisions. For some, the standards are seen as a strong indicator of the introduction of New Public Management approaches in the universal Danish welfare state model and as a movement from "quality as standardization to quality as consumerism" (Dahl, 2012, p. 147). The label "quality standard" therefore seems misleading except when the number of minutes of support one gets can be seen as an understanding of what quality is.

Still, the development of the Danish long-term care system has shown continually improved professionalisation (Dahl and Burau, 2013), although in recent years, focus on home care and expectation of informal care have arguably reduced this. It has been argued that 1994 to 2007 was a time of "substantial change through restructuring rather than retrenchment" (Dahl and Burau, 2013, p. 92); the changes were the increased focus on marketization, free-choice, common language and standards as central to the provision of long-term care.

There have been different commissions in Denmark in the area, as mentioned earlier. In 2012, the elderly commission continued the recommendation for prevention, reablement and focus on those most in need, but they also argued that quality would revolve around influence on one's own life, respect for diversity, a good daily life and focus on human interaction. Finally, they also touched upon a dignified end to life (Ældrekommissionen, 2012). In 2013, *Hjemmehjælpskommissionen* focused on rehabilitation so that the welfare services could focus on how to help the individual elderly. In the political agreement on the Finance Bill for the year 2016, 1 billion Danish Kroner were set aside so the municipalities could form a so-called dignity policy; by this they meant that there should be more staff, but that amount can only provide a limited number of staff relative to the increasing number of elderly in need of care.

A central development in all Nordic countries has been this path towards more marketization of care both within the public sector and by including private agents in the delivery of care. There is in general only limited evidence of the impact of using marketization. What seems to be the case is that there is some tendency toward higher transaction costs, but also, at least in first generation contracts for residential care, toward saving of money in Sweden. At the same time, there has been a lower staff ratio, but also better focus in the involvement of the elderly in the care plan and risk assessment, but no indication of higher user satisfaction. For home-care services, the Danish case seems to indicate higher user satisfaction with the practical help in the individual's own home (Meagher and Szebehely, 2013). Part of this development has been the ability for the elderly to buy extra support together with the public financed support. Buying extra support seems to still only have a limited size, at least in both Sweden and Denmark, so this subject is therefore left out of this article (Brogaard and Hjelmar, 2014).

Overall, the picture of the development is not clear and seemingly depends on the specific focus of the study. If choice is seen as a positive quality indicator (for a discussion see Greve, 2010), then the development has implied higher quality, but this is at the cost of a larger degree of inequality, as not all elderly will be able to make a choice. With the number of people with dementia expected to increase, this can pose new problems for care delivery.

Furthermore, the lack of clear central quality standards might make it difficult to find and ensure good quality, long-term care, and elements thereof must be included when making contracts with private providers. An overview indicates that the impact of more private for-profit providers in Sweden indicates no clear differences in the outcomes (Stolt, Blomqvist, and Winblad, 2011), although if focus is on staff, there is "a significantly lower staff to resident ratio" (p. 566).

The blurring picture of the development is due to healthy ageing and also increased focus on prevention, including rehabilitation that prevents further reduction in the individual's ability to take care of him-/herself. Use of welfare technology and ways to reenable people, early detection of frailty and age-friendly environments are part of the process for ensuring better life standards for elderly persons. Furthermore, the ability to combine work and informal caring has gradually come more to the front of the debate.

Finally, despite the expectation that marketization should imply at least the same care for a lower amount of money, there is overall no clear evidence in support of this or of better service quality (Petersen and Hjelmar, 2014).

## 11.6 Conclusions: reformulation of welfare mix

The development of long-term care has not moved away from a universalistic approach by making it possible for people in need of long-term care to get this based on an evaluation of what types of needs they have. Tendencies have been to provide more help at home and, if possible, to avoid institutionalisation, but there are still options for formal care either in home or at institutions. Increasingly, focus has been on rehabilitation, enablement and use of new technologies as ways of both increasing quality of life for the elderly and reducing the cost pressure on the public sector. At the same time, there has been an increase in the pressure on spouses/partners and families to provide informal care, which indicates a lesser involvement of the welfare state in the care for the elderly in the future; however,

## 182 Bent Greve

information does not indicate that people are buying more care services from private providers or seeking it from public providers.

Overall, the data do not lend support to retrenchment in the area, but more to change in focus and structure. In real terms, for elderly above the age of 75, more resources have been devoted to the area, and given active ageing with more healthy life years, this implies that retrenchment has not been on the agenda. Still, the higher focus on care in the home indicates that professionalisation might be less strong than it used to be.

There is still no clear and precise definition of what good quality in long-term care means. There is an interest in, or at least an argument for, quality care being provided. The marketization of care has implied more care being delivered by private for-profit companies. Whether this can be interpreted as a strong movement away from the universal Nordic model is still open for debate. The welfare states decide and pay the cost of care, so it is only the delivery that has changed.

In Nordic countries, delivery has changed (e.g. more marketization) and things are moving in a less universalistic direction; this opens up the possibility for more individual payments and the possibility that the more affluent people will be able to buy more service than low-income groups. In this way a reformulation has taken place, but at the same time the informal sector also plays a role, albeit without any clear change in the development. Focus on reablement, rehabilitation and use of new technology might further imply a new path towards a less universalistic approach for the Nordic welfare states unless the welfare states support and help with acquiring these technologies.

The development of free choice and higher involvement of private companies in a more market-led approach has changed delivery, but whether this is an end to universalism is still open for interpretation.

## Note

1 See, for example, *Social Policy & Administration*, vol. 48, no. 4, Regional issue on the impact of the financial crisis on small European welfare states.

## References

Barr, N. (2010), Long-term care: A suitable case for social insurance, *Social Policy & Administration* 44(4): 359–374.

Brogaard, L. and Hjelmar, U. (2014), *Tilkøbsydelser på ældreområdet: En systematisk analyse af litteratur på området*. København: KORA.

Bruigiavini, A., Buia, R., Pasini, G. and Zantonio, F. (2013), Long-term care and reciprocity: Does helping with grandchildren result in the receipt of more help at older ages? In A. Börsch-Supan et al. (ed) *Active Ageing and Solidarity between Generations in Europe*, Amsterdam: De Gruyter, pp. 369–378.

Claid Dale, M., St John, S. and Hanna, J. (2013), *Financing of long-term care and long-term care insurance for the aged: A literature-based comparison of Seven OECD-countries*, RPRC Working Paper 2012, 2.

Council of European Union (2014), Adequate social protection for long-term care needs in an ageing society. Report Jointly prepared by the Social Protection Committee and the European Commission services. Brussels, SOC 403, ECOFIN 525.

## Long-term care in Denmark    183

Dahl, H.M. (2012), Who can be against quality? A new Story about home-based care: NPM and Governmentality. In C. Ceci, K. Bjørnsdottir and M. Purkis (eds) *Perspectives on Care at Home for Older People*, Oxon, Routledge, pp. 139–157.

Dahl, H.M. and Bureau, V. (2013), Trajectories of change in Danish long term care policies. In C. Ranci and E. Pavolini (eds) *Reforms in Long-Term Care Policies in Europe*, New York: Springer, pp. 79–95.

De la Masioneuve, C. and Martins, J.O. (2014), The future of health and long-term care spending, OECD, *Journal Economic Studies* 1: 61–96.

Farnsworth, K. and Irving, Z. (2011), *Social Policy in Challenging Times: Economic Crisis and Welfare Systems*, Bristol: Policy Press.

Greve, B. (2002), *Vouchers. Nye styrings- og leveringsmåder i velfærdsstaten*, København: Jurist- og Økonomforbundets Forlag.

Greve, B. (2010), *Choice: Challenges and Perspectives for the European Welfare States*, Oxford, Wiley-Blackwell.

Greve, B. (2012), *Reconciliation of Work and Family Life in Four Different Welfare States*. NEUJOBS Working Paper D 5.5.

Greve, B. (2015), *Den sociale og innovative velfærdsstat*, København: Hans Reitzel.

Heger, D (2014), *Work and Well-Being of Informal Caregivers in Europe*. Essen, RWI.

Hjemmehjælpskommissionen (2013), Fremtidens hjemmehjælp, København, Hjemmehjælpskommission.

Jacobzone, S. (1999), *Ageing and Care for Frail Elderly Persons: An Overview of International Perspectives*, Labour Market and Social Policy Occasional Papers no. 38, Paris: OECD.

Meagher, G. and Szebehely, M. (ed) (2013), *Marketisation in Nordic Eldercare: A Research Report on Legislation, Oversight, Extent and Consequences*, Stockholm: Stockholm University.

Mot, E., Faber, R., Geerts, J. and Willemé, P. (eds) (2012), *Performance of long-term care systems in Europe*. Enepri Research Report no. 117.

OECD (2011), *Help Wanted? Providing and Paying for Long-Term Care*, Paris: OECD.

OECD (2013a), A good life in old age? Monitoring and improving quality in long-term care, OECD Health Policy Studies, Paris: OECD.

OECD (2013b), *A Good Life in Old Age? Monitoring and Improving Quality in Long-Term Care, Policy Brief*, Paris: OECD.

OECD (2013c), *Health at a Glance*, Paris: OECD.

Pavolini, E. and Ranci, C. (2008), Restructuring the welfare state: Reforms in long-term care in Western European countries, *Journal of European Social Policy*, 18(3): 246–259.

Petersen, J.H., Petersen, K. and Christiansen, N. (2014), *Hvor glider vi hen? Dansk Velfærdshistorie, bind 6, 1993–2014*. Odense: Syddansk Universitetsforlag.

Petersen, O.H. and Hjelmar, U. (2014), Marketization of welfare services in Scandinavia: A review of Danish and Swedish experiences, *Scandinavian Journal of Public Administration*, 17(4): 3–20.

Ragin, C. (1987), *The Comparative Model: Moving beyond Qualitative and Quantitative Strategies*, Berkeley: University of California Press.

Schubert, K., Villota, P. and Kuhlmann, J. (2015), *Challenges to European Welfare Systems*, Berlin: Springer.

Stolt, R., Blomqvist, P. and Winblad, U. (2011), Privatization of social services: Quality differences in Swedish elderly care, *Social Science & Medicine* 72: 560–567.

Swartz, K. (2013), Searching for a balance of responsibilities: OECD countries changing elderly assistance policies, *Annual Review of Public Health* 34: 397–412.

## 184   Bent Greve

Ulmanen, P. and Szebehely, M. (2015), From the state to the family or to the market? Consequences of reduced residential eldercare in Sweden, *International Journal of Social Welfare* 24: 81–92.

Verbakel, E. (2014), Informal caregiving and well-being in Europe: What can ease the negative consequences for caregivers? *Journal of European Social Policy* 24(5): 424–441.

Vis, B. (2013), How to analyze welfare states and their development. In B. Greve (ed.), *The Routledge Handbook of the Welfare State*, New York and London: Routledge, pp. 274–282.

Werne, K. and Unsgaard, O. (2014), *Den stora omvandlingen: En granskning af välfärdsmarknaden*, Stockholm: Leopold Forläg.

Ældrekommissionen (2012), *Livskvalitet og selvbestemmelse på plejehjem*, København: Social- og integrationsministeriet.

# 12  Some concluding reflections

*Bent Greve*

## 12.1 Introduction

This chapter will try to sum up and make a short comparative analysis of the trends and developments in long-term care in the countries included in the book. This chapter will try to shed light on whether the development is common among countries belonging to different welfare regimes while still acknowledging the diversity in delivery and financing of long-term care. The chapter will not in great detail deal with the expected future development and possible pressures on spending in the field of long-term care; this is important, however, in trying to understand some of the developments as the rising number of elderly might imply a pressure on public spending, especially if the civil society will provide care to a lesser extent. On the other hand, the possible use of new welfare technology and a more healthy ageing process might reduce the possible economic pressure on the welfare states.

The chapter is structured so that the next section will present a general overview of spending on long-term care and some information on the informal care. This is then followed by a general overview of trends in long-term care since the financial crisis. This is done by looking at five different themes, which are also shown in Table 12.4, in order to synthesize recent developments in long-term care. There will be five short sections (12.3 through 12.7) on each of these themes, followed by a short concluding section.

Keep in mind that long-term care is not necessarily structured in the same way in all the countries. The boundaries between health care and long-term care are blurred; the interaction between state, market and civil societies is varied among the countries; and strong and systematic comparable data not always are available.

## 12.2 Synthesis of development in long-term care

This chapter aims at a synthesis of the development and a comparison of the countries studied in the book. Table 12.1 shows expenditures split between health and social long-term care.

Before commenting on the data, it is important to stress that there are severe delimitations for data in this area due to national differences in organisations and

## 186 *Bent Greve*

*Table 12.1* Long-term care public expenditure (health and social components), as share of GDP, 2013 (or nearest year)

|  | Health LTC | Social LTC | Total | Annual Real growth rate 2005–2013 |
|---|---|---|---|---|
| Denmark | 2.3 |  | 2.3 | 1.8 |
| Finland | 0.6 | 1.6 | 2.2 | 3.8 |
| Germany | 1.0 |  | 1.0 | 2.4 |
| Portugal | 0.2 | 0.4 | 0.5 | 10.8 |
| Poland (2012) | 0.4 | 0.0 | 0.4 | 2.3 |
| Hungary | 0.2 |  | 0.2 | −0.3 |
| Greece | 0.0 |  | 0.0 | n/a |
| Italy |  |  | 1.8 | n/a |
| Lithuania |  |  | 0.9 | n/a |
| UK |  |  | 1.2 | n/a |

Source: OECD Health Statistics 2015, http://dx.doi.org/10.1787/health-data-en. This did not include any data for Lithuania, Italy and UK; these are from http://ec.europa.eu/economy_finance/publications/european_economy/2015/ee3_en.htm.

due to where expenditures are entered in the accounting within each of the systems. In some countries, long-term care is mainly in the health care area, and in others it is a separate branch. In some, cash benefits play a role. Furthermore, the reliance on informal care, including family, is different among countries, although data here is also scarce. It is worth noting that some of these national figures obscure major within-country variations. Moreover, the full costs of long-term care should, in principle, include the (largely privately borne) costs of informal caregiving.

Table 12.1 indicates that the countries in the more universal welfare state (Finland and Denmark) spend more on formal long-term care, with the continental and liberal welfare states (Germany and the UK) spending a lower amount, and with Eastern and Southern Europe, with Italy as an exception, spending an even lower amount. From 2005 to 2013, there has been a strong increase in the level of spending, especially in Portugal, but in Finland a clear increase has been seen. Hungary is the only country in this sample with a negative growth development. Naturally, a problem with data of this kind is that development in spending does not necessarily reflect change in needs of care, as this might be difficult to measure. It is not easy to define exactly what need is and what quality of care is. The data is furthermore not corrected for the development in the number of elderly, thus implying that despite an increase in the overall level of spending, there might have been reductions for individual persons through an overall lower level of spending per inhabitant.

Overall, although the data in a way confirm the often classical way of making a portrait of the welfare states around in Europe, the differences are not always that large. This because some of the differences might reflect possible differences in demography and also in the expectation of that the civil society will play a more central role in some countries than in other countries. The information regarding the size of the informal sector is limited.

Table 12.2 provides information on informal carers in some of the countries.

The table indicates the stronger role of civil society in the liberal, continental and Southern European welfare states, but the difference to the Nordic welfare state of Denmark is not that large. In all welfare states, as can be witnessed also from the individual country chapters, women seem to do the main part of the care, although in Denmark the difference is not that big. In addition, many of those providing care will presumably be spouses or cohabiting persons when care is on daily basis, whereas care on weekly basis might be provided by other family members. The growing life expectancy might also imply that an increasing number of men do informal care.

Another question revolves around how many can get access to institutional care and how many workers are employed in this field. In Table 12.3 some central information is presented.

*Table 12.2* Informal care: a few data for 2013 (or nearest year)

| | *Population aged 50 and over reporting to be informal carers* | *Share of women among all informal carers aged 50 and over* | *Frequency of care provided by informal carers* | |
| --- | --- | --- | --- | --- |
| | | | *Daily* | *Weekly* |
| Denmark | 12.3 | 55.9 | 67 | 33 |
| Germany | 14.4 | 59.0 | 71 | 29 |
| Italy | 15.4 | 63.2 | 77 | 23 |
| UK | 17.5 | 61.7 | n/a | n/a |

Source: OECD Health Statistics 2015, http://dx.doi.org/10.1787/health-data-en.

*Table 12.3* Workers and proportion receiving long-term care in 2013 (or nearest year)

| | *Long-term care workers per 100 people aged 65 and over* | | | *Proportion of population receiving long-term care* | | | |
| --- | --- | --- | --- | --- | --- | --- | --- |
| | *Institutions* | *Home* | *Total* | *65–79* | *80+* | *Total* | *Total (2000 or nearest year)* |
| Denmark | 5.2 | 3.3 | 8.5 | 1.4 | 0.9 | 3.2 | 3.1 |
| Finland | n/a | n/a | n/a | 0.7 | 1.5 | 2.7 | 2.2 |
| Germany | 3 | 1.7 | 4.7 | 0.9 | 1.7 | 3.3 | 2.3 |
| Hungary | 1.4 | 1 | 2.4 | 0.8 | 0.9 | 3.2 | 1.4 |
| Italy | n/a | n/a | n/a | n/a | n/a | 2.0 | 0.8 |
| Portugal | 0.5 | 0.1 | 0.6 | 0.1 | 0.2 | 0.4 | n/a |
| Poland | n/a | n/a | n/a | 0.1 | 0.1 | 0.3 | 0.2 |

Source: OECD Health Statistics 2015, http://dx.doi.org/10.1787/health-data-en.

Note: The reason that the totals do not add up is that people younger than age 65 might be in need of long-term care.

188    *Bent Greve*

The data in Table 12.3 indicate a clear division in the number of long-term care workers and the proportion of the population receiving long-term care with the highest in the more universal and continental welfare states and the least in Southern and Eastern Europe. However, in all countries there has been an increase in the proportion receiving long-term care, thus implying a possible pressure on welfare state spending. Also, despite the growing spending level, as reported in Table 12.1, there might have been a reduction in the overall level of service for individuals in need of care. There is further a strong deviation in the use of institutions in the provision of long-term care, although it looks like in all countries the trend has been towards a higher focus on support in the individual's own home.

Recent years have seen rapid developments in the field of long-term care. Table 12.4 shows a synthesis of trends and status in long-term care in the countries included in the book. The authors of the different chapters kindly commented on and supplemented this table.

## 12.3  Trends in marketization of long-term care

Despite that marketization and privatization have been part of the development of welfare states around Europe, this is seemingly less the case in the area of long-term care, with possible exceptions in the Nordic countries and the UK, where marketization has been an explicit policy objective since major reforms were enacted in 1993. Marketization can be understood in different ways: in financing or in delivery. Here the focus is on who is actually delivering the long-term care, less on who is financing it, although it seems that financing is still mainly with the state regarding the delivered care, albeit this does not include the value of the care delivered by the informal sector, nor what is delivered and paid for in the hidden economy. The knowledge on financing of workers in the hidden economy is not clearly known, so if illegal migrants are working and living with the elderly (as seems to be the case in at least Italy and Poland), then there is not detailed information about this, and thus more use of workers in the "grey economy" can be the impact hereof, thereby making the data less precise.

Part of the reason for this development reflects that long-term care has not been as institutionalised like other welfare services; to a large degree it has been taken care of by the civil society, especially the family. Furthermore, long-term care is a latecomer to social policy because the need for long-term care is only recognised as a pressing issue within social policy now that life expectancy has increased. This is indicated by the relatively low overall level of spending within the long-term care area from as low as 0.11 % of GDP in Greece to 2.5 % in Denmark in 2013 (Greve, 2016).

Still, in the Nordic countries, there have been tendencies to use private companies to deliver especially cleaning and personal care services. It is difficult to know how strong the trend is, given that the boundaries between health care and long-term care are blurred. The implication has been that some in need of long-term care are placed, for example, in long-term medicine sections of hospitals. Thus, they might get some services; however, this is not counted as long-term care.

*Table 12.4* Long-term care synthesis of trends and status in long-term care

| Country | Trends in marketization of long-term care | Role of civil society | Austerity measures/ change in financing | Rehabilitation/reablement and other investments in the field | Quality measures, including quality of life. |
|---|---|---|---|---|---|
| Denmark | Yes, especially for practical home help | Important | Limited, but can vary locally as long-term care services are, within limits, decided in the municipalities | Yes, stronger focus on rehabilitation and use of welfare technology | Up to local level to specify what they will do, therefore no central overview |
| Finland | Yes, in part of the care system | Important | Limited as there has been increase in spending | Yes, there is a strong emphasis in quality recommendations to include rehabilitation as part of services provided for older people | To a large degree a local issue; quality recommendations are provided to help local decision makers assess and develop quality of services for older people |
| Germany | Important | Important | Limited | Some increased attention since 2008 | Obligatory quality management in professional care providers since 2002 |
| Greece | Limited | Very important | Limited | Limited | No clear and precise definition |
| Hungary | Limited | Very important | Some (see Table 12.1); the only country with negative development in spending | Only more limited in this field | No clear and precise definition |
| Italy | Limited, but a "grey" market is important | Very important, including also NGOs and not-for-profit institutions' involvement | Some | Limited, with some regional variation in the approach to and use of this | No clear and precise definition |

(*Continued*)

*Table 12.4* (Continued)

| Country | Trends in marketization of long-term care | Role of civil society | Austerity measures/ change in financing | Rehabilitation/reablement and other investments in the field | Quality measures, including quality of life. |
|---|---|---|---|---|---|
| Lithuania | Limited, especially due to low involvement | Strong, with expectation that elderly will stay as long as possible in their own homes | Limited, due to low public sector involvement | No, this has so far not really been on the agenda | No national clear guidelines |
| Poland | Limited for historical reasons and overlap to health care | Very important, especially family, but also migrant workers | Some | Limited and still in infancy | No, and with risk of low quality due to working conditions within the area |
| Portugal | Limited | Very important | No, there has been a large increase in spending | Limited | No central definition |
| UK | Marketization of long-term care has been a clear policy objective since major reforms implemented in 1993. Martketisation has been extended and deepened during the first decade of the 21st century with the promotion of personalised funding models; the aim is that individual service users should become economic market actors rather than relying on purchase by proxy professionals. | The prevalence of informal caregiving has grown during the period of austerity | Yes, especially since 2010 with increasingly significant cuts in local authority budgets | Yes, extensive service redesign and some new investments in the area | There are major concerns about the quality of care – both domiciliary and institutional – in the context of increasingly severe funding constraints |

*Some concluding reflections* 191

The risk of marketization, even if it is only the delivery aspect, is more inequality in access to care. Due to that, there might be user charges attached to using the private sector for long-term care. Charges can be in different forms. They can be copayments (which can be calculated in more or less progressive/regressive ways). People might also purchase services privately with their own funds because the services they need are no longer provided by the state. Thus, use of the market if it opens for buying more by private providers thus implies higher overall cost for long-term care. Also, within a publicly provided system, there is the option of asking for copayment. Still, user charges tend to have a negative impact on access to service.

Other risks have been worsening work conditions and less quality in the delivery (see also section 12.8). Marketization also has implications, often negative, for those employed in the sector; this is, however, not the focus here.

Finally, if the increase in use of the market as a provider also includes changes and higher user charges, this implies inequality in access to services and that for some, no care will be available. Thus, user charges, as well as choice, can have negative effects on quality and access to long-term care.

## 12.4 Role of civil society

There might be a trade-off between the role of civil society and the states' and markets' roles in relation to long-term care. Good family contact might reduce the need for state intervention, and this seems to be the case, although also with deviant cases (Haynes, Hill, and Banks, 2010). In all welfare states included in this book, the civil society plays a very central role (naturally with differences), and it is less important in the Nordic welfare states than in the other countries. Still, the expectation that a spouse/partner will help take care of a frail mate might imply a gender inequality in all countries; given that women live longer, they less frequently have spouses/partners to take care of them if they become dependent. Still, as argued earlier, increasingly men will also be informal carers.

This implies a pressure on children and other relatives. Some do not have children/relatives close when they are in need of assistance, which puts them at a disadvantage.

Thus, despite all the positive implications of having and using civil society in the delivery of long-term care, there is a risk that some will not have care or will at least have less care than they might need when they are frail. Inequality in access to care is seemingly a common problem across welfare states in Europe. Overall, also in this book, there seem to be converging trends (Gori et al., 2016) in Europe in the use of informal care through the civil society as a way of providing long-term care.

The conflicting perspective on the role of civil society thus still prevails. Civil society is extremely important in order to ensure at least a minimum of care for many; however, it creates inequality for who can get long-term care – a type of inequality related to both income and gender.

A considerable risk is that there will be negative repercussion on labour market participation when relatives have to take care of family members; thus, the

192    *Bent Greve*

alternative cost for society by not providing care is less activity on the labour market and an inequality between men and women. A further issue relates to the possible quality of care (see also later).

## 12.5  Austerity measures/change in financing

Recent years have seen pressure on most welfare states' abilities to finance spending on welfare state policies. In the area of long-term care, there has at the same time, due to demographic changes, been an increased pressure in all countries. Thus, despite the fact that spending on elderly often has a high level of legitimacy because the elderly are often seen as deserving, there is an ambition (that varies by area) to curb the expenditures within the area of LTC and to reduce the future pressure on spending for LTC.

Naturally, given the existing size of spending on LTC, there might be measures to reduce spending, but in some countries that will be limited. There are only limited options to further curb spending. Therefore, there is a risk that the measures taken seem stronger in the welfare states with higher levels of spending than in countries with already low levels.

A further problem in comparing is that, at least theoretically, the elderly might be healthier than earlier generations; thus, an absolute or relative decline in spending may not be due to austerity but to better living conditions.

At the same time, the unchanged level of spending might reflect austerity measures if the number of elderly in need of care is increasing. Interpretation of data is not straightforward, and (as seen in Table 12.1) there has, with the exception of Hungary, been an increase in the level of spending on long-term care in the countries where data are available. Still, most of the contributors to this book point to retrenchment in the field of long-term care in their countries.

Therefore, even if austerity not has been so strong in the field of long-term care as in other social policy areas, because the legitimacy of long-term care often is high, a gradual reduction of the state's role seems prevalent.

## 12.6  Rehabilitation and/or reablement: new trends

Use of new technologies and ambitions to try to help the elderly be able to continue their daily lives in their own homes has (with different emphasis) been part of the development, especially in the Nordic countries and in England and Scotland.

The general idea is that rehabilitation and/or reablement will make it possible for individuals to be better able to live independent lives with only limited care (or perhaps none). The same idea lies behind the use of welfare technology. Several means of welfare technology should help ensure that even if, for example, an elderly is no longer able to do cleaning, cooking or other daily activities, the technology can help. Thus, the ability to live an independent life can continue longer than earlier.

Further, the use of new technologies might also help alleviate loneliness among elderly, as they might be able to be more in contact with family or friends when they are no longer able to leave the home as much as they used to.

Use of new technologies might improve quality of life and reduce public sector spending on long-term care, but there will be a need to invest before the possible reduction in public/private spending on long-term care is possible.

## 12.7 Quality measures including quality of life

Defining quality in long-term care is not an easy task, especially given that, as in health care, it will presumably not be possible to go back to the situation before the needs arises. Therefore, service has to focus on how to make it possible to cope with changes in abilities.

Asking the users about the quality of the service can often be difficult, especially given that those in homes for the elderly are often very frail and sometimes have dementia. This reduces the ability to get subjective information on the development of quality in care, including indicators for the quality of life.

The lack of strong and clear indicators of the quality of care also make the evaluation and discussion of the development in long-term care very difficult. This is also made difficult by the many and varied ways of providing long-term care and the differences in and varied preferences among users of long-term care.

The lack of strong and simple quality measurement criteria also opens for a debate on how to measure the need for long-term care. Further, the issue of retrenchment/austerity measures can be difficult to depict; for example, a reduction in spending is not necessarily the same as retrenchment if the reduction is the result of the elderly living longer with better health and rehabilitation measures having a positive impact on the daily living of the elderly.

## 12.8 Final concluding remarks

Long-term care is a central and important social policy area given the ageing population and the importance of ensuring good lives for older people. How to balance living in one's own home and being able to get the necessary support and how to combine the support from the civil society with the state support is still an open question.

Countries around Europe have used different ways and different measures to cope with these changes. The information in this book does not point to one solution that is better than another. It points more towards the idea that there are dilemmas and that there are risks of inequality in access to care in different countries.

The balance between individually tailored solutions, the ability to stay as long as possible in one's own home, and a continued social life without hindering a spouse or relative will also be challenges for long-term care in the future.

## References

Gori, C., Fernandez, J. and Wittenberg, R. (2016), *Long-Term Care Reforms in OECD Countries: Successes and Failures*, Bristol: Policy Press.

Greve, B. (2016), *The Long-Term Care Resourcing Landscape*, Sprint-Deliverable D.2.4.

Haynes, P., Hill, M. and Banks, L. (2010), Older people's family contacts and long-term care expenditure in OECD countries: A comparative approach using qualitative comparative analysis, *Social Policy & Administration* 44(1): 67–84

# Index

activities of daily living (ADL) 13, 16, 45
added worker effect 104
ADL *see* activities of daily living (ADL)
ageing projections 20–1, 81–3, 104–5, 150–2
Ageing Report 13, 20
Augustyn, Mieczyslaw 54
austerity policies 192; in Germany 126–7; in Greece 99–103; in Italy 76, 79, 84; in the United Kingdom 114–21
Avolio, M. 19

Barthel scale 29, 45
Belgium 177

Casanova, G. 19
civil society 49–50, 80–1, 191–2
contract culture 136

Dandi, R. 19
De Belvis, A. G. 19
demand and supply, long-term care: in Hungary 14–19; in Italy 79; in Lithuania 25–32; in Poland 40–51
demographic projections 20–1, 81–3, 104–5, 150–2
Denmark 3, 5–6, 181–2, 186, 187; central issues of long-term care in 169–70; development in elder-care policies in 178–81; quality of long-term care in 171–2; welfare state 168–9, 172–7, *178*
Dilnot, Andrew 112
disabled children 49

eligibility for long-term care: in Hungary 12; in Lithuania 27–9; in Poland 45, 51; in Portugal 62; in the United Kingdom 112
England *see* United Kingdom

European Health Interview Survey (EHIS) 13
expenditures on long-term care: in Finland 145, 152–60; in Germany 126–7; in Greece 98; in Hungary 20; in Lithuania 25, 32; in Poland 48–9

Faber, R. 3
familism 76, 81–3; in Denmark 169–70; in Germany 133–4; in Italy 75, 76; in Portugal 60–1; in the United Kingdom 119–20; *see also* informal market for long-term care
financing of long-term care: in Finland 147–8, 160–2; in Hungary 16–19; in Lithuania 32; in Poland 38–40, 46, 48, 51–3; in Portugal 68–70; in the United Kingdom 108–21; *see also* austerity policies
Finland 3, 145, 163, 179, 186; demographic development in 150–2; economic and demographic development in 148–52; expenditures on long-term care in 152–60; financing of long-term care in 160–2; long-term care and services for older people in 146–7; organisation and financing of services for older people in 147–8; public sector surplus in 149–50; recent policy initiatives in 162–3; welfare state in 177
France 78, 79

Geerts, J. 3
Germany 3, 5, 78, 79, 186; austerity measures in 126–7; characteristics and governance structures in long-term care in 133–7; design of unwieldy long-term care system in 128–33; familism in

133–4; question of long-term care expansion in 126–8; role of the market in long-term care in 134–5

Greece 4, 5, 93–4, 188; crisis and care economy in 99–103; long-term care towards the end of the crisis in 103–5; mixed system before the crisis in 94–9

Hungary 4, 8; aging projections in 20–1; available benefits and services in 13–14; being old in 9–11; eligibility for long-term care in 12; financing of long-term care in 16–19; informal market for long-term care services in 19; institutionalisation in 11; long-term care demand and supply in 12–19; long-term care system overview 8–9; needs assessment in 12; supply of public care in 14–19; time transfers in retired households in 10–11

IADL *see* instrumental activities of daily living (IADL)
informal market for long-term care 187; in Denmark 169–70; in Finland 146–7; in Greece 94–9; in Hungary 19; in Italy 81–3; in Lithuania 23–4, 33–4; in Poland 41–2; in Portugal 60–5; in the United Kingdom 119–20
instrumental activities of daily living (IADL) 13, 16
International Labor Organization (ILO) 70–1
Italy 4, 5, 75–7, 89–90; developments in long-term care policies in 77–80; familism in 75, 76, 81–3; long-term care amid increasing individual needs and diminishing family capacity in 81–3; migrant care workers in long-term care system in 83–5; quality measures in 88–9; role of civil society in long-term care delivery in 80–1; use of rehabilitation and welfare technology in 85–8

Lillini, R. 19
Lithuania 4, 23, 34–5; boundaries between state and civil society in the approach to delivery of care in 33; formal long-term care for the elderly in 25–32; informal care in 33–4; organisations of long-term care in 23–5; use of rehabilitation and welfare technology in 34

Little Brothers of the Poor 50–1
Litwin, H. 19
long-term care (LTC): changing demographics in Europe and 20–1, 81–3, 104–5, 150–2; in choice of countries studied 3–6; civil society role in 49–50, 80–1, 191–2; components of 2–3; demand and supply (*see* demand and supply, long-term care); for disabled children 49; eligibility for (*see* eligibility for long-term care); expenditures on (*see* expenditures on long-term care); familism in 60–1, 75, 76, 81–3, 119–20, 133–4, 169–70; financing of (*see* financing of long-term care); importance of addressing 1–2; informal market for (*see* informal market for long-term care); migrant care workers in 83–5; public *vs.* private (*see* public versus private long-term care); quality 2–3, 51–3, 70–1, 88–9, 171–2; reforms (*see* reforms, long-term care); role of civil society in 49–50; staff shortages 70–1; synthesis of development in 185–8; trends in marketization of 188–91
Luxembourg 177
Lyberaki, A. 98

Malta 177
marketization trends in long-term care 188–91
migrant care workers in Italy 83–5
Mot, E. 3

National Audit Office of Lithuania 30
needs assessment 13, 62; instrumental activities of daily living (IADL); *see also* activities of daily living (ADL)
nongovernmental organizations (NGOs) 49–51

OECD (Organisation for Economic Co-operation and Development) 3, 60, 65, 97, 169, 171–2

palliative care services 25
Pavolini, E. 135
Pelone, F. 19
Poland 4, 38, 55–6; administration, financing and quality of long-term care in 51–3; debate and reform proposals in 53–5; demand for long-term care

## 196    Index

in 40–1; families as care providers in 41–2; new welfare state institutional context in 38–40; private sector and NGOs in the long-term care market in 49–51; public sector long-term care in 42–5; social sector of long-term care in 45–9; supply of long-term care in 41–51
Polish Committee of Social Assistance 50
Polish Red Cross 50
PolSenior 41
Portugal 4, 59–60, 72, 186; critical challenges for formal care provision in 70–1; familism in 60–1; financials of care provision in 68–70; historical trends in consolidation of social care for dependent elderly in 60–1; long-term care in contemporary 61–5; national network for long-term care in 65–8
post-communist countries 50
public versus private long-term care: in Finland 157–60; in Greece 94–9; in Hungary 14–19; in Italy 76, 83–5; in Lithuania 33; in Poland 41–51; in Portugal 60–5; in the United Kingdom 119–21

quality, long-term care: administration and law in 51–3; in Denmark 171–2; measures including quality of life 193; measures in Italy 88–9; quest for 2–3; staff shortages and 70–1; use of rehabilitation and welfare technology as ways to improve 34
quasi-privatization of care 60–1

Ranci, C. 135
reablement 107, 111–12, 174, 178, 180–2, 192–3
reforms, long-term care: in Finland 162–3; in Greece 101–3; in Poland 53–5; in Portugal 65–8; in the United Kingdom 112–13, 137–9
rehabilitation and welfare technology: in Italy 85–8; in Lithuania 34; trends in 192–3; in the United Kingdom 111–12
Robot-Era 87
Roman Catholic Church 50, 60–1

social investment 127–8, 140, 177

spending on long-term care *see* financing of long-term care
Statistics Lithuania 27
Stoeckel, K. J. 19
Streeck, W. 75, 78
Survey of Health, Ageing, and Retirement in Europe (SHARE) 19
Swartz, K. 169
Sweden 174–5, 177, 179
Syntomia 50–1

Thelen, K. 75, 78
time transfers, intergenerational 10–11

United Kingdom, the 3, 5, 79, 107–8, 121–2, 139–41, 186; austerity impacts on care markets in 120–1; austerity impacts on family caregivers in 119–20; austerity impacts on long-term care services in 117–18; austerity impacts on older people in 118–19; austerity impacts on private care markets in 119; familism in 119–20; fragmented responsibilities of long-term care in 108–9; governance of long-term care in 135–7; implementation of austerity policies in 114–16; long-term care insurance funds in 136–7; modernizing long-term care in 139; personalisation and personal budgets in 110–11; recent developments in long-term care in 109–13; recent long-term care reforms in 137–9; reforming social care law and funding in 112–13; rehabilitation and reablement in 111–12

Volpe, M. 19

welfare state 187; in Denmark 168–9; institutional context in Poland 38–40; in Italy 76; recent developments in the Nordic 172–7, *178*
welfare technology 4, 6, 34, 72, 85–8, 174, 181, 185, 192
Willeme, P. 3
workers, long-term care: migrant, in Italy 83–5; shortage in Portugal 83–5

Year for Active Aging and Solidarity Between Generations 55